"A book written with the artful grace and subtle mystique the Spirit deserves...like a refreshing ballet amid the hustle and bustle of postmodern theologizing."

Shane Claiborne
author of *The Irresistible Revolution* (Zondervan, 2006), activist, and recovering sinner

"There is music everywhere if you stop and listen. Oden has heard the beat and started into the dance. In this book, Oden has truth and fiction twirling together in a beautiful waltz. Once you hear the music, you can never go without it. Join the dance."

Neil Cole
church starter and wineskin architect, author of *Organic Church: Growing Faith Where Life Happens* (Jossey-Bass, 2005)

"*It's a Dance* is a conversation more than a book. It's a lively discussion through which we develop a fluid, organic, shifting, growing awareness of the unmistakable and missional work of the Holy Spirit. It's a conversation that the emerging church definitely needs to have and we are indebted to Patrick Oden for starting it."

Michael Frost
founding director of Centre for Evangelism and Global Mission at Morling Theological College, Sydney, Australia; author of *Exiles* (Hendrickson, 2006) and coauthor of *The Shaping of Things to Come* (Hendrickson, 2003)

"The theoretical principles of the emerging-church phenomena only reach a limited audience of pastors and students. Patrick Oden's storytelling approach makes those insights far more attractive and accessible to a wider audience, which needs to be part of the conversation. He has done an excellent job not only of popularizing the key concepts but of adding insights of his own."

Eddie Gibbs
senior professor, School of Intercultural Studies, Fuller Theological Seminary, Pasadena, California

"While books on pneumatology—the doctrine and spirituality of the Holy Spirit—abound in these days, there is no work comparable to that of *It's a Dance: Moving with the Holy Spirit*. This pneumatological narrative indeed is a dance with the Spirit, an invitation to the Divine Ball, a feast of pneumatology. It not only breaks new ground in combining creatively biblical, pastoral, theological, and literary elements. It also points to the future of doing theology in a postmodern world, consulting spiritual experiences in the community and everyday life along with best insights of theological tradition and contemporary constructive thinking."

Veli-Matti Kärkkäinen

professor of systematic theology, Fuller
Theological Seminary, Pasadena, California;
docent of ecumenics, University of Helsinki, Finland

"An imaginative book for people who have been touched by the Spirit of God and want to know more. It introduces key biblical passages and doctrines on the Holy Spirit in a painless way, and gently widens perceptions of where and how the Spirit is at work."

Kirsteen Kim

honorary lecturer, University of Birmingham, U.K.;
vice-moderator of the World Council of Churches'
Commission on World Mission and Evangelism;
author of *The Holy Spirit in the World* (Orbis, 2007)

"What an encouraging, inspiring, and refreshing book to read! Often we forget the critical importance of acknowledging the role of the Holy Spirit in our lives that this book strongly reminds us of."

Dan Kimball

a pastor at Vintage Faith Church in Santa Cruz, California;
author of *They Like Jesus but Not the Church* (Zondervan, 2007), and *The Emerging Church* (Zondervan, 2003)

"What a great idea: theology through table talk! Patrick Oden invites the reader to listen in on a series of fictional conversations about the life of the Holy Spirit. The result is an invitation to focus on Jesus and to follow him by participating, and inviting others to participate, in the creative dance of the Holy Trinity. There is no dry or abstract theologizing here, only a highly-readable guide to the Holy Spirit that everyone will truly enjoy, from the seasoned pastor to the new Christian."

Frank D. Macchia
professor of theology, Vanguard University of Southern California, Costa Mesa; author of *Baptized in the Spirit: A Global Pentecostal Theology* (Zondervan, 2006)

"I read Patrick Oden's book with growing admiration. This new style of theology is a surprise from chapter to chapter. One is drawn into a proceeding conversation and is 'in' all of a sudden. I like chapter 9 on inciting creativity. The whole book is inspired by the creativity of the Spirit. It's a 'dance' in the vividness of the Spirit. Let this dance never end!"

Jürgen Moltmann
professor of theology, University of Tübingen, Germany

"Among the myriad new books on the emergent church that have appeared lately, Patrick Oden's book is different. It's a compelling dialogue, solid theology, and insightful biblical studies all rolled into one. Oden's book is an amazing combination of a Quaker understanding of the Holy Spirit with revolutionary insight for the renewal of the church in our time. This book is a great gift to the Friends Church and beyond. I plan to use this book as one of the required texts in my Theology and Culture class because it provides ready access to how critical thinking about the doctrine of the Holy Spirit interfaces with the role and function of the church in a missional context."

Carole Spencer
adjunct professor of church history and spiritual formation, George Fox Evangelical Seminary, Portland, Oregon

IT'S A DANCE

moving with the Holy Spirit

BY PATRICK ODEN

BARCLAY PRESS

Newberg, Oregon

IT'S A DANCE
Moving with the Holy Spirit

© 2007 by Patrick Oden

Published by
Barclay Press
211 N. Meridian St., #101
Newberg, OR 97132
800.962.4014
www.barclaypress.com

BOOK WEB SITE
www.itsadance.net

ISBN 978-1-59498-012-1

All Scripture quotations, unless otherwise noted, are taken from the
Holy Bible, New International Version ®. *NIV*®. Copyright © 1973,
1978, 1984 by International Bible Society. Used by permission of
Zondervan. All rights reserved.

Scripture quotations marked *KJV* are taken from the
King James Version.

Cover design by Darryl Brown

Acknowledgments & Dedication

Fifteen years ago John and Denise Fehlen put together a wonderful youth group and showed me light during a season of absolute darkness. They helped the seed of the Spirit blossom in my life, and reignited my passion for the broad work of God in this world. They renewed my love for the dance.

Following this I attended an unusual church—NewSong in San Dimas, California. It was the first "GenX" church. Dieter Zander was the head pastor, and his leadership brought some of the most dynamic and passionate young men and women together. From him I learned that the old patterns of church weren't set in stone. I learned new, life-changing ways God could reach me and those like me. At NewSong I got involved with a small group that still exemplifies Christian community in my mind. I saw there was something to church that extended way past sermons and singing. Thanks to Dieter and those in the Claremont Care Group, I knew God was doing something profound in the church, if we just stepped aside and let God do it. They taught me to enjoy dancing.

They taught me so well I wanted to know more. I went first to Wheaton College and then to Fuller Seminary. Both of these institutions provided a profound, reshaping influence that moved my heart, soul, and mind toward Christ and his kingdom. A few names stand out among the many influences. Dr. J. Julius Scott awakened my mind to church history—an awakening that has utterly transformed every part of my faith. Also shaping my mind were wonderful professors of the history department: Dr. Maas, Dr. Long, Dr. Rapp, and Dr. Noll who helped me understand history as a story worth knowing. Dr. Burge, Dr. Schultz, and others in the Bible/theology department helped me encounter

Scripture in a powerful way, helping me embrace it while diving deeper. Their faithful pursuit of God's revelation sparked a love for Scripture that I carried into this book.

At Fuller my first class was with Eddie Gibbs and his teaching assistant Ryan Bolger. This class opened my eyes to the study of the present church. Fuller is rich in professors with a deep knowledge of their discipline coupled with great experience in practical ministry, leading to class after class of development and sharpening. However, this book would not have been written without the influence and teaching of Veli-Matti Kärkkäinen. At Wheaton and at Fuller I learned the steps of the dance.

I was given new opportunities to lead and explore during my time at Fuller. Much of this came as I took on new roles at NewSong Church. Dennis Bachman and Eric Herron were particularly helpful. The space they gave, the times we participated together, the conversations we had, and the questions that arose, helped bring an urgency to my heart. God was not distant or passive. He was eager to move in the lives of his people. Those not on staff I worked among helped me find something more in ministry and taught me so much as I saw the Spirit working in them. Thanks to those at NewSong I learned how to lead in this dance.

I have been warned about publishers and the need to be wary. Yet, I was blessed beyond measure when Barclay Press accepted this manuscript. They are not just the publishers, they shared my excitement and from the beginning tracked with my goals and thoughts. Their suggestions and editing honed my writing and took it to a new level. Dan and Sierra, as well as others involved, helped make this process a sign of God's participation. They joined with me in the dance.

Others entered this process. Their support and friendship during the last few years were more valued than I likely ever expressed. They stuck by me and our conversations helped me sort through persistent questions. Their pursuit of God was a constant example and an encouragement. Izabela, Peter, Maria, Susan, Jon, my writers group, and others were my community, near and far, as I sought the dance.

Two people believed in me when no one else did. They encouraged me when I struggled. They supported me when I was in need. They taught me to love God and to wrestle with the depths. They talked with me and counseled me. They sacrificed, they prayed, they loved, they hoped, and they trusted that God was working in my life. In word and action they exemplified the work of the Spirit from my earliest days. They are my friends. They are my best teachers. This book is dedicated to them—my parents, Dave and Marie Oden—the best dancers I know.

Contents

Foreword \ xii

1. Looking for Something New \ 1

2. Focusing on Jesus \ 7

3. Breaking the Boundaries between Sacred and Secular \ 33

4. Drawing Us into Community \ 59

5. Empowering for Right Living \ 91

6. Welcoming Strangers \ 117

7. Spurring Us to Give \ 141

8. Provoking Participation \ 167

9. Inciting Creativity \ 193

10. Leading as a Body \ 217

11. Uniting Us through Worship \ 241

Bibliography \ 263

About these sources \ 265

Foreword

The book in your hands represents a very unusual and, dare I say, somewhat postmodern way of exploring a very complex and much-debated topic for the church—*pneumatology*. The doctrine of the Holy Spirit is a subject not often explored in so-called Emerging Missional Church (EMC) circles. But that is precisely the problem. This is *exactly* what we need at the moment—an approach to understanding the Holy Spirit that fits neatly into the ecclesial and spiritual exploration that is going on in the emerging church. The truth is that I can't think of one text from the ever-increasing EMC stable that even gets close to addressing the issues touched on in this sensitive work by Patrick Oden. Sure, there are the standard, heavy theological books on the subject, but none of them (as far as I am aware) pays specific attention to the particularity going on in the creative edges of the church. It's time the insiders of the movement began openly exploring the phenomenon of the Holy Spirit and appropriating the many gifts the Spirit brings to us.

Here we have an exploration of the role and power of the Holy Spirit that actually gets us beyond the caricatures that so readily suggest themselves to us. Using a narrative approach—rather than the more conventional concept-based approach to theologizing—Patrick ably guides us beyond rigid fundamentalism, wet-noodle liberalism, and technique-based ecclesiology to a kind of direct engagement with the Spirit that is as wholesome as it is life-transforming. To do this, he has adopted the excellent framework set out by

Eddie Gibbs and Ryan K. Bolger in their definitive book *Emerging Churches,* and has cleverly woven his story around it. Or perhaps it has woven its influence into Patrick's story. In a strange way this mutuality of framework and story provides an inadvertent metaphor of the role of Holy Spirit in our lives and/or ours in his. The title, *It's a Dance,* gives us both the feel of the book as well as what it means to truly walk in the Spirit.

Let me admit that I write this foreword as a clandestine Pentecostal. I have been touched, and therefore forever changed, by the divine flame of God. But why "clandestine" then? The last fifteen years have been a self-imposed exile from the movement in which I came to faith in Jesus. This was brought on by sheer disgust in the distortions of Christianity so evident in the excesses of the Pentecostal-Charismatic movement, currently enamoured with technique-based fundamentalism and TBN-type manipulations. In the meantime I have made a wonderful and rather cozy ecclesiological home among the EMC tribe that is only beginning to influence the direction of the church in the West. I love my tribe and I really believe it contains the seeds of the future of Christianity in the West. But I have to confess that I have long felt that an elusive *something* is still missing. A circle has yet to be completed and a torch has yet to be kindled.

I have thought long and hard about this and have to say that the only way I can understand this lack, this spiritual deficiency, is that we are missing that sacred fire that is the Spirit of God. For all the good theology, sociology, missiology, ecclesiology, and every other possible "ology," there has been precious little pneumatology going down in the EMC. Great ideas, serious discussion, and brave experimentation are just good ideas, words, and wilful human effort, until the Spirit breathes and gives them life. With this book by Patrick Oden, we have at last started the journey.

Alan Hirsch, author of *The Forgotten Ways*
and *The Shaping of Things to Come*
and founding director of
Forge Mission Training Network

" I want to know what makes people get up on a Sunday morning, put on their nice clothes, and go to a fancy building," [says Luke's editor, Mitch]. I want to know what they're looking for, why they think their particular place of worship answers their questions. I want to know what these people are looking for and whether or not they are finding it."

"All I'm seeing so far looks to me like all the same thing, just packaged differently," I tell Mitch. "But I'll keep looking."

"Well that's a great idea," he answers. Mitchell Orion Moffett III is a stocky man, no taller than five feet six inches and no lighter than two hundred pounds. He's sixty-eight years old, almost entirely bald. The hair on his head must have decided to migrate south, for he has the most amazing mustache—a mustache that would have made Mark Twain jealous. About forty years ago, in honor of his pioneer roots, he decided to start a weekly magazine highlighting the peculiarities of Southern California life. The first issue of the *California Clarion* was published five months later. He's kept at it ever since.

"Maybe a series?" I continue.

"A series, eh? Well, that's something right there. Yeah—you could tour around the area and visit different churches. Talk to the clergy, see what they believe. Find out what religion looks like in our neck of the woods."

Mitch is entirely nonreligious. But it is the old kind of nonreligious—the kind entirely uninterested in anything spiritual while retaining the utmost respect for the institution of religion. He thinks the same way about baseball.

"What kind of approach should I take?" I ask.

"Well, I mean it's your story—so whatever you want to do. We'll make it a regular feature for a few months—maybe more if it gets a good reaction. Now if it were me I'd try to write it from the perspective of someone looking for a church. Nothing too critical, but honest, you see. Something for our religious readers to get a kick out of. We've done too many restaurants and exposés. Everyone does celebrity weddings and divorces. If we start doing those we might as well pack up right now because our mission is over. We don't want that. We need to do different and interesting. I want to stick with what we do best. That means getting to the heart of real life around here. Churches are part of the culture, more so than restaurants and starlets. Frank over at the *Review*—you remember him—told me

1

Looking for Something New

"So what are churches like in this area?" my editor, N
one spring afternoon, just as I am wrapping up an
local mechanics who cheat their customers.

It is a big story, with heroes and villains, victim
quishers. At least that's how I decided to write it.
mundane so I spiced up the narrative with a little mec
There are magicians among us, who wield arcane kno
our benefit. Or our abuse.

"Uh, well, that depends on the church,"
"Churches are all different. It's like asking what resta
like in this area."

"We've done that," he responds. "About twe1
Now I think it's time to see what kind of religion is
around here."

I'm fairly certain he asked me because I am a
Only I don't know how much of an insider I am any
been a long time since I've gone to church on a Sunda
whatever it is I am supposed to feel.

"Do you want me to write about this, Mitch?" I a

the other day about a really big religious movement that started not too far from here. What's the one with the dancing and hand raising and wild talk?"

"Pentecostals," I reply, and laugh. He could be quite innocently offensive at times.

"Yeah. Big movement. Started here, Frank said, then went all over the world. I never knew that. I felt really stupid when I had to plead ignorance. I hate feeling stupid. I especially hate feeling stupid in front of Frank. I'm supposed to make him feel stupid. It's a tradition. I like traditions. Fact is everyone in our business is afraid of talking religion now. Frank knows something, but won't write about it. He's too busy talking about celebrities. Too many people think of Hollywood and movie stars when they think of L.A. They don't think of spirituality. I want to change that. Religion is a big topic in this world, Luke. It's a big topic here too. I want to learn what we're doing these days. I'd get a kick out of that."

My questions about what to do next are answered.

"Not just the big churches, Luke. I want to know all sorts, even some of the kooky ones. But don't describe them like that. Let the reader decide. Visit the Cathedral—the big glass church in Orange County—other big ones too, but try to be—what's the word?"

"Diverse?"

"Ecumenical. Visit all types. I want to learn something. Something Frank doesn't know. And I want both our religious readers and the nonreligious ones to get something they will enjoy reading. I realize this will keep you from going to your church, is that okay? Well, you can use your church too. But only once. I don't want to show partiality. I can have someone else do this series, if this is a problem."

"No," I answer. "It's not a problem at all."

"Okay. Run with it."

He walks away and leaves me to my new task.

Some of the choices are obvious. I make the right calls and get interviews with pastors. The series turns out to be popular and Mitch encourages me to continue.

"Keep looking for something new," he tells me each time I see him. "Something that would match what Frank talked about. Did you know that William Randolph Hearst helped bring Billy Graham to the attention of the world in the 1950s? That's huge. Imagine if we got a scoop like that? I like what you've been doing, but I don't feel like we've hit gold yet. Keep digging. Dig deeper. I want to know what's going on but I also want to know something Frank doesn't know. I want to know what makes people get up on a Sunday morning, put on their nice clothes, and go to a fancy building. I want to know what they're looking for, why they think their particular place of worship answers their questions. I want to know what these people are looking for and whether or not they are finding it."

"All I'm seeing so far looks to me like all the same thing, just packaged differently," I tell Mitch. "But I'll keep looking."

"You do that," he says.

I continue to visit different denominations and traditions. I don't find anything Mitch or Frank would really consider gold.

"Luke," Phyllis the receptionist calls to me as I walk out of the office on a bright Tuesday afternoon.

"Yeah," I reply and stop at her desk. She's been a fixture in the office since Mitch started. I doubt there is anyone of any importance in Southern California who she can't call within ten minutes. Phyllis is the secret weapon of the *Clarion*.

"My niece has a suggestion about a church you should visit. The Upper Room is its name."

"What kind of church is it?" I ask. Phyllis is an entrenched Presbyterian herself. I had already visited five different Presbyterian churches and had that approach pretty well covered.

"The kind my niece finds interesting. She gave me the phone number and told me I should tell you about it. She says it's really different. *I* wouldn't visit, that's for certain. But I told her you might be willing to try it out."

"Alright," I say. "I'm definitely willing to try something out of the ordinary."

She gives me the number. I call the next day.

"Hi, this is Jennifer," a woman answers.

"I'm calling about the Upper Room," I say, then proceed to tell her about my series and ask if I can meet with the pastor before attending the service.

Jennifer laughs and says, "Sure. Are you free at ten tomorrow morning?"

"The pastor will be free?"

"I'm sure he can find some space in his schedule," she replies. "You have our address, right?"

"Yeah."

"Ten o'clock then," she says.

"Should I meet him in his office?"

She laughs again. "No, just come through our main doors; he'll meet you there."

I hang up and wonder why she was laughing.

" *The Spirit always focuses on Jesus. We focus through the Spirit on Jesus. If we're distracted from Jesus we've lost the Spirit. It's the same Spirit, don't you see? That's the brilliance of it all. Instead of pursuing Jesus through the Spirit we do all sorts of other things to replace the Spirit. In doing this we miss Jesus. We'd rather do what we think makes total sense and seems right to our logic. Scripture says that's not the way it goes—scandal to the Jews and foolishness to the Greeks, as Paul put it.*"

2

Focusing on Jesus

"Hunting truth is no easy task; we must look everywhere for its tracks." I forget who first said this but the words have stayed with me since college. I decided to be a journalist when I heard this quote. It was in a religion class, but it didn't lead me to pursue religion. Instead I wanted to get out into the world. I wanted to be someone who could tell others the truth about things and find where it led. Maybe that's why this series on churches became so interesting for me. Yet I still couldn't quite see the tracks. I think I lost the trail in some proverbial river and now find myself on the other side trying to pick it up again. I keep poking around the brush, looking under rocks, taking steps down various paths. There is something. I know it. There has to be something out there that answers the whispers in my soul and leads me to a deeper truth.

"No pressure," I say to myself. "Only my soul."

I laugh at my private sarcasm as I pull my Jetta into a parking garage not too far from the church. Taking this stuff too seriously was likely the worst thing for my soul.

I lock the car and walk down the block. I don't see a church or anything that suggests a church, only restaurants, bookstores, even a small art gallery. I don't see anything suggesting sacred space. Maybe I heard the street name wrong. I get worried when the large white numbers on a canvas awning match those on my Post-it Note.

I've learned by now that steeples and crosses aren't very common, especially with smaller churches. And space is hard to come by in Pasadena. If a community of faith hadn't found a nice plot of land sometime in the earlier part of the twentieth century, it likely had to do something a little more, well, makeshift.

Over the last weeks I've seen churches in gyms, in rented space in shopping centers, and occupying the basements of larger churches. I've been in all sorts of curious locations that at least once a week host a pastor, a congregation, and a worship band. Churches often pop up wherever space can be foraged.

Still, this address must be wrong. What I see is very nice. Only it definitely isn't a church. The dark green canopy over the outdoor patio in front reads "The Columba Pub & Restaurant." It's an all-brick building, an old-looking building, or at least what passes for old in Southern California, which means it may date as far back as the 1920s. The pub itself has dark green outdoor furniture on the patio, with light padded chairs and metal tables matching the canopy above. Two heaters stand between the tables to provide warmth on cool evenings. Inside, the furniture is dark, heavy wood; the room is decorated in the model of a European pub. It is very inviting, even if it is not particularly Sunday-morning inviting.

Most of the tables are empty. It's early yet. A man and woman sit close together away from the door, not paying attention to the world around them. Near the entrance another man sits with a cup of coffee in front of him and a newspaper in his hands. I dare say he's reading the people walking by more than the print on the page. He stares at me for a moment, then looks past me. Apparently he finds the two older women carrying large Macy's bags more interesting.

I look around some more and see a sign in another doorway of the pub. The sign reads "Upper Room." An arrow points up the stairs.

A tall, thin man with a five o'clock shadow comes through the doorway and says to me, "Hey, I'm Nate."

"From the Upper Room?" I ask, pointing to the sign.

"Yeah," he says. "Are you Luke?"

"How did you know?"

"You look lost. I've seen that look before when people are given our address and little else."

His dark hair falls over his forehead in a particularly ordered mess. Instead of a suit and tie, he's wearing a T-shirt with a red and yellow square covering the front. His expression is familiar—a combination of earnest interest and probing assessment. I've seen many pastors with this look, yet there is a different quality to Nate's demeanor. I can see it right away. It is both unsettling and curious.

His posture seems unhurried and relaxed, not qualities I have associated with many pastors. Only two, now that I think about it. Both were older men, nearing retirement. Nate is young, in his early thirties.

"So what brings you by, Luke?" he asks.

We sit down in the deep seats of the heavy wood booth.

"I'm doing a series of articles, Nate. On churches."

"Ah, right. Very interesting stuff."

"You've been following along?"

"You've made quite a stir in the church world," he laughs. "Free advertising is hard to come by. As is positive coverage these days."

"I'm trying to be fair and see with open eyes."

"That's quite a trick," Nate replies. "What have you seen? Anything stand out?"

"Not really. Nothing unexpected."

"No tips for me?" he asks. "I'm trying to get a feel for the competition. Anything to improve our market share would be great."

"Who do you see as your competition?"

"I'm kidding," he laughs. "We're not competing with anyone. We're just here doing our thing, praying for our souls, watching for people who might share our passion."

"What is your passion?"

"The world, Luke. The world. How about you? What is your passion?"

"I'm not sure I have a passion," I reply and laugh. "Only deadlines."

"Well, that does keep a person going. Do you go to church or are you an explorer deep in the rainforest, marveling at the strange new plants and animals while watching out for poisonous snakes and restless natives?"

"No. I've attended church pretty regularly, ever since high school. This is a lot more like doing an article on extended family. I don't know all the details, but I do know the agenda."

"How's the family doing? It's been a while since we got everyone together for a potluck."

"Yeah," I laugh. "Good and bad, like all families. But I'm trying to focus on the good. There's more than enough out there about the bad. To be honest, I'm also trying to find something."

"Something for yourself?"

"Yeah. I guess. I'm a little church weary, to be honest. Not just because of this series. Before I started. Burnout or something. So, I'm researching. This series came at a good time for me. Hopefully."

I've found that framing conversations in terms of my personal journey helps bring out a little more from pastors. They become more open. It's a ploy, but not an altogether dishonest one.

"If you don't mind my asking," Nate responds, "Why *hopefully*?"

"I want to find that spark again. I fell into a rut. I don't even know where to start."

"Starting is the hardest bit. Well, that and the muddy middle, and sometimes getting to the end is pretty rough too. It is a worthwhile trip, though. Have any new insights about your quest?"

"I suppose a few, but not as many as I'd like. Which is why I'm eager to hear what others think. What have you found?" I ask. "Do you have anything to help a fellow traveler find his way in a complicated world?"

"Ah, keeping me on focus," he replies and laughs. "I tend to avoid talking about myself if I can. Other people seem a lot more interesting so I want to hear who they are and what they're up to, you know. I'm just a guy, sitting in a pub."

"Who apparently heads a church. At least that's what I'm told."

"I'm told that too," he laughs. "Sometimes. But, since you're here for a story I guess I should oblige. What do you want to know?"

"Tell me about your church. And don't try to turn the conversation back around to me. I'm wise to the ways of pastors."

We both laugh. The waitress comes by with a glass of water.

"Anything to drink or eat?" she asks.

"A Coke would be great," I say.

The waitress smiles and walks off.

"Alright," Nate says, "You want to know about the Upper Room. Anything particular?"

"How about starting with the most basic? I'm still pretty confused about where you all meet. Your church is upstairs, above a pub?"

"No," he replies.

"It isn't? So where is your church? In someone's home? Somewhere nearby?"

"No, the pub isn't downstairs from the church because this is the church, upstairs and downstairs. It's all part of who we are."

"The pub is part of the church?"

"Yeah, the place we eat and drink is infused with the rest of our activities. Upstairs is our more purposeful area of prayer, worship, and discussion. It's also where I sleep, but that's beside the point. Downstairs is where we participate with everyone. We also run the coffee shop/bookstore next door. For, um, coffee and books. Our hope is to have places where people can gather and feel comfortable."

"So the Upper Room is what?" I ask.

"Just that, an upper room—upstairs. The first week we were here, before the Columba opened for business, we were sitting around a table trying to think of a name for our community. Jen, one of our founding members—you spoke with her on the phone I think—said she was tired of talking and was going to go to the upper room to pray about it. We realized the symbolism, so we started calling it that. We had our name. Soon after that we had our Web site" (www.itsadance.net).

"Why this approach? Why here? Is this about being trendy or relevant?"

"I ask myself the same question every day," Nate says with a chuckle. "Really, it all came down to Jesus."

"Jesus told you to start a new church in a pub?" I ask.

"No, though that would make a better story. I was looking for Jesus. It seems he wanted me to find him here, because that's how the Holy Spirit worked things out."

"What do you mean?" I ask.

"I was an assistant minister in charge of spiritual formation. You know, Christian education stuff. I led Bible studies, taught classes on Scripture and on theology. Did a lot of discipling. I had been in this position for about six months when everything started to feel really dry. I was supposed to be in charge of helping people find maturity, but I felt I was just babysitting. I couldn't shake the feeling I had no right to be the babysitter. I realized how much I didn't know. I had a seminary education. I'd spent my whole life in church and leading church ministries. But that wasn't enough. Everything looked wrong. I couldn't shake the feeling I was missing something important."

"Was it that bad?"

"Once I started seeing it this way I couldn't see anything else. Most people would have said our church was thriving. We had all sorts of programs. Thousands of people came each week. My classes were filled. We had the best high school group in town. We were evangelizing. Our worship team put out a CD. Everything seemed great. Some weeks I didn't take a day off because there was so much going on. But it felt dry and empty. The feeling wouldn't leave. All I saw were people going through the motions."

"So what did you do?"

"I started praying. I mean real, honest prayer. After a few weeks of this I felt even worse. Can you believe it? So I had a talk with some of my friends—folks I trusted to pray for me and be honest with me. We started to pray together. It was funny because when I shared how I felt, they all admitted feeling the same way. Only they never admitted this to anyone else. They thought everyone else seemed excited about the church. Turns out people were excited because they assumed others were excited. We realized there was a turnover, in which folks were excited, got burned out and left after a few years, to be replaced by new people. So the ministries seemed steady. Just different faces. I guess there were people genuinely excited, only God didn't lead me to talk with them, or lead them to talk with me."

I nod and say, "A couple of churches I've been to are dealing with this. Well, not always exactly this. Some are not getting any new folks to fill in. It's the same small group of people doing all the work. Getting excited but then always following it with disappointment when no one else steps up."

"I bet they were exhausted."

"They didn't say it, but I could see a weariness and hear the frustration. So what did you do? Did you pray for guidance?"

"No," Nate answers, "that's the funny thing. At first I prayed for guidance but that felt so selfish. It wasn't about me, you know; I was feeling for the church. So I started praying for the church—for all the other pastors and for the congregation. The small group of us started praying like this, praying for the Holy Spirit to really do something. I needed someone to take away the dryness and give us real life. God needed to be the leader."

"Did your prayers make a difference?"

"Well after about a month I was thumbing through my Bible, without any real purpose, just because it was there. I began reading Isaiah. I couldn't stop. That had never happened, you know. I read it all the way through. Sixty-six chapters. Took me all day. Then I felt like just reading Matthew. The next day I finished Matthew and started Mark. It all seemed so totally new to me. I can't explain it. I'd grown up in the church and suddenly I felt like I had never read these stories before. Each little interaction seemed totally new and fresh. Parts of Jesus' teaching and the images in his parables stood out. I had never noticed some of this stuff before, even though I had preached on it. Now it seemed so obvious."

"What do you think it was?"

"For whatever reason, this Jesus character grabbed me. I don't mean that disrespectfully. He just never seemed a real person before. I know I talked about Jesus, lots of times. But it wasn't from my heart. When I finished John I couldn't stop talking about Jesus in a new way."

"So you prayed for the Holy Spirit to come and you became fixated on Jesus?"

"Yeah," Nate answers. "Funny isn't it? Like it all was translated from a totally different language. I didn't get it before, and then it became so totally clear. That changed everything. It was my Pentecost."

> **When the** day of Pentecost came, they were all together in one place. Suddenly a sound like the blowing of a violent wind came from heaven and filled the whole house where they were sitting. They saw what seemed to be tongues of fire that separated and came to

rest on each of them. All of them were filled with the Holy Spirit and began to speak in other tongues as the Spirit enabled them.

Now there were staying in Jerusalem God-fearing Jews from every nation under heaven. When they heard this sound, a crowd came together in bewilderment, because each one heard them speaking in his own language. Utterly amazed, they asked: "Are not all these men who are speaking Galileans? Then how is it that each of us hears them in his own native language? Parthians, Medes and Elamites; residents of Mesopotamia, Judea and Cappadocia, Pontus and Asia, Phrygia and Pamphylia, Egypt and the parts of Libya near Cyrene; visitors from Rome (both Jews and converts to Judaism) Cretans and Arabs—we hear them declaring the wonders of God in our own tongues!" Amazed and perplexed, they asked one another, "What does this mean?"

Some, however, made fun of them and said, "They have had too much wine." *(Acts 2:1-13)*

"So what exactly changed?" I ask. "Did you see fire over your head?"

He laughs, then says, "Well, no fire over my head. It was a fire inside. Everything changed. I realized I had been spending my life telling people about Christ, but not of Christ, you know what I mean?"

"No."

"Jesus was this person I knew about, but didn't really know. Jesus saves, right? But what does that mean? Salvation isn't just pie in the sky, Luke. It's everything. Jesus saves. So what? Saves me from what? If nothing changes, if there's not a difference in my life, what does 'Jesus saves' mean? What does that mean to me, to my life, to the lives of my friends now? What does that mean to people who are really struggling, like the people Jesus met on the street and who were desperate to touch him? They didn't want some eternal salvation. They wanted to be saved, saved from their present. I realized I didn't know how Jesus saves."

"Eternal salvation," I suggest. "Cleansed from your sins, your name written in the Book of Life."

"Of course, yeah, that's part of it. But, here's what got to me—eternal salvation is just part of it and we've made it all of it."

To be honest I'm still not sure what to make of Nate. He seems very passionate, but passion isn't always a sign of being right. I like him. He's very personable. But that worries me a little bit. Each time he speaks I expect that's when he's going to say something really off-the-wall, maybe heretical. But he hasn't. I feel like he's walking the line without crossing it, though maybe I just need to push a little to see it.

"What more is there?" I ask.

"We have seen Jesus at the gate, and nothing else. That's our whole message. Get saved. Save others. Jesus was about something greater. It's a lot more than what we think, but we've lost sight of a holistic understanding of salvation because we've lost sight of Jesus. We've made him into someone we can manage and control."

"So you are saying we don't know Jesus?" I ask.

"No, not really. Well, maybe. That's not a slam. I mean that's a funny part of the Gospels. Even the disciples never really knew Jesus. They kept asking him if they could be his best friend, or if this was when he was going to restore the physical kingdom of Israel, or other really off-the-wall questions. I'm sure Jesus hit his head at how totally clueless they were on occasion. No one really got Jesus. Maybe a few people did, like the centurion, or some of the lepers, or Mary."

"Which one?"

"Which Mary?" Nate laughs. "Well, I'm talking about Mary of Mary and Martha fame. I mean even Jesus' mother knew who he was, but she didn't get him. Not for a while at least. She would say, 'Stop all this bother, Jesus, and either get to work or come home and be a good son.' The other Mary sat at his feet and listened, you know. Which means even if she didn't understand who Jesus really was, she at least had the good sense to realize it. We don't. Pastors don't. Other people don't. We're all Pharisees in a way, committed to our version of the Law, and making Jesus our standard bearer. We make our own Jesus and insist everyone take our word for it."

"Whatever cause we value becomes Jesus' cause, right?" I had a conversation about this earlier in the week with an old friend from college, a friend who had just left his church because of political disagreements.

"Yeah. We've made ourselves the lord of our Lord, putting him to work doing whatever it is we think he should do, and making him support everything we support. He's become this icon for our own beliefs. We're supposed to be icons of his beliefs, but that's too much work for us. Too much of a challenge."

"He demands too much?" I ask.

"No, it's too much of a challenge to admit that we're not Jesus. Our egos don't want to admit that Jesus really was his own person. That's what the disciples ran into. That's what the Pharisees and the Sadducees ran into. That's what they all ran into. Jesus was his own man, he was *the* Man. A person had to deal with him as he was. Jesus didn't adapt. He fulfilled the Law but broke the law of the Pharisees. He welcomed the sinners, ate with them, laughed with them, but at the same time held to a very strict code of holiness and demanded others follow the same. No one could pin him down. Those who thought they could were blasted. Only the folks who let him be himself found his favor, you know. He was the most real person ever—more real than anyone else. More real than the culture. He defined his own culture. People had to either accept him or deny him. They couldn't reshape him, so they crucified him."

"You're saying they crucified Jesus because he wouldn't play their game?"

"Exactly. Faced with the fact Jesus didn't play to their pet causes, these people realized that his reality was a lot more subversive than anything they had met. Everything, anything, can be used as a tool. But if that tool won't be used, then it's better off destroyed."

"I think I get what you're saying," I reply.

"Now we aren't faced with Jesus in the flesh. We have doctrine and theology. We have our version of the gospel, which never really has to encounter Jesus for who he is. We have words with lots of syllables and all sorts of doctrines we argue about to prove we are champions of God. We can use him and abuse him, putting him to work for our own pet projects, always getting him to support our structures, or power, or values."

"We make Jesus into our own image. Except for the sin."

"Except for the sin, of course. But that's the really funny thing. Our obsession with sin becomes itself sin. We make sin into such a huge thing that's all we can see."

"I don't get what you're saying, Nate."

"That's why Jesus had a problem with the Pharisees. Jesus condemned the lot of them. Not because they sinned, but because they missed the point and made God into a reflection of their own emphases. They talked. They didn't listen. They were busy about their business, like Martha, but didn't sit and listen like Mary. The Law became their focus. Jesus was interested in where the Law was pointing, not the Law itself. Jesus is about pointing toward the Father, not pointing toward sin."

"The disciples finally got it, and passed it on through the New Testament."

"Yeah, they did," Nate says. "Of course they did; that's why you and I are sitting here talking about it now. In a way this makes it more difficult. It's the subtle things—being right, but not being totally right. Or emphasizing parts, but missing a whole lot of other parts. I love the story of the upstart Paul who had to correct the chosen disciple, Peter, for missing the mark when he began to insist on kosher food laws again.* That's a warning to all of us really."

"So how do we get past making Jesus into ourselves? If we can't get past misusing Jesus, how do we know what to do? What can people depend on? What's our model? Do we depend on church tradition? The examples of pastors? Good preaching? Jesus is not here, so where do we get our answers?"

"Ah, Luke, that's where you're wrong. Well, yeah, he's not here, but he *is* here. He told us he would be here, and he told us exactly how he would be here. Only it's not what so many of us have decided to teach."

"What did he say? How do we know him?"

"The Spirit. It's in the Gospel of John. Jesus tells us we can know him. We have the gift of knowing him. We have the joy of knowing him. All of us, Luke. We can all know him. The Spirit teaches us all things. That's the beauty of it all. I had missed Jesus because I was busy like Martha and forgot to listen to what Jesus was saying. I forgot to listen to Jesus' words in John 15."

When the Counselor comes, whom I will send to you from the Father, the Spirit of truth who goes out from the Father, he will testify about me. And you also must testify, for you have been with me from the beginning.

All this I have told you so that you will not go astray. They will put you out of the synagogue; in fact, a time is coming when anyone who kills you will think he is offering a service to God. They will do such things

---

* *Galatians 2:11-21*

because they have not known the Father or me. I have told you this, so that when the time comes you will remember that I warned you. I did not tell you this at first because I was with you.

Now I am going to him who sent me, yet none of you asks me, 'Where are you going?' Because I have said these things, you are filled with grief. But I tell you the truth: It is for your good that I am going away. Unless I go away, the Counselor will not come to you; but if I go, I will send him to you. When he comes, he will convict the world of guilt in regard to sin and righteousness and judgment: in regard to sin, because men do not believe in me; in regard to righteousness, because I am going to the Father, where you can see me no longer; and in regard to judgment, because the prince of this world now stands condemned.

I have much more to say to you, more than you can now bear. But when he, the Spirit of truth, comes, he will guide you into all truth. He will not speak on his own; he will speak only what he hears, and he will tell you what is yet to come. He will bring glory to me by taking from what is mine and making it known to you. All that belongs to the Father is mine. That is why I said the Spirit will take from what is mine and make it known to you.

In a little while you will see me no more, and then after a little while you will see me. *(John 15:26—16:16)*

"We have an opportunity to see Jesus, Luke. The Spirit is our access to Jesus. The Spirit is here calling us to pursue Jesus. This is what Jesus said. This is what he told us. This is our path to life."

"How do we know Jesus through the Spirit? Are you talking about something different than Scripture?"

"The disciples had a real, living memory of Jesus and they were given the Holy Spirit," Nate says. "They still stumbled at times. We have the Holy Spirit but we also have Scripture and our own discernment. Folks who know the Scriptures the absolute best still make major errors with their interpretations. This was true in Jesus' time and it's true now. We make similar mistakes today because we don't use what we've been given. We don't tap into our real authority."

"The Holy Spirit?"

"We forget about the Spirit, Luke. We have the Spirit doing tricks or thrown on like tinsel around our Christmas tree. But, we don't know the Spirit or how the Spirit works. Because of this we have no idea who Jesus is, or what he is about. So we've been preaching an anemic gospel. It is so filled with our own expectations and interests it has only a fraction of the power we see in Pentecost. We still wallow in all our sins and frustrations because we have forgotten the work of God is significantly more than salvation. We're not just saved, Luke. We have been called heirs. What is it that heirs do?"

"Wait for the inheritance," I reply.

"They wait and they watch, learning what it is they have inherited and learning how to live in a way that honors the inheritance."

"How do we live like that now?"

"What does Paul say?" Nate prods.

"We're justified by faith in Christ Jesus."

"Is that all?"

"What else?"

"He adds to that in other places. Take his letter to Titus for instance."

> **At one** time we too were foolish, disobedient, deceived and enslaved by all kinds of passions and pleasures. We lived in malice and envy, being hated and hating one another. But when the kindness and love of God our

Savior appeared, he saved us, not because of righteous things we had done, but because of his mercy. He saved us through the washing of rebirth and renewal by the Holy Spirit, whom he poured out on us generously through Jesus Christ our Savior, so that, having been justified by his grace, we might become heirs having the hope of eternal life. This is a trustworthy saying. And I want you to stress these things, so that those who have trusted in God may be careful to devote themselves to doing what is good. These things are excellent and profitable for everyone. *(Titus 3:3-8)*

"We have been reborn and renewed by the Holy Spirit," Nate continues, "who does more than save us from death. The Spirit renews us so that we can finally learn how to live—how to live like Jesus lived. That's all through Paul. You're saved, so now go do what it is you are called to do."

"So we need to focus on the Spirit?"

"No, that's the great thing. We need to focus on Jesus. The Spirit always focuses on Jesus. We focus through the Spirit on Jesus. If we're distracted from Jesus we've lost the Spirit. It's the same Spirit, don't you see? That's the brilliance of it all. Instead of pursuing Jesus through the Spirit we do all sorts of other things to replace the Spirit. In doing this we miss Jesus. We'd rather do what we think makes total sense and seems right to our logic. Scripture says that's not the way it goes—scandal to the Jews and foolishness to the Greeks, as Paul put it."

"No one is happy," I say. "People want their religion to make sense. Is that what you are saying?"

"Yes! Now all we want is acceptable and sensible. We want order and systems and patterns all which, oddly enough, make the Spirit extraneous. Not in doctrine. No, we keep the Spirit language. We might even speak in tongues, but all too often it's an addition, an extra, which isn't at the core of who we are. The Spirit is dangerous, you see, just as Jesus is dangerous. When we become really in tune with the Spirit we become increasingly like Jesus, and that upsets all sorts of order and power structures."

"So, this is why you couldn't stay at your church?" I ask, trying to hold on to the interview.

"Maybe. I don't know. I think I could have stayed but that's not how things worked out. I wanted to experiment a little bit. I wanted to see exactly what it would be like if we built a church based on something deeper. What if we took some of the great stuff that's being discussed in theological circles and really threw ourselves into discovering what the Holy Spirit is doing? A group of us asked that. Things worked out. Here we are, still working that out."

"A Holy Spirit church, right."

"Yeah. Which sounds obvious in a way and off track in another way. Of course, the church needs the Spirit, but the church is the church of Christ, right? This is why at the heart of our talking about the Spirit we keep in mind the Spirit is always leading a person toward Jesus. The Spirit is the only way anyone can find Jesus."

"So what does it mean to have the Spirit lead you toward Jesus? How does that look any different from what everyone else is doing? Or maybe I should ask an even more foundational question: Why do you say the Holy Spirit focuses us on Jesus? I thought it was Jesus who led us to the Holy Spirit. Once we find Christ we find all the gifts and the fruit of the Spirit. That's what I've been taught."

"That's what I thought too. Ephesians says something like that."

> And you also were included in Christ when you heard the word of truth, the gospel of your salvation. Having believed, you were marked in him with a seal, the promised Holy Spirit, who is a deposit guaranteeing

our inheritance until the redemption of those who are
God's possession—to the praise of his glory.
(Ephesians 1:13-14)

"So what we thought does seem right," he adds. "Only it's
not all Paul says on this subject. He continues in chapter three."

In reading this, then, you will be able to understand
my insight into the mystery of Christ, which was not
made known to men in other generations as it has now
been revealed by the Spirit to God's holy apostles and
prophets. *(Ephesians 3:4-5)*

"Paul is talking about his call to the Gentiles here," Nate
continues, "but what he is saying goes beyond that topic. The
mystery of Christ was revealed by the Spirit. This was true
when John baptized Jesus and it is still true. Jesus is revealed by
the Spirit. We know Christ through the Spirit. We know Christ
only through the Spirit. We think we know Jesus first, and that
through Jesus we can discover the Spirit. That has totally im-
pacted our entire philosophy of church, and not for the better
because it's not following what Jesus himself said, nor what any
of the apostles said. This is one of those curious times in which
really complex theological discussions have totally important,
practical results."

"What do you mean?"

"Well, the church, a thousand years ago, put in a little
phrase in the Nicene Creed, and this caused the united church to
make its first real split into two different parts, East and West."

"What did they add?"

"You know in the last section of the Nicene Creed—'We
believe in the Holy Spirit'? They added 'and the Son' to 'who
proceeds from the Father,' making it 'We believe in the Holy
Spirit who proceeds from the Father and the Son.'"

"Wow, that seems terrible. How could they possibly do such an awful thing?"

"I know! I appreciate your enthusiasm even if it's not sincere."

"So, what does it mean?"

"Basically, they put the Holy Spirit underneath Christ, making Jesus the source of the Spirit, and in doing this they essentially made the church the authority over the Spirit because they saw the church as the primary representative of Jesus."

This is getting deep and I'm not sure what to say. Nate's comments feel uncomfortably close to a religious conspiracy theory.

"Who can argue against Jesus having priority?" Nate continues. "Jesus revealed himself in a specific way. This sometimes differs from how the church has taught about Jesus, often putting too much emphasis on him alone. We have to respect what Jesus said, respect what Paul said about Jesus and the Spirit in Ephesians. Jesus is the priority. The Father and the Spirit are equally the priorities. That's the Trinity. When Jesus is placed ahead we get distorted priorities and distorted representation. But the Gospels seem to indicate that this isn't the case at all. Jesus did send the Spirit, but it was the Spirit who sent Jesus too."

"That is getting complicated."

"Totally, but beautiful in a way. What it means is that the church doesn't control the Spirit, and it doesn't control Jesus. The church is a gift to us from God. It is a way to gather and grow together, but it is not the authority. All because the Spirit isn't owned by the church."

"Can we do whatever we want and call it the Spirit?"

"No, I'm not suggesting anarchy," Nate says and laughs. "I'm suggesting humility. If even Jesus—and thus the whole church—is empowered by the work of the Spirit, then all our assumed authority over each other is a sham. The Spirit doesn't need any of us, and any one of us can be empowered to be in charge. God chose Saul to be king of Israel, then chucked Saul out the window. David replaced him. Control and power can become a heresy of sorts because in trying to hold onto our power structures we deny the broader work of the Spirit in this world. In doing that we lose out on a significant amount of our own power and message. By asserting power we lose power."

"Explain."

"Deb," Nate calls out to the waitress. "What's the Christian life without the Spirit?"

"Like a car without a battery, Nate," Deb hollers back without stopping on her way from a table to the kitchen.

He looks back at me and smiles, then repeats, "Like a car without a battery. You can have all the features in the world: comfortable seats, leather interior, great stereo with satellite radio, GPS, seat warmers, fast engine, great paint job. But without a battery, nothing turns on and you don't go anywhere. A lot of the church, Luke, is like that. They take you to their car show and tell you all about the wonderful features. But the car doesn't go anywhere because instead of a battery they have a cardboard box."

"So you're saying the church has gotten it all wrong then? That's a pretty arrogant thing to say."

"Well," Nate says, "it might be a little arrogant but if it is, it's not my arrogance. It's in Scripture. Peter himself said, 'For Christ died for sins once for all, the righteous for the unrighteous, to bring you to God. He was put to death in the body but made alive by the Spirit.'* Jesus was born by the Spirit. Jesus was killed by men. Jesus was brought to life again by the Spirit. Do you get this?"

"People get Jesus wrong and so do the wrong things. It is the Spirit who brings life to it all. Is that it?"

---

* *1 Peter 3:18*

"It's not that they got it totally wrong, it's more that they missed out on a good bit. This comes from reading Scripture with a purpose or a filter."

"So, tell me how it is you say the Spirit sent Jesus as much as Jesus sent the Spirit?"

"Don't let me tell you, Luke; let's look in the Bible. Matthew chapter one establishes the identity of Jesus. The rest of the Bible assumes a lot, but this first chapter of the New Testament puts Jesus into history. It shows us where he was placed, how he was placed, and who he was placed with. Most people skip the genealogy bits, but these are really important because they tie together what happened already. The entire Old Testament can be discovered in this genealogy. Matthew 1 acts as a funnel of sorts, pouring the whole narrative into one person: the person of Jesus."

A record of the genealogy of Jesus Christ the son of David, the son of Abraham:

Abraham was the father of Isaac,
Isaac the father of Jacob,
Jacob the father of Judah and his brothers,
Judah the father of Perez and Zerah, whose mother was Tamar,
Perez the father of Hezron,
Hezron the father of Ram,
Ram the father of Amminadab,
Amminadab the father of Nahshon,
Nahshon the father of Salmon,
Salmon the father of Boaz, whose mother was Rahab,
Boaz the father of Obed, whose mother was Ruth,
Obed the father of Jesse,
and Jesse the father of King David.

David was the father of Solomon, whose mother had been Uriah's wife,
Solomon the father of Rehoboam,
Rehoboam the father of Abijah,
Abijah the father of Asa,

Asa the father of Jehoshaphat,
Jehoshaphat the father of Jehoram,
Jehoram the father of Uzziah,
Uzziah the father of Jotham,
Jotham the father of Ahaz,
Ahaz the father of Hezekiah,
Hezekiah the father of Manasseh,
Manasseh the father of Amon,
Amon the father of Josiah,
and Josiah the father of Jeconiah and his brothers at the
time of the exile to Babylon.

After the exile to Babylon:
Jeconiah was the father of Shealtiel,
Shealtiel the father of Zerubbabel,
Zerubbabel the father of Abiud,
Abiud the father of Eliakim,
Eliakim the father of Azor,
Azor the father of Zadok,
Zadok the father of Akim,
Akim the father of Eliud,
Eliud the father of Eleazar,
Eleazar the father of Matthan,
Matthan the father of Jacob,
and Jacob the father of Joseph, the husband of Mary, of
whom was born Jesus, who is called Christ.

Thus there were fourteen generations in all from Abraham to David, fourteen from David to the exile to Babylon, and fourteen from the exile to the Christ.

This is how the birth of Jesus Christ came about: His mother Mary was pledged to be married to Joseph, but before they came together, she was found to be with child through the Holy Spirit. Because Joseph her husband was a righteous man and did not want to expose her to public disgrace, he had in mind to divorce her quietly.

But after he had considered this, an angel of the Lord appeared to him in a dream and said, "Joseph son of David, do not be afraid to take Mary home as your wife, because what is conceived in her is from the Holy Spirit. She will give birth to a son, and you are to give

him the name Jesus, because he will save his people
from their sins."

All this took place to fulfill what the Lord had said
through the prophet: "The virgin will be with child and
will give birth to a son, and they will call him Imman-
uel"—which means, "God with us."

When Joseph woke up, he did what the angel of the
Lord had commanded him and took Mary home as his
wife. But he had no union with her until she gave birth
to a son. And he gave him the name Jesus.
(Matthew 1:1-25)

"We're told that Jesus was a man," Nate continues, "a man
who arrived in a line filled with all sorts of other important men
and the occasional woman. Then in the second section we're
told about his birth. The Holy Spirit is in charge of that. Here in
the first chapter we get the first emphasis on the Holy Spirit, but
who in this chapter has the church emphasized?"

"Mary."

"Yeah, Mary. The focus moves from the Holy Spirit as the
one who essentially fathered Jesus, toward Mary, who received
the Holy Spirit and gave birth to Christ in this world."

"She received the Spirit before Pentecost?"

"Yes. After Pentecost the Spirit came on everyone. Before
Pentecost the Spirit seemed to be more particular. Here in Matthew chapter one we are introduced to Jesus the Messiah, conceived by the Holy Spirit. The Virgin gave birth to the son, but
only because of the Holy Spirit. This is the same Spirit who
came upon the church at Pentecost. The Spirit sent the Son,
don't you see? The Spirit is still doing the same exact thing now.
It is only the Holy Spirit who can conceive Jesus in anyone."

I'm not quite following him anymore. He sounds like he's
starting to drift a little from what I was taught. "This is a little
confusing," I say.

"I know. But it's worth wrestling with. In terms of chronology, we can't say the Spirit came after Jesus. The Spirit started it all and still starts it all, giving birth to Jesus, and still giving birth to Jesus in and through each of us. That's the core of the Spirit's work. What the Spirit did in Mary is still going on. We are all called to rebirth, and we are all called to bring forth Christ in this world. That's a miracle, and a miracle for which we'll all be called most blessed."

"I see that," I say, though it is still a little confusing to me.

"So what is the first work of the Holy Spirit in the New Testament?"

"The conception of Jesus?" I answer.

"Yes! We always think of Pentecost, or maybe the baptism with the dove, but the first work of the Holy Spirit in the New Testament is bringing forth Jesus, and that's why when I prayed for the Holy Spirit to really pour out over us we became intensely interested in who Jesus was and is. He became more than just a name or a goal. The Spirit made the man, and we are called to know the man, and be like the man, and follow this man Jesus to the end of our own days. We know we are walking with Jesus because of the Spirit who lives in us, as 1 John 3:24 says. Along with that we know *how* to walk with Jesus because of the Spirit who lives in us. We know we *must* walk with Jesus because of the Spirit who lives in us. It's all tied together."

"So what happened at Pentecost?"

"Everything, Luke. Pentecost was when people found the power of Christ and what it means to truly reflect Christ to this world. Pentecost was the moment God empowered the church to act. But that's a whole new topic, and I've really got to use the bathroom. Feel free to look around."

He smiles, then gets up and walks to the back of the building. I follow Nate's advice and take a look around the Columba Pub and Restaurant. It is indeed a very interesting place.

" When we create barriers—when we make divisions between something spiritual and something not spiritual, or something sacred and something secular—we have a good chance to completely miss what the Spirit is doing. The Spirit is often in what we would call secular. It's all through the Bible. And the Spirit is often missing in what we would call sacred. The prophets reminded the people of that. It's still true."

3

Breaking the Boundaries
between Sacred and Secular

Following what seems to be the restaurant décor trend these days, the walls of the Columba are covered with all sorts of knickknacks, which blend together and make a busy ambience. Presumably, people are supposed to feel like they're eating in the dining room of a particularly cluttered friend. Now that I look around with more attention, it all seems curious.

Candles on high shelves cast a faint glow along the ceiling. I think they are the electric kind, not real flame, but they create a nice effect. Framed art—pictures of doves and icons of saints—lines the walls. This creates a vaguely religious feel, though certainly not in a way that immediately strikes me as being Christian. There are no inspirational verses.

A rock fountain in the corner pours water into a small pond. The top of the fountain is near the ceiling, and there are four levels, each with a larger pool. Rocks encircle the bottom pool. I can see silver glints beneath the surface of the water. Someone has been making wishes. The tinkling of water reminds me of a lazy mountain stream. Very soothing. The

Columba is definitely different than the Lutheran church I visited last week.

Everything here is decorated in dark reds and browns. The chairs all have dark green cushions. It appears there are three main rooms. The front room has high, small tables and high chairs. The middle room is about half again as big, and has normal tables and booths, with the bar and the kitchen on the right as you walk in. From what I can tell, the back room is about the same size but I can only see one large table. For banquets maybe.

It's getting close to noon and I wonder how much more time I should spend with Nate today.

"What do you think?" Nate asks as he pulls out his chair and sits down again.

"It's cozy. Reminds me of some pubs I visited in Scotland."

"Yeah, that's sort of the model we were hoping for. We're trying for more of a community pub sort of place, where people can come and hang out. We want it to be a place where worlds blend, where people come to relax and find themselves, not lose themselves. Food and drink have the ability to encourage that, and we want to encourage the food and drink. Architecture has always been a theological tool. We're trying to look at that from the perspective of a place of business."

"I can see that, I think, but it's not real obvious."

"That's sort of the point. We aren't wanting to make this into a chapel. It's a place to gather, and the way everything is framed contributes to an atmosphere."

"What kind of atmosphere?"

"We're all so caught up in creating something useful we don't think about what it is we're creating. That's what I like about the great cathedrals. Everything is so intentional. Everything is so purposeful. It's functional, yeah, but it all has a meaning, even if we don't know the meaning, and that pushes us."

"Pushes us to find the meaning?"

"Exactly, even when we don't realize it. Our minds are working. Our souls are working."

"So this place is supposed to be like a cathedral?"

"No, not at all. We're nothing like a cathedral. Our decorative abilities aren't that good and we certainly don't have the budget. I mean, I did think about making all the windows out of alabaster. Didn't work out."

"What stopped you?" I joked.

"Well, I went to check and didn't know which aisle to look in. I even asked the man in the orange vest, but it turns out Home Depot doesn't stock transparent rock. They didn't have any great bronze doors either. I was very disappointed to say the least."

"I bet." I smiled. "I like your fountain, though."

"Isn't that great? One of the guys here—Steve—has a side business selling pool supplies and stuff like that. He got a great deal on that. Makes the whole place for me. I love sitting and listening to the water after we close. It cleanses my soul somehow. It's like the sound is washing through me."

"I think I know what you mean," I replied. "So, you decorate purposefully, but you don't want to be a cathedral—which is pretty clear."

"Luke, those kinds of churches have a different goal. They are like a throne room of God, meant to provoke the hearts of people heavenward as the people walk in. It is a liturgical space where heaven itself can be better realized. You can tell how visions of faith and heaven have changed over the centuries, by the way. So, people are gathered together there, like they were gathered at the tabernacle. They meet God and see what God is like. They come and they go away. That's what the cathedral is about."

"So what are you about?"

"Seashores."

"Seashores?"

"And dawn."

"Is this something I should understand?"

"The ancient Celts had an understanding of sorts. They tended to be very fluid in their understanding of spirituality, not limiting it to one realm, or one moment, or one place. The two worlds blended together in a curious sort of way."

"Interesting."

"Yeah, you can see it in their art. All the whorls and swirls and complex knots are a contrast to the more standard patterns we see elsewhere. They were expressing a complexity of this world, and not just the world we see but also the world we don't see. It's all intermingled in an infinitely complex reality."

"So what does that have to do with dawn, or dusk, or seashores?"

"Besides being pretty?" Nate asks, and laughs. "Though they saw everything intermingling, there were certain times and places that were especially connected. Off-ramps and on-ramps, maybe. They were places of connection, neither here nor there. Both places at once."

"And that's how you see this place?"

"No," Nate says. He pauses and thinks a moment. "Well maybe. But, it's not like it's about this place. We try to capture something but it's not about capturing it. You know what I mean?"

"I have no idea."

"I'm not sure I do either. That's my trouble sometimes," he says and laughs. "Are you hungry, by the way?"

"A little bit, I suppose," I reply.

"Debbie," he calls to the nearby waitress.

"What?" she shouts back, in mock irritation.

He picks up the same tone and yells, "Chicken wings."

"Whatever you say!"

That stops him for a moment, then he laughs.

"I would have thought you were a vegetarian or something," I say.

"Really? Because that's the thing to do? Shop at Whole Foods for our daily grazing?"

"Something like that," I laugh.

"I think there's something to that, except for the fact I really do like meat and I really don't like vegetables."

"So your passions overcome your desire to do what is right?"

"Yeah," he laughs, "I do what I shouldn't, and don't do what I should. The great moral quandaries of life, right?"

"People have to face the worst of themselves, I guess."

"This reminds me of an old Quaker adage for folks who can't quite give up their violence: 'Wear your sword as long as you can.' Meaning the Spirit will convict each person of what is right, given enough time."

"So, dip your wings as long as you can, Nate," I say.

"And so I shall," he replies, just as the wings arrive.

"Here you go." Debbie sets down the plate of wings, ranch dressing, and celery.

"Thanks so much for your kind and gracious service," Nate laughs as she walks away. "So where were we?"

"Celts, swirls, and the intermingling of natural and supernatural."

"Oh, right," Nate says. "Acts 10."

"Acts 10?"

"Yeah, that's what always comes to mind when I think of the Celts, and what I'm trying to get at when you ask about what we're doing here."

"What happened in Acts 10?" I ask.

After a lifetime in the church I should probably know, but don't.

𝔄t 𝕮aesarea there was a man named Cornelius, a centurion in what was known as the Italian Regiment. He and all his family were devout and God-fearing; he gave generously to those in need and prayed to God regularly. One day at about three in the afternoon he had a vision. He distinctly saw an angel of God, who came to him and said, "Cornelius!"

Cornelius stared at him in fear. "What is it, Lord?" he asked.

The angel answered, "Your prayers and gifts to the poor have come up as a memorial offering before God. Now send men to Joppa to bring back a man named Simon who is called Peter. He is staying with Simon the tanner, whose house is by the sea."

When the angel who spoke to him had gone, Cornelius called two of his servants and a devout soldier who was one of his attendants. He told them everything that had happened and sent them to Joppa.

About noon the following day as they were on their journey and approaching the city, Peter went up on the roof to pray. He became hungry and wanted something to eat, and while the meal was being prepared, he fell into a trance. He saw heaven opened and something like a large sheet being let down to earth by its four corners. It contained all kinds of four-footed animals, as well as reptiles of the earth and birds of the air. Then a voice told him, "Get up, Peter. Kill and eat."

"Surely not, Lord!" Peter replied. "I have never eaten anything impure or unclean."

The voice spoke to him a second time, "Do not call anything impure that God has made clean."

This happened three times, and immediately the sheet was taken back to heaven.

While Peter was wondering about the meaning of the vision, the men sent by Cornelius found out where Simon's house was and stopped at the gate. They called out, asking if Simon who was known as Peter was staying there.

While Peter was still thinking about the vision, the Spirit said to him, "Simon, three men are looking for you. So get up and go downstairs. Do not hesitate to go with them, for I have sent them."

Peter went down and said to the men, "I'm the one you're looking for. Why have you come?"

The men replied, "We have come from Cornelius the centurion. He is a righteous and God-fearing man, who is respected by all the Jewish people. A holy angel told him to have you come to his house so that he could hear what you have to say." Then Peter invited the men into the house to be his guests.

The next day Peter started out with them, and some of the brothers from Joppa went along. The following day he arrived in Caesarea. Cornelius was expecting them and had called together his relatives and close friends. As Peter entered the house, Cornelius met him and fell at his feet in reverence. But Peter made him get up. "Stand up," he said, "I am only a man myself."

Talking with him, Peter went inside and found a large gathering of people. He said to them: "You are well aware that it is against our law for a Jew to associate with a Gentile or visit him. But God has shown me that I should not call any man impure or unclean. So when I was sent for, I came without raising any objection. May I ask why you sent for me?"

Cornelius answered: "Four days ago I was in my house praying at this hour, at three in the afternoon. Suddenly a man in shining clothes stood before me and said, 'Cornelius, God has heard your prayer and remembered your gifts to the poor. Send to Joppa for Simon who is called Peter. He is a guest in the home of Simon the tanner, who lives by the sea.' So I sent for you immediately, and it was good of you to come. Now we are all here in the presence of God to listen to everything the Lord has commanded you to tell us."

Then Peter began to speak: "I now realize how true it is that God does not show favoritism but accepts men from every nation who fear him and do what is right. You know the message God sent to the people of Israel, telling the good news of peace through Jesus Christ, who is Lord of all. You know what has happened throughout Judea, beginning in Galilee after the baptism that John preached—how God anointed Jesus of Nazareth with the Holy Spirit and power, and how he went around doing good and healing all who were under the power of the devil, because God was with him.

"We are witnesses of everything he did in the country of the Jews and in Jerusalem. They killed him by hanging him on a tree, but God raised him from the dead on the third day and caused him to be seen. He was not seen by all the people, but by witnesses whom God had already chosen—by us who ate and drank with him after he rose from the dead. He commanded us to preach to the people and to testify that he is the one whom God appointed as judge of the living and the dead. All the prophets testify about him that everyone who believes in him receives forgiveness of sins through his name."

> While Peter was still speaking these words, the Holy Spirit came on all who heard the message. The circumcised believers who had come with Peter were astonished that the gift of the Holy Spirit had been poured out even on the Gentiles. For they heard them speaking in tongues and praising God.
>
> Then Peter said, "Can anyone keep these people from being baptized with water? They have received the Holy Spirit just as we have." So he ordered that they be baptized in the name of Jesus Christ. Then they asked Peter to stay with them for a few days. *(Acts 10:1-48)*

"Peter and the Centurion," Nate says. "You remember. I'm sure you've heard this story. Peter has a vision and the vision causes him do something which is entirely religiously wrong, except that God himself commands it. A guy who isn't altogether religiously right also has a vision, and that vision tells him that God is pleased, even though the religion says he shouldn't be. God tells this guy to wait. He's sending someone his way. Not just anyone, Peter himself, fresh off the raising-the-dead tour there in Joppa, which is Tel-Aviv now, if you pay attention to such things."

"So what does this have to do with anything you've said so far? I'm trying to get it, Nate, but right now I'm feeling like I'm being tossed around by waves."

"No problem," Nate says and laughs. "I get going and lose myself sometimes. Which can be really inconvenient when I think there's a good point somewhere. This is one of the most important and most brilliant passages in the entire Bible, if you think about it. Right here, in Acts 10, everything goes out of whack. Up to now, God has pretty much been sticking to the plan. Now, the plan is thrown out. Peter is called into the mix. He's not given any choice about it. Just told to go. Cornelius is told to invite him. Crazy, isn't it?"

"What's so crazy about it?"

"Everything, Luke. The whole story should be cut out of the Bible and left off to the side. It doesn't fit. It doesn't make sense."

"I'm not catching what you're saying."

"Peter, who is one of the most important guys in the early church, has a vision to go against everything he has stood for, and lived for, throughout his whole life. Cornelius is supposed to wait for Peter. Right where he's at. Peter comes. The Spirit comes and blesses the whole household. The Spirit blesses it all."

"In what way?"

"There are no more food laws. There's no more separation of nations. There are no more barriers. Cornelius didn't have to go to a church, or a synagogue, or the Temple, or even to Peter. Peter came to him, and the Spirit came to him. Where he was. The Spirit did what Jesus did."

"Which was?"

"Make every place a place of holiness. Where the Spirit is we can find God. And the Spirit can be just about anywhere."

He stops and eats a chicken wing, then continues, "We find the Spirit doing all sorts of things, in all sorts of places. The early apostles kept having to chase down wherever the Spirit erupted next. They met in particular places, but they kept having to go somewhere else. They had to go wherever the Spirit pulled them. The Spirit was doing the work. They didn't have a place, you know, where they had to go to find God. The Spirit was moving. Not up in his throne room looking down. He was—and is—here and there. Like the wind. Always like the wind."

"So how do you see this working out here in the Columba?"

"This is a hub, Luke, nothing more. A place where all sorts of people can come together in relative ease, and as we come together we get to see the Spirit who has brought us, and is with us, and doing a work. Acts 10 means flexibility. It means we can worship God here, upstairs, wherever we're at, not limited to certain laws. We have to know who Jesus is, but we don't have to do a whole list of things anymore. Where the Spirit is, there is the kingdom of God. Where the Spirit is, there is freedom. We're called to go, not stay, to be out in the mix—always worshiping, always watching, always waiting, always ready to give an answer for the hope that is in us."

"Now that's a good religious sentence," I laugh. "What do you mean by that?"

"We go out to people. We live our lives where people can see us, and where they can see there's something hopeful about us. I know what you're saying about sounding religious, because people think going out means doing some kind of formal, standardized evangelism. But we see it differently. It's not just about packing up the picnic basket with our religious tidbits and handing out morsels to the passersby. So many missionary trips to spread the gospel in foreign lands remind me of submarine voyages. We go into the depths of a foreign culture and peek out through our periscope. We put on scuba gear and wetsuits and protective equipment to venture out, always scurrying back into our self-contained worlds whenever we run out of air, which is fairly quickly."

"Always making sure to watch out for the giant squid."

"Ha! Yeah, gotta watch out for those and the sharks."

"I think you're saying Christians need to engage the culture around them. Is that it?"

"Let's go back to Scripture to see what the Spirit is about. In this way can we see what *we* should be about. There is a great distinction in the Bible, especially in the Old Testament, between clean and unclean. This isn't about sin. Well, sometimes it is, but it relates to a lot more than sin. Like skin diseases, menstruating women, dealing with dead bodies, or going to the bathroom. All sorts of stuff that is just part of living this life. Being unclean prevented you from contact with God. It kept you out of the temple. That's why the priest and the Levite ignored the man beat up on the side of the road. He might have been dead and was certainly unclean. By helping him they would have made themselves ritually unclean, unable to serve God as they were called to."

"So to serve God they refused to serve God."

"Yeah, that was exactly Jesus' point in the Good Samaritan story. To serve God they refused to serve God, because they had this expectation of God. They thought he would be in a certain place, doing certain things. They thought he demanded all the people go to the temple. They were wrong."

"But didn't he give all sorts of laws for this?"

"Yeah, yeah he did, but I get the feeling he regretted doing that. Or, maybe that's not the right word, even if some passages do talk about God feeling regret. Maybe it's more the fact that he got the sense everyone was missing the point. It was never about going to the temple. That was for the people; God commanded it in order to help people feel like they were doing something to honor him.

"God wants people to live right, to do what is right, within whatever context we find ourselves, you know. We get in our cars, and drive on the freeways past our neighbors, past our neighborhoods, and go to our special place of worship on a Sunday, thinking this is where we do our God service, where we get away from the world and go renew our sacred hearts. But, really, who are we like when we think this?"

"The Pharisees?" I answer.

"Exactly, we're a lot more like the Pharisees than we would ever want to admit."

"We don't want to admit it because they're the villains?"

"Kind of. Only I never really think of them as the villains. When you study you find out what these guys were really like. They were zealous for God, you know. They did all the things they did because they had read the Prophets. They knew their history, and they knew Israel had a major burden to stay right with God. They were dedicated to staying right with God. They were dedicated to the Scriptures they had been given and dedicated to all the traditions that had developed which would lead them to a right understanding. They were so dedicated they missed him."

"They missed Jesus?"

"They missed everything. They became so worried and so nervous, they closed themselves off. They thought there was safety in that box. They thought God would stay in there with them. You know what they did? They prayed, and gave the Spirit a multiple-choice test. The Spirit was allowed to do A, B, C, or D, and as long as the Spirit did those things, as long as God worked in the expected ways, then they would allow that work. The church has done that exact same thing. The church has limited the Spirit to a Scantron test, giving the Spirit a specific set of contexts in which to bubble in the right answer. The Spirit can only work through a sermon; or with the Eucharist; or in a church building; or with just the right singing or recitation of words, spoken by the right sort of person. But that's not true at all. We only believe that so we can keep a handle on what the Spirit does. But the Spirit—the Spirit is doing all sorts of things in all sorts of places whether we like it or not. Whether we approve of it or not, the Spirit is drawing people to God where we are. We don't have to go where we might think we should go. That's the point about Cornelius in Acts 10, or the Ethiopian and Philip in Acts 8."

Now an angel of the Lord said to Philip, "Go south to the road—the desert road—that goes down from Jerusalem to Gaza." So he started out, and on his way he met an Ethiopian eunuch, an important official in charge of all the treasury of Candace, queen of the Ethiopians. This man had gone to Jerusalem to worship, and on his way home was sitting in his chariot reading the book of Isaiah the prophet. The Spirit told Philip, "Go to that chariot and stay near it."

Then Philip ran up to the chariot and heard the man reading Isaiah the prophet. "Do you understand what you are reading?" Philip asked.

"How can I," he said, "unless someone explains it to me?" So he invited Philip to come up and sit with him.

The eunuch was reading this passage of Scripture:

"He was led like a sheep to the slaughter,
and as a lamb before the shearer is silent,
so he did not open his mouth.
In his humiliation he was deprived of justice.
Who can speak of his descendants?
For his life was taken from the earth."

The eunuch asked Philip, "Tell me, please, who is the prophet talking about, himself or someone else?" Then Philip began with that very passage of Scripture and told him the good news about Jesus.

As they traveled along the road, they came to some water and the eunuch said, "Look, here is water. Why shouldn't I be baptized?" And he gave orders to stop the chariot. Then both Philip and the eunuch went down into the water and Philip baptized him. When they came up out of the water, the Spirit of the Lord suddenly took Philip away, and the eunuch did not see him again, but went on his way rejoicing.
(Acts 8:26-39)

"Philip," Nate continues, "is told by an angel to go for a walk on a specific road. When he does that the Holy Spirit tells him to go up to this chariot passing by. Philip likely doesn't have a clue who is in this fancy chariot. But the Spirit does, and the Spirit has been doing a work all along."

"Working completely outside of the church."

"Yeah. We don't have any idea what the real story is. It's like in *The Chronicles of Narnia*, you know, where Lucy asks about the older children, and Aslan tells her he doesn't tell other people's stories. The eunuch is reading the book of Isaiah, after spending a bit of time in Jerusalem for worship. We don't know who he is, or anything about his story, but we meet him where he intersects with Philip. Philip is doing what the Spirit wants him to do, there on the road from Jerusalem. It isn't exactly what you would consider an ideal religious setting. We don't know anything more than Philip. All the religious walls are broken down here. There's no clear line between sacred and secular. There's no official control of the interpretation of Scripture."

"Even baptism isn't being limited."

"Even baptism, that's right. Philip, after all, wasn't an apostle."

"I thought Philip was a disciple."

"Different Philip. This Philip was chosen by the disciples to do all the dirty work in Acts 6. The disciples were getting complaints. They wanted to pray and 'serve the word,' but there were needs in the community. So they chose seven men to do the work—waiting tables as Luke says."

"A noble profession," Debbie says as she walks by, hands filled with dirty plates.

We laugh.

"Absolutely," Nate replies. "So they chose these guys who were filled with the Holy Spirit, to do the standard, non-religious sort of stuff, leaving the disciples to get on with the business of spirituality. But then a crazy thing happened. The Spirit was working everywhere. In the next chapter we see that

Stephen became the first martyr. We're not told why he was picked up instead of any of the rest. But I think it has to do with the fact he was out there, doing all that mundane work—service stuff. He talked with people. I can imagine Stephen bringing food or clothes to an old widow, maybe helping out by fixing a table for her or mending her roof. Then her son, a busy religious man, shows up and begins talking.

"Then Stephen gets to talking back," Nate continues. "While the mother is a new Christian, the son is, say, a devout member of the Synagogue of the Freedmen. So he gets his cronies, Saul included, to stir up trouble. Stephen is a waiter, a waiter doing great wonders and miraculous signs among the people. He's arrested for it, and condemned to die. Before he dies, he gives this great testimony. Instead of being contrite he accuses his accusers. What is Stephen's accusation? The Jewish leaders resist the Holy Spirit. They persecuted anyone who didn't fit. They killed the prophets, and Stephen, for telling it like it is."

"It sounds to me like following the Spirit can be dangerous," I observe.

"Stephen was the first martyr and one of the better preachers. He wasn't anyone special, except for the fact he was filled with the Holy Spirit. He let himself be led by the Holy Spirit. He embraced the Holy Spirit instead of resisting the Spirit. His testimony echoes even to our day. The Spirit was doing something special in him and in Philip, and likely the rest of them. What's funny is that we don't hear about a good number of the disciples. They fall out of the story, but these guys, the waiters, get a lot of play. It's because, as Stephen made clear, God isn't limited to a particular context. What is it that Stephen says? He says the leaders didn't understand God because they thought God had to be found in a certain place or setting. They were totally wrong, and didn't understand God at all. The Spirit made all things, and is everywhere."

Our forefathers had the tabernacle of the Testimony with them in the desert. It had been made as God directed Moses, according to the pattern he had seen. Having received the tabernacle, our fathers under Joshua brought it with them when they took the land from the nations God drove out before them. It remained in the land until the time of David, who enjoyed God's favor and asked that he might provide a dwelling place for the God of Jacob. But it was Solomon who built the house for him.

However, the Most High does not live in houses made by men. As the prophet says:

"Heaven is my throne, and the earth is my footstool. What kind of house will you build for me? says the Lord. Or where will my resting place be? Has not my hand made all these things?" *(Acts 7:44-50)*

"We want to keep God in particular settings too, right?" I ask. "Is that what you're saying?"

"We have our big buildings, our big programs, our big gatherings, our own culture. We live in a bubble and we've created an understanding of the Holy Spirit that expects the Spirit to follow our lead. Only, the Spirit has never changed. The Spirit is still out there on the highway, out serving people, out among the crowds. The Spirit is doing a work in stories we don't even know and never learn because we're too often not like Philip. We're not willing to go out and see what's happening. We miss that work of the Spirit. We've sought to honor God, honor the Spirit, by having all these sacred bits, and trying to make sure we stay away from all the secular bits. But, the Spirit is in it all. The Spirit doesn't recognize any of these divisions. They're utterly false because the Spirit goes all sorts of places we might not expect. Wherever the Spirit goes, that place is made sacred. By not paying attention to the sacred and secular boundaries others held to, Philip encountered the Ethiopian. We don't know what happened after they parted ways. We're told only this small part—the part we need to know. It's the Spirit's story, and by being in the mix of things we begin to participate in the Spirit's story, even when we don't know the beginning or the end."

"Is this pub a sacred space?"

"It's outside the normal bounds and a place where we want the Spirit to show up. It's a place to gather and stay flexible. We're free to react to the situation—which might involve going somewhere and doing something, or it might involve going nowhere and staying still. There's a looseness about our pub and our church that doesn't insist on one meaning. Each person brings who they are. People bring their own story, and we, hopefully, can share who we are just as Philip did. Like Jesus and the lepers.

"Lepers?"

"They saw him, and he saw them, precisely because he didn't limit his ministry to the so-called sacred places. This brings me back to what I said before about clean and unclean. That's a lot like our secular and sacred division. The division really has nothing to do with true holiness. It's a division meant to be a division for its own sake. It creates this line between what we think is of God and what we think is apart from God. The unclean is what is apart from God. The secular is what is apart from God."

"But God created everything. How can anything be apart from God?"

"Excellent point," Nate says. "God instituted the Law in order to draw a sharply defined line between what was of God and what was not of God. There was the morality, but there was more than that, just as there's more to God. The clean and the unclean tell us a lot about God and a lot about how he views his own holiness. So you have Leviticus 13 talking about how people suffering from leprosy would have to announce their uncleanness to everyone, and live outside the camp. But then you have Jesus going out to meet these lepers. That's the brilliance of it. Jesus was so clean, you see—he was so entirely right about everything and perfectly in tune with God, being the very image of God and God—that instead of being made unclean himself by the uncleanness, he made clean that which was unclean."

"The Pharisees and the Law were concerned with keeping clean, and to keep clean one had to separate from the unclean things," I add, to show Nate I'm following, "which is what the Law told them to do. And it told them exactly how to do it, ad nauseam."

"And the nausea was unclean, which created a vicious cycle," Nate says, and laughs. "You said it right. The Law described only the limits, the divisions, so the people could relate to God as God himself ordered. But Jesus came and acted differently because he was the new image of God, completing the Law and continuing its goals. He was clean and he made all things clean. His touch, his power, was not going to be corrupted, for he was incorruptible. So incorruptible, in fact, he reversed the process, just as he reversed all the processes of corruption and decay."

"Overcoming the barrier of the unclean, then, is like his rising from the dead."

"Death being the ultimate uncleanness. Death is the antithesis of God. God brings life to death, clean to unclean. That's what Peter is told in the vision we read about in Acts 10. The vision is about food, the message is about life, and in drawing the lines that Peter had drawn—even though they were initially from God—he was, in effect, keeping life from Cornelius and the other Gentiles."

"Well, Peter himself wasn't."

"No, that's true," Nate says. "Peter wasn't. It's just that Peter was part of the whole process. The church had to reach out to what the Spirit was doing, so that all the Spirit's work would find unity. Like I said before, it was the Spirit who brought Jesus to life, and it is still the Spirit bringing all sorts of people to life, with or without our cooperation. If we don't cooperate and instead insist the Spirit work in a particular way, we create division. That leads to a whole mess of confusion erupting everywhere."

"Like history has shown."

"Like the present shows. Jesus came to break down those barriers. The Spirit continues the process of breaking down the barriers—those artificial, religious barriers that have nothing to do with good and evil, but only with our preferences and comfort in relating to God. Church is comfortable. We choose a church that is comfortable for our religious selves, a place where we can make God into who we think God should be. Where we have God do those sorts of things we think God should do, and where we act in those ways we think are proper responses to God's grace. Peter was told in a vision. Then, when the Spirit came down onto the household, Peter was given evidence he couldn't deny. To move with the Spirit we have to move past all the lines, past all the rules we set up, past all those things that seem so much like church to us, because there isn't any of that any more. The Spirit moves everywhere. To track with the Spirit we have to move everywhere as well."

"Like Jesus," I say.

"We have the Spirit of Christ, you see. The same Spirit. We move fluidly, without the Law of the Jews or any of our own more recent versions of the Law, because the Spirit is erupting in all sorts of places, doing a work in all sorts of people, with or without our involvement. Paul says this in Romans 7:6, 'But now, by dying to what once bound us, we have been released from the law so that we serve in the new way of the Spirit, and not in the old way of the written code.' If we're in the mix we're not limiting Christ to churchy things."

Nate continues, "Where did a first-century Jew see Jesus? Maybe a synagogue, sometimes the temple. But not *just* in those places. The crowds found him by a seashore. They found him on the lake. They came up to him on the streets, at parties, and while shopping, eating, and working. They found him during the day and they found him at night. Jesus was even found in places no respectable Jewish teacher would be found. He ate with tax collectors and talked with scandalous women. He touched lepers and treated beggars with respect. He was even willing to be in the presence of the dead. He brought healing and life everywhere he went. The Spirit is about the same kind of work, in all sorts of places.

"He's the father always running after us. We have to run with him, to meet and greet the ones he's welcoming home. The old way was him telling us how to come. The new way of the Spirit is active, seeking people out. It's a freedom and flexibility. The chains of restrictions have been broken off with our old life. We don't need to have the established structure because the Spirit is out and about doing something new. You know, the earliest church in Acts called itself 'The Way,' and I think Paul's message here—Romans 7:6—says what that is: It's the new way of the Spirit. Our churches have tried to hold onto the old ways—the restrictive and binding ways—because they are safe and controllable. But the Spirit is never safe nor controllable. So the new way is about doing something different."

I ask, "But isn't there something to church—something holy and good about having that central, dedicated place of worship?"

"Yeah, I think there is something to that," Nate acknowledges. "The earliest church had its upper room. And we have our upper room, where we have our place of prayer, and more focused worship activities, but that's not our primary space, you know. We don't think of that as our sacred space. It's just a functional place where we can have a bit more quiet. It's an oasis in the city. Where we worship is where the Spirit is, and where the Spirit is has no boundaries.

"I think there's a difference between functional locations and places or forms endowed with more meaning. I remember in college we had movie nights once a month. The screen would come down in our big chapel, and a good many people would spend the evening watching this movie, having a good time with friends. Well, one night there was a movie—I forget what it was—and it had a bit of cussing in it. A friend of mine was really mad afterward. 'I don't think they should have that sort of language in a place we worship God,' he said. Others got into a discussion about how it was okay because the building served many functions, but he stayed angry. I didn't say anything because I didn't feel like saying anything, but it was funny to me. This was a guy who certainly didn't hold back his own tongue, letting loose the choice word or three on regular occasions. But he was offended that in a chapel there would be a movie that had cussing."

"So was it okay or was it wrong?"

"My point is that if it were wrong in a chapel, because that's where we worship God, then it's wrong everywhere. We are always responsible for worshiping God and we ourselves are God's Temple. This guy had a split in his head between sacred space and secular space. He thought he could do whatever he wanted, watch whatever he wanted, on his own time, as long as he found something good and religious when he went to a chapel."

"What's the Scripture about us being God's temple and his Spirit living in us?"

"It's in Paul's first letter to the Corinthians," Nate says. "God's Spirit lives in us. God's Spirit goes everywhere. God's Spirit is doing all sorts of things in all sorts of people. Peter heard this. Philip experienced this. The Spirit confirmed it all by coming down and blessing all of it. There are no barriers anymore. When we create barriers—when we make divisions between something spiritual and something not spiritual, or something sacred and something secular—we have a good chance to completely miss what the Spirit is doing. The Spirit is often in what we would call secular. It's all through the Bible. And the Spirit is often missing in what we would call sacred. The prophets reminded the people of that. It's still true. The Spirit is like fire, or water, or wind—not able to be constrained. Even if constraining the Spirit is more convenient to us, even if it makes the Spirit easier for us to understand, the Spirit won't be constrained. Even if our theology insists the Spirit be appropriate and proper, the Spirit doesn't care. The only way to deal with the Spirit is to be loose with it all. Sometimes we even intentionally need to get these worlds mingling, in whorls and swirls."

"Staying within our little boundaries is kind of like being wallflowers then?"

"Wallflowers!" Nate exclaims. "That's a great description. We need to get out on the dance floor! We need to invite others to dance."

"So what are you two talking about so seriously?" Debbie asks, grabbing the seat next to me and sitting down. "It must be something terribly interesting."

Debbie is about average height, with bleached hair that reaches to her shoulders. She has a wry, crooked smile. It's the kind of smile that one could use to show a rare joy, or use as a weapon.

"Why do you say that?" Nate asks, then laughs. "When am I ever interesting?"

"Oh, you're generally interesting," she says, still with that wry, crooked smile.

She turns to me and says, "It's more that Nate is a bit of a lazy conversationalist. Interesting, but lazy."

"What does that mean?" Nate asks.

"He usually has the other person doing most of the talking," she says to me. "Nate, you see, is very good about seeming to have a conversation, but he always lets the other person do all the talking. It took me a long time to notice that. Not that I mind, of course. It's kind of sweet, until you realize you're doing all the work. So what are you talking about?"

"Your community and your church," I answer. "And you might be surprised. I'm hardly saying a word."

"Oh," she says, her smile growing a tad less crooked, "that's why he seemed so excited. Nothing gets him going like talking about what's going on here in the Columba. Though, I personally hate the word *church*. Don't use that word; it doesn't really match what we're doing, I think."

"Why doesn't it match?" I ask.

"Well, maybe it does. My problem is when I turned eighteen I swore to myself, to God, and to everyone around me that I would never step into a church again for the rest of my life. So if this is a church, I'm a bit of a fraud and liar. It can't be a church, you see."

She smiles that crooked smile again, and stares at me. I feel like she's looking inside of me. She pauses for a moment, then adds, "For the sake of my integrity. Hey, did he talk about the seashore yet?"

"Yeah."

"Did you get what he was saying?" Debbie asks.

"I think so, yeah."

"Could you explain it to me? I think I get the rest, but I'm not so sure what seashores have to do with any of this."

Nate laughs.

"So if it's not a church, what would you call it?" I ask.

"What would I call it?" Debbie replies. "I don't know. I don't really want to call it anything. Names bring all sorts of official meaning and structure and expectations. Nouns have power, and I hate some of the power those nouns bring. That's not why I'm here. I'm not here for the nouns."

"Why are you here?"

"For the verbs," she says, and smiles.

"Such as?" I ask.

"Such as...community," she replies.

"That's not a verb."

"It is here."

" *Community—real and total community—is the profound work of the Spirit in our midst. We have always seen it as a separate thing. We think it is something we are supposed to manage or create. That's not it at all. The whole point—like we're shown in Acts—is to get out of the way. Get our barriers out of the way. Get our pride and ambitions out of the way. The Spirit will do the work.*"

4

Drawing Us into Community

It is about two o'clock now. The lunch crowd has nearly emptied out. Those who remain talk with each other over their now-empty plates. Most of them are laughing, except for one couple in the back corner. Her plate is more than half full still. She pokes at her food while he talks. This is a serious and private moment for them. They are in public but are hidden by the fun everyone else is having.

Debbie glances at the group of men laughing near the front door, the group out on the patio, and the couple in the back. No one needs any service, so Debbie takes a break and continues to sit with us.

Twenty minutes ago some men and women came into the pub in ones, twos, and threes. They wandered up the stairs, where I guessed the more formal parts of the church were located. Just now they walk back down together—serene smiles on their faces, they share quiet conversations as they walk out. A few come over and briefly say hi to Nate and Debbie before going back to wherever they came from.

"See what I mean?" Debbie asks.

"What?" I ask back, not sure what she is talking about.

"Community," she says. "People coming by in the middle of the day, doing the prayer thing. Saying hi. Like it's all part of regular life. Like we're normal people."

"I'm a normal person," Nate says.

"Oh, who are you kidding?" Debbie replies and laughs. "You're the king of the misfits. What kind of self-respecting pastor would hang out in a pub all day?"

"And all night," Nate agrees.

"All night?" I have to ask.

"I live upstairs. There's a small—"

"Very small," Debbie interrupts.

"—very small apartment upstairs. Small bathroom with a shower, small living area. Enough for a bed, a desk, and some other stuff."

"It's quite cozy," Debbie says.

"I've had to, um, reduce my lifestyle a little bit," Nate laughs.

"Reduce it to about a teaspoon," Debbie adds, "but it's nice always knowing where he is, or should be. Keeps him out of trouble."

"By the way," Nate says to me. "I never really got to one of your earlier questions, how I came to be here, and really how *here* came to be. We started talking about the Spirit, and that got me going."

"So how did you get the Upper Room started?"

"My fiancée left me about a month before we were going to get married."

"So you couldn't stay at church, had to move above a pub, and start a new church?"

Nate laughs before saying, "Some people might have thought that. It was a hard, terrible, awful time. But that's not why I walked into the head pastor's office on a hot August day and told him I couldn't stay. Well, maybe that's part of it, just not the core of it."

"What was it? If you don't mind me asking."

"Maybe it was her, at least at first. I mean she left me for one of the guitar players in the worship band. Neither felt any real interest in leaving the church. It seemed odd, but I couldn't force them out. Which left me in a bit of a bind."

"No one saw any problems with what happened?"

"We weren't married yet and she's, you know, a pretty convincing woman when it comes to doing what she wants to do. She has a way of explaining so that people take her side. I don't want to say anything against her, because she really has a good heart."

"I'll say something," Debbie adds.

"Yeah, Deb will say two or three things," Nate says and laughs, "none of which should go into anything you're writing. What I didn't know then, that I know now, is how words don't always go down deep. They can be like buoys floating on the ocean. When it's calm you don't know which are tied down, and which are floating free."

"Your fiancée wasn't tied down?"

"I didn't know that. But everything we had together, all the promises, were cast adrift in a moment of her own dissatisfaction."

"What did she say?"

"She said it wasn't meant to be."

"She liked musicians," Debbie says. "Though I can't blame her for that."

"It wasn't meant to be? Better she said that before the wedding, I suppose," I say.

"I think she was wrong. That's the problem. Everything in me said she was wrong, that we were right. She wasn't willing to press past her fleeting interests. She only saw what was right in front of her, what grabbed her heart in that moment. She leaped at it, and dropped me. When I realized she wasn't going to change her mind...."

"When she and the guitar player got engaged a month later," Debbie adds.

Nate continues, "Something hit me. It wasn't them. I really do think if I saw what she was talking about I would be okay. Or more than that, if there was something else, something bigger, something that gave me perspective I would have been okay. But there was suddenly nothing. A very palpable, heavy, oppressive *nothing*. You know? It surrounded me. In the same way I thought my faith surrounded me before, this darkness, this void, surrounded me. I couldn't get away from it. It was everywhere I looked, in everything I did, covering everyone I looked at."

"Sounds like depression."

"Oh, it was certainly that. No doubt. Which made the other pastors on staff really worried because that's how they diagnosed it. I knew it wasn't just depression. It was all darkness, but in that darkness I began to see, and I began to feel, and even as it tore me all apart, somehow it pulled me all together. It's hard to explain. I found a wholeness. I was empty, soul crushingly empty, but I had found a wholeness."

"You embraced your depression?"

"No. No, not at all. I rejected it entirely. It was a veil, you see, a veil that lied and deceived and misdirected. But behind it...behind it was something. When that veil tore, I saw."

"Saw what?"

Nate leans in toward me and says, "Everyone was like her. All of them. All of us. We are all like her. Grasping at our whims. It's just that some of us have more acceptable whims than other people. At our core it's all the same. I knew something was not right when I saw in the senior pastor the same spirit I saw in her. Maybe that's why no one got mad at her. Something was wrong and I had to figure out what it was, and I couldn't figure it out there without causing a lot more distraction."

"Why not?" I ask.

"Because when I see that same spirit in me I am willing to stare at it and fix it, whatever it takes. Other people may not be at that point—of either wanting to see or caring to do anything about it. Church is a business like any other and there are ways of doing things, ways of getting ahead, ways of playing the politics and jumping through the hoops."

"You didn't want to jump through the hoops anymore?"

"I wanted to dismantle all the hoops. Take them down, shutter the business, end the show. I had some feeler conversations with a couple key folks and realized if I tried to even start any change of direction there would be something nasty happening. I didn't want to do that. I didn't want to put the church through that."

"A split?"

"At the very least there would have been power grabs and a shuffling of influence sought in the church. This could have even provoked a church split. Or something more kosher in name. Luke, I didn't have it figured out myself. God was calling me, you see, but I realized if others weren't seeing it, it wasn't my job to be the Holy Spirit for them. I had to find the Holy Spirit for myself, to see what the Spirit was doing, and only then could I be safe. If God was calling me he would bring others along. I had to trust that and stay safe."

"Safe from what?" I ask.

"Myself, oddly enough. You get a passion, a vision for something, and all sorts of nasty influences can get in and work out a whole bunch of vices, most of them quite culturally acceptable. And even within the church we expect to see pride, envy, and greed. But the Spirit was showing me another way."

"So you left the church you were at, but how did you come to live above a pub?"

"Oh, this is a good story," Debbie laughs. "Nate the prophet."

"Nothing like that," Nate replies. "Nate the easily influenced, I think. Well, I won't get into the story of how we got a hold of this place."

"It's long and complicated," Debbie says.

"Or at least complicated. But for me it was a number of things coming together all at once. Here I am, which seems to be entirely God's work."

"Here we all are," Debbie adds.

I ask, "What were the 'number of things,' if you don't mind me asking?"

"You keep at it," Nate says and laughs. "I could learn from you. Well all of a sudden I wasn't married. I mean I never was married, but for eight months I had thought of myself as going to be married. We had decided to buy a house together. I had a decent steady income. She is a pretty successful advertising executive. So we found a place we liked and bought it. I was going to move in the week before our wedding, she was going to move in the week after."

"After their honeymoon," Debbie adds, though I had picked that up.

"And," Nate continues, "when she called the wedding off she also decided she didn't want to move, leaving me with a house of my own. I didn't really think anything of it, to be honest. Most people I know own their own homes now, and so I figured it was time. It would stretch me a bit more than I wanted, but I could afford it. I thought it would be a great place to host small groups and other get-togethers."

"Like a twelve-step group on recovering from evil fiancées," Debbie says.

"Yeah, I probably needed that one."

"What happened, then?" I ask.

"I was in my car driving out to sign yet more paperwork. Had the radio on and happened to go by a Christian station, one that spends a bit of the day—like five minutes in the morning and again in the afternoon—reading Scripture. They were on Matthew 8."

"Which says?" I ask.

Nate leans back and closes his eyes, like he's reading his memory, "When Jesus saw the crowd around him, he gave orders to cross to the other side of the lake. Then a teacher of the law came to him and said, 'Teacher, I will follow you wherever you go.' Jesus replied, 'Foxes have holes and birds of the air have nests, but the Son of Man has no place to lay his head.' Another disciple said to him, 'Lord, first let me go and bury my father.' But Jesus told him, 'Follow me, and let the dead bury their own dead.'"

"What did that mean for you?"

"Have you heard of Anthony of Egypt?" Nate asks. "He was this guy, this rich kid whose parents died and left him a bit of a fortune when he was in his late teens or so. He was walking by a church and heard a preacher talking about the rich young ruler, who Jesus told needed to give away all his possessions so the ruler could find perfection. The rich young ruler couldn't do it, and that made Jesus sad."

"Anthony did it?" I ask.

"Yeah, Anthony did it. He gave away everything he owned and eventually moved into an abandoned fort where he became the first great Christian hermit and had a major impact on the Christian world because of his decision. He was called to move in with Christ, and later when Christ called him back to the world he was this immensely wise, humble, spiritual man. Instead of worrying about wealth he worried about prayer. Instead of thinking about investments, he thought about overcoming temptations and fasting."

"Investments in a different world," Debbie adds.

"We don't think in such terms anymore," Nate says. "We make sure everything is in order, then we'll go out and do what is right for Christ. Have the family, the home, the kids, the minivan, the right entertainment, the right friends, the safe investments for a safe retirement. When I heard that verse read on the radio it hit me, and it hit me so hard I pulled to the side of the freeway. I can't explain it other than to say it was like this cloud of light covered me. It filled me. It inspired me. Suddenly I saw order. I was given a glimpse of God's order, and those verses on the radio were tying it all together for me."

"How so?" I ask.

"Here I was going to buy what by any rational consideration is a very expensive house, and Jesus didn't have a place to lay his head. Here I was asking the Spirit to lead me toward some sort of truth in my life, and I felt I had to deal with all the issues of my past experiences—bury the dead relationships. Luke, I realized in that instant I was stuck, and getting myself more stuck. Buying that house was playing by society's rules, but I couldn't do it. I couldn't hear those verses and keep going in the directions that were at the core of my problems. My fiancée wasn't the issue, you see. She was a symptom. So I got off the freeway, turned around, and went back to my apartment—which I had for only another two weeks before the lease expired. It was already rented out to new people."

"You decided not to take the house?"

"That's the thing. I didn't make that decision. It wasn't a choice. I couldn't go that direction. I had to turn around. It wasn't a decision, Luke. It was the Spirit working and pushing me. All this time as I had been praying for the Spirit to do a work, to pour out over people, my own instincts were being reshaped. I got a better feel for the whispers and prodding of the Spirit through my wrestling, so that when the moment of a supposed decision came, the Spirit made a decision."

"Because of a verse on the radio, you walked away from buying the house?"

"The house was neither here nor there. It was extraneous. Didn't matter. What the Spirit was doing was something different. I was being led into community. That house would have been a fifteen-minute drive from here. It was a barrier, you see. It would have been an excuse. Kept being an excuse. Now, I sleep five seconds from this table. Let me tell you, with community it's not about the intentional times of planning or scheduling or services. It's presence. It's being here when someone doesn't even know they need you, and being around someone else when you don't even know you need them just as much. It's that thing I thought I was going to find in marriage—trust and companionship. That was fleeting. Romance was fleeting. The Spirit is about something more thorough and a lot more complex."

"Which is?" I ask.

"I came across a Princeton professor recently—James Loder. In his book he talks about human development and faith development working together.* He writes that as babies we instinctively respond and desire the face of our parents. We are comforted by this face, but this face goes away. We don't understand then, and we don't really understand now. What we want, Luke, is that face that will never go away—that face of the Father as seen in Christ through the Spirit. All our other yearnings, everything we do out of ambition or lust or desire is all seeking to meet this core need. Except these things never can meet that need. It's the Spirit's call in us, and it's the Spirit who has to answer. Have you read Acts 2? The end of it, I mean?"

"Peter's speech before the crowd?"

"After that even."

They devoted themselves to the apostles' teaching and to the fellowship, to the breaking of bread and to prayer. Everyone was filled with awe, and many wonders and miraculous signs were done by the apostles. All the believers were together and had everything in common. Selling their possessions and goods, they gave to anyone as he had need. Every day they continued to meet together in the temple courts. They broke bread in their homes and ate together with glad and sincere hearts, praising God and enjoying the favor of all the people. And the Lord added to their number daily those who were being saved. *(Acts 2:42-47)*

"So we're supposed to do all these things and we'll find the Spirit?" I ask.

"No, it's the other way around. We find the Spirit, we really find the Spirit, and we will do these things. We can't help but do these things. Do you mind a little history lesson?"

"Not at all," I say.

---

*The Logic of the Spirit: Human Development in Theological Perspective *(San Francisco, CA: Jossey-Bass, 1998)*

"I do," Debbie says, and gets up, though I think it was because a new group of people had walked in.

"In the early 1900s a group of students in Topeka, Kansas, decided they would figure out the evidence of the Holy Spirit. They started in Acts and didn't have to get very far. Tongues, they said. The sign of the Spirit's coming is the gift of tongues. To prove it they all started speaking in tongues. Which was something of a curiosity, of course. Mostly because it seems they weren't the ones sparking the speaking. The Spirit had done a work confirming it. This confirmation began to spread, coming—like all interesting things—to Los Angeles, where the Azusa Street Revival helped turn this work into a movement. The most dynamic movement in a very, very long time. Pentecostalism."

"Interesting."

"Yeah, except that group of students got it wrong. Well, not the bits wrong that most people, most conservatives, accuse them of getting wrong. They weren't wrong in what they said. They were wrong in stopping too early."

"Stopping too early?"

"They didn't read the whole chapter, Luke. It's at the end of the chapter, not the beginning, that we see what the Spirit's real work is about. Tongues can be a sign; that's true. It's all through history, and whenever the Spirit comes down especially powerfully upon a group of people, there's going to be an ecstatic expression because people aren't used to that sort of power."

"Like Saul among the prophets?"*

"Yes! Exactly like that, and the passage in Exodus where we read Moses anoints the new leaders and they get filled with the Spirit. Even the ones who were late to the meeting got

---

* *1 Samuel 10:1-12*

turned into prophets. The power came over them, and they burst with the filling."

"So tongues is a sign of the Spirit's coming?"

"It can be. Hundreds of millions of people around the world are a difficult testimony to argue against. Others might be up for it, and make good arguments, but I'm not going to join in. Tongues can be a sign of the Spirit's coming, but something else is a sign of the Spirit's staying."

"Which is?"

"Community, Luke. It's all in Acts. If you read the Epistles, the whole lot of them, it's the same thing. Community—real and total community—is the profound work of the Spirit in our midst. We have always seen it as a separate thing. We think it is something we are supposed to manage or create. That's not it at all. The whole point—like we're shown in Acts—is to get out of the way. Get our barriers out of the way. Get our pride and ambitions out of the way. The Spirit will do the work."

"The real evidence of the Spirit is community instead of tongues?"

"According to Scripture, there's no doubt about it," Nate replies. "All the rest are the tools the Spirit uses for this goal, tongues included. Which is why Paul went on the little tirade we read about in 1 Corinthians. They began getting focused on the evidence rather than the purpose. Christ is the head of the body. The body is the purpose. The Spirit joins it together."

"I always hear how we should be just like the church in Acts," I say, "and it's always some sort of idealistic dream. Don't you think this is something that has been tried a lot over the years, generally dissolving into some sort of mess?"

"Yeah, absolutely," Nate replies. "That's the whole thing, don't you see? It's been tried. It's been institutionalized. It's been systematized. Like Communism. That's the trouble. I'm not talking about something prescriptive, like 'Go out and be like these people' or 'Everyone do what I say and share the gospel the way I tell you to share it.' What I'm saying is when the fullness of the Spirit is present, this is what happens. It's a sign of the Spirit, not a sign of our power or authority. It's not that people have to make these sacrificial decisions to do something they don't want to do—like four-year-olds putting money into the offering plate. It's like parents at Christmas; the joy of the holiday is in the giving—finding the right gift, the right present, seeing their kids' eyes light up. The kids only want to receive, and can't imagine enjoying giving. That's where most of us are in life. But parents don't care as much what they get because they have discovered that the higher joy, the more profound joy, is in the giving. The Spirit makes all of life like this, so that it is a joy to give, a joy to do, a joy to be something for someone else."

"So we don't have to do anything? You make it sound so easy. So automatic. The Spirit will just make us into giving sorts of people?"

"Well, kind of. The Spirit will make us into that kind of person. But it's a process. It's a journey. We will taste now only a little of what we will experience in full later. Really, the New Testament is mostly about our not being people like this in our present lives. Luke, the Spirit doesn't manhandle us. We don't become slaves of the Spirit, or pawns of the Spirit. The Spirit enables, focuses, and empowers, but we work with the Spirit. This isn't about salvation, you know. That's the common misconception with a topic like this. Christ and the Spirit work in salvation through grace. It's all on their end. Once saved, however, we are called to participate, and our willingness to participate frees us up for even greater service."

"Describe how we participate."

"The goal of our lives isn't to go out and do all those things they talk about in Acts," Nate explains. "That's the Spirit working, and if we try to do it with our own power we lose heart and are totally ineffective. Our goal is to break down the barriers and sharpen our spiritual ears so we listen and so our instincts are shaped by the power of the Spirit to make us into people who naturally live in a way that forms community. We don't do these things at first; instead we begin to mature and tap into the power that allows us and encourages us to do all of this."

"How do we break down barriers?"

"We create a context by giving things up—attitudes, fixtures, whatever. Then the Spirit moves in. The house was a barrier and I needed to let it go. Not just as a house, but as a symbol. It represented a place to lay my head. Giving it up represented my desire to go out and bury my dead—my dead experiences and relationships. I had to let it all go. In letting it go the Spirit opened the door for me to find and experience a real freedom, a freedom I could never have managed, even if my goals were the same. Letting things go is the most profound spiritual act we can do, because all that stuff—our possessions, ambitions, sins, whatever—becomes a substitute for the Spirit."

"How do we know what we need to give up?"

"Look for anything that is a barrier. Some things we just need to let go. Let go trying to control. Let go being controlled. This can even apply to good things, because by letting go of demands we can gain perspective. If we hold too tightly then these form our identity. We even let spiritual leaders or tradition or good influences be the Spirit for us. These things are not and can never be our Holy Spirit. Each of those things—good and bad—whisper to us, and in the cacophony of whispers we get confused about which is the real Holy Spirit. We have to abandon it all, and then we find it all, and we find each other. Because when we let go, then the Spirit works in us and in others to create this profound bond, this profound reality in which our greatest joy is to serve and help and live for others. That's the nature of the kingdom. That's the discovery of God and heaven in this present."

"Does everyone need to do what you did?"

"Do what I did? No. That would mean everyone was just like me. We all have different things we need to let go. We all have different ways we try to form our identity apart from Christ. We all have different barriers to our finding free and full relationships with others."

"So we move toward God and we find community?" I ask.

"God is drawing us toward him. Part of that process is drawing all people toward him. To grow closer to him we have to grow closer together. Think of it like we're all climbing a mountain starting from separate spots. The closer we get to the top, the closer we all climb with each other. It just happens. Our goal is the peak, but in going there, each step we take draws us together, so at the top, there can only be the bunch of us gathered together, all at the same goal."

"I don't get this. I mean I understand community is good, but you seem to be raising it to this new sort of level. Like a cult might do, where everyone has to strictly conform to the particularities of their community rules for it to work. I guess I see those sorts of communities as being really exclusive. How do you find the balance?"

"The balance is found by realizing diverse individuals can value each other and maintain unity instead of uniformity. That is the essence of the Spirit, Luke. But to keep it up we have to listen to each other, valuing both our differences and our contributions. I can't assert my own ideas all the time. I have to listen. We talk about issues and concerns. We work out what it means, not in a settled plan but in a continual process of discernment. It's because I value the community that I value the individuals here, value them enough to take their worries and ideas seriously. In doing that, and never stopping doing that, we can find a balanced community. "

"Is such a thing achievable? To be a really perfect community, like the Acts community, I mean? Is that what you want? It seems like this is the most common, most never-achieved goal. Have you seen it?"

"Most 'never-achieved'?"

"You know what I mean," I say and laugh.

"No, I've never seen it. But, you know what else I haven't seen? I have never seen anyone raised from the dead. I've never seen a person who can't walk get up like nothing had ever been wrong. I've never seen a lot of the things we are told we should see when the Spirit comes upon a group of people. Why is that?"

"You tell me."

"I was hoping you would know!" Nate laughs. "To be honest, I don't know. Not in full, at least. But that's the whole point of what we are trying to be about. The Christian life, Luke, isn't about getting all the structures in a row and coming up with a good business plan, making sure to climb the ladder of ecclesial success. It's not about being perfect, then abandoning the quest if things don't match up to the goals right away. There's something more to it and that something more is seen all through Paul's epistles and definitely in Acts. My praying spurred some sort of instinct in me, where I was seeing only one path to walk down and seeing the rest increasingly barricaded. That led me to this place. But it's not enough to trust our feelings. That's dangerous. That is precisely what has led to so many false starts over the years. So I took my feelings, took my stirrings to help create a new sort of gathering, and I prayed about them. And I studied Scripture."

"It was confirmed?"

"Well, not really. That's the thing. You ask if we are wanting to be the same sort of community as found in Acts. Yes and no. We're not living in the first-century Roman Empire now. We're not coming out of the same kinds of backgrounds and cultures and religions. We have different baggage, you know, and society around us has different realities. What is clear is that the Spirit is not about mimicry. There's no creativity in mimicry. The Spirit is always doing something creative, always doing something new, always reimagining the world, encouraging us and allowing us to participate in what is going on."

"So why is that hard to see?"

"Because we're not as creative, Luke. We don't really have faith. We say we believe in Christ, but we really don't. We see Jesus walking on the sea and we stay in the boat instead of walking toward him. We believe in things that make sense. Nothing about Jesus makes sense. We believe in security. We believe in our own talents, and doing a lot of work, and good organizational principles."

"Those aren't bad things, Nate."

"No, of course not. They're not inherently bad. But they are terrible when they become substitutes for the Holy Spirit, and that's what the church has done throughout its history. That's what I was doing when I was working at a church. The Spirit is elusive. Like wind and fire. Wind and fire destroy all those things we want to put together. We try to manage them and end up creating chaos. So, we replace the Spirit. We come up with really formal theology and comprehensive liturgy. What would Paul think if he saw all the things we came up with, which we insist others follow?"

"I don't know."

"He'd assume the Judaizers he was always arguing against had won," Nate says. "Paul realized that Christ had begun something new. Something new not only for salvation but also in the very foundations of how we relate to God. God isn't this foreign potentate. He's Our Father. God isn't this formal king. He's Abba. In keeping the rules and building fences around the rules in our worry that we might somehow offend God, we end up rejecting the very things he said we are supposed to do. That's what got Paul so terribly frustrated. 'Read the Scriptures!' he yelled in his letters. We would be yelled at in the same way, because we miss the mark in the exact same ways. We gloss over what God says, and what God is saying through the Holy Spirit. We mutter, 'That can't be right' because it doesn't make sense to us, and doesn't have a clear order or flowchart."

"So are you saying everyone is wrong, and you've finally figured it all out?"

"If you think I've figured it all out, I need to introduce you to everyone else in our community," Nate says and laughs. "They'll set you straight. I haven't figured a lot of things out. Most things, some might say. I'm a novice, that's what I realized. So much of what I thought I knew, I really don't."

"Why do you think that is? I mean you're talking a lot about the Spirit in the New Testament, and it sounds all new to me. Sounds new to you too. If this stuff is so clear why has it been missed, or at least hard to find? Why does this sound new?"

"It's certainly not new. The more I read the more I realize there have been men and women throughout the centuries who have brought these things up. Maybe not the same way, in the same setting, but a lot of my present confidence comes from the fact that while it all was new to me, it's not new. But it's inconvenient, you know. It's a little disordering too. So it was skipped over. Other parts were emphasized. Take Luther, for instance. His pressing problem was sin and grace. He read Scripture and found an answer to his particular questions. Then he shaped a church around those answers. He emphasized the parts that really addressed his problems. The church always does that."

"Are you doing that too?"

"Yeah," Nate laughs. "I probably am. That's likely why I'm really emphasizing the Holy Spirit now. My questions have to do with broken community. With incomplete Christian lives. I understand the sin and grace thing, but I had no idea what to do next. It is the Holy Spirit who fills that out. Maybe now that others have answered some foundational questions we can get to the questions I'm asking, and others in our era are asking."

"How do you find the answers?"

"I need other people, not to preach at but to preach with. People hear us talk about this stuff, and they assume we are accusing other people of being totally wrong. That's missing the Spirit in another way—making it seem like the Spirit is dependent on us to do things exactly right to get things done."

"Which isn't the case?"

"Of course not," Nate says. "The only reason you and I are sitting here together now is because for the last two thousand years the story has been working in the lives of men and women who feel the power of God in their lives and know there is light to be found in Christ. The Spirit has continued to work. The gospel changed lives in the first century and has continued to change lives. It isn't always the official governments of the church that do this, but it's the people in the church who find it and live it and share it. That's how the Spirit has continued to work. We are helpful, but we're all far from necessary so even in our profound imperfections the Spirit takes what we do and forms a work out of it. What I'm *not* saying is that everyone has to do things the way I want to do them. I *am* saying that the way we do things generally isn't the Spirit's concern. The Spirit has a mission in this world and it's not to be the hall monitor.

It's to draw all people, all of creation, to Christ, and fill them so they encounter God with the fullness intended from the beginning."

"How do we encounter God, then?"

"That's the question, isn't it? What do the Scriptures say?"

"Is he still talking about history?" Debbie asks, sitting back down at the table.

"I think he might be starting up again," I laugh.

"No, we're talking about Scripture now. You're okay with Scripture?"

"Scripture's okay," she says. "I suppose. What are you talking about?

"How do we encounter God, Debbie?" Nate asks her.

"Through and with other people," she says, then looks at me and adds, "it's all in Scripture."

I laugh. "That's what he said. You two make a good tag team."

"Really, it's true. And not just because Nate and I both said it. The fact I'm sitting right here, the fact I think about God in a positive way at all—that's what we're talking about. This didn't happen because I sang the right hymns or went to the right services every week. I grew up with all that, and you know what it got me?"

"What?"

"Hatred. Hatred of other people. Hatred of God. Hatred of myself. It got me running away from church because church represented something. It represented power-hungry, dirty men wanting to control every little bit of everyone else's life. They got their hands on me, and no one would listen, no one cared because these were men who did all the right things, were great speakers and leaders, and put a lot of stinking money in the collection plate. They were elders and deacons and pastors. What was I? I was a rebellious little girl who was always asking for it. It all made me sick. It still does. So much that I swore I would never go to church again, because I saw what church was like, and it destroyed my soul."

She stops and stares outside. I don't know what to say. I'm not sure where that came from.

Nate jumps in, "When we first moved in here we decided to hire staff who weren't related to what we were doing. We wanted to make sure this was a business, and a context, but for most of us the business part wouldn't be our main priority. In doing that we also decided we didn't want a split reality here. So with everyone who came we were very upfront about what we were doing. When we got to that point of the interview, Debbie got up and walked out. She didn't say a word, but just left. Chris—Chris Patterson, our manager here and part of the core community—was going to hire her, but she walked out when she heard we had a spiritual interest."

"I didn't want to be part of any religious stupidity," Debbie says. "And it sounded a bit like a cult."

"It did?" Nate asks her.

"Yeah, it did. Kinda still does."

"Anyway, Debbie called back later that afternoon and asked if she got the job. Chris had mentioned it, and I was caught by surprise so I said yes. She came back and we three had a long talk."

"I had to explain myself," Debbie adds.

"She put us on probation," Nate laughs. "We had to show her we weren't a bunch of fanatics."

"It was the only way I was going to take the job."

"Why did you do that? Was there nothing else out there?"

"Maybe. I don't know. I had to take it. That's what I'm saying. I left, thinking this was a cult, and everything in me ordered me to call back. From the moment I left, it was like I couldn't leave. I wasn't supposed to leave. I left but I couldn't stick with it. That same pull that always made me leave before, made me come back. I had to know."

"Know what?" I ask.

"If it could really be different."

"Was it?"

"I stayed."

"So what was it?" I ask.

"It took me a while to realize the difference," Debbie says. "Why did things seem more whole? Then I realized it was the fact they weren't wanting to take from me. Everyone else— every other religious person I came across my whole life— wanted to take something. Freedom. My soul. My money. My body. I know not all churches are like that. I know most churches aren't like that now. But growing up that was what I was around. All the worst tendencies and temptations of churches were given free reign where I was, so I became intensely sensitive to any hints of it. They were all like leeches wanting to suck something out of me so they could fill themselves with whatever poison they preferred. Vampires. They were all like vampires. Not alive, not dead, but feasting off anyone they could get under their power. I ran away from that, because I wasn't going to feed them any longer.

"I've got to help that table." Debbie stands up and walks over to a table on the other side of the room.

"She gets intense sometimes," Nate says. "Sorry about that. She's not the most agreeable person to talk with about church things. I suggest music as a more healthy conversation topic with her."

"You can't argue with personal experience, can you?"

"I never went through what she went through, and that makes a difference. Church was always just the opposite for me. It's where I found approval and success, ever since I was young. I was always a leader, though when I hear her talk I always begin to distrust myself." He laughs, then gets serious again.

"But yeah, she has a point," he continues. "That's what I was saying about Scripture, why community stuff is all the way through. It's not about the forms and the structures and the pop psychology stuff that's so common now, even though that's always where contemporary Acts 2 conversations stray. It's what Debbie said about people—religious people—always wanting and taking something. Which is precisely what Jesus seems to rail against when attacking the Pharisees. They were interested in religion, so that wasn't their problem. Their problem was that their religion wasn't interested in the same things God is interested in."

"People."

"Always people. The Prodigal Son and stuff like that. When you read Acts all the way through and not broken up into the usual bite-sized bits, you get to see a pattern. Luke himself has divided the story into increasingly larger chunks as he takes us from the resurrection of Jesus to the trial of Paul, stepping us through the early formational experiences of the church. He breaks it up with a curious phrasing, the same sort of description he used at the end of Acts 2 that I mentioned before."

After they prayed, the place where they were meeting was shaken. And they were all filled with the Holy Spirit and spoke the word of God boldly.

All the believers were one in heart and mind. No one claimed that any of his possessions was his own, but they shared everything they had. With great power the apostles continued to testify to the resurrection of the

Lord Jesus, and much grace was upon them all. There were no needy persons among them. For from time to time those who owned lands or houses sold them, brought the money from the sales and put it at the apostles' feet, and it was distributed to anyone as he had need.

Joseph, a Levite from Cyprus, whom the apostles called Barnabas (which means Son of Encouragement), sold a field he owned and brought the money and put it at the apostles' feet. *(Acts 4:31-37)*

"People separate the paragraphs following Acts 4:31," Nate continues. "They see they prayed, that the Holy Spirit came upon the people and spurred them to speak the word of God boldly. But then they don't continue to see what else the Holy Spirit was about. Verses thirty-two and onward aren't a description of how the early church was communist in principle. They are verses which describe the natural outworking of the Holy Spirit in a group of people truly committed to freeing themselves for the Spirit's work. These are people who saw the risen Jesus. So they held nothing back. They believed. They really believed in the things they talked about and let everything else go. In letting everything else go they opened their lives to the fluidity of the Spirit to do a work. The Spirit worked by spurring them to let go of everything they claimed and to reach out to others, in word and in deed. Acts 2 was not a fluke, it was a pattern that continued."

"People surrendered themselves when the Holy Spirit worked."

"Yes, that's why Ananias and Sapphira got into so much trouble.* It wasn't just that they were deceptive. What was it that Peter said? He said they lied to the Holy Spirit. The Holy Spirit was the one spurring the actions, and these two thought it would be okay to act like they were following. The only prob-

---

* *Acts 5:1-11*

lem was they were not really doing what the Holy Spirit was suggesting. They put on a show for everyone else. They acted like they were these great Christians. They wanted the best of all the worlds. The Spirit wouldn't have any of that. The Spirit doesn't mind if we are weak. The Spirit does mind if we're not honest. To take hold of the Spirit, to find the blessings of the Spirit, they had to release themselves and all they had, holding back nothing. The Spirit wouldn't make them. We're not turned into slaves. But the Spirit does react to our actions and motives. We can't play like we love people or pretend we want people to find their fullness when we really want them to feed into our fullness. That's what runs all through the New Testament. We have to let go of everything. I mean everything. In letting go of it all the Spirit takes hold of us and spurs us to become something—something as individuals and something as a community."

"I think I'm getting this. When we stop focusing on ourselves, the Spirit brings others who will focus on us, so that it becomes a circle."

"Yes! That's it. A circle. That's the whirls and knots of the Celtic designs. The endless knot where everything is complicated and interlinked."

Debbie sits down again at the table, sighing as she sits.

"Do you mind a bit of theology?" Nate asks me.

Debbie gets up and walks into the kitchen.

"Go ahead," I say.

"I'm trying to get my brain around a couple of terms that describe the nature of the Trinity. One way of viewing the Trinity is as the Community of God, a relationship that is flowing and eternal."

"I don't know what that means."

Nate laughs and says, "I'm not sure I do either. But I think there's something worthwhile there. Anyway, one of the words used to describe how the Trinity relates is *perichoresis*."

"Peri- what?"

"Perichoresis. Basically, Luke, the Trinity is a bit of a problem. It's hard to explain, or understand. It's so bad most people would much rather believe in it while completely ignoring what's going on."

"Like me."

"But if that's who God is, as all Christian theology suggests, then it should mean something. Who we are affects how we relate to this world."

"So who God is affects how God relates to this world, which is quite a lot of relating?"

"Yeah, all the universe is affected by how God relates to creation. So people have tried to come up with ways of understanding that would gather together all the various forms of God's revelation and help us understand what it means that three are one. There are a lot of ways of doing this. Some folks have come up with a hierarchy, thinking the Father is number one, the Son is number two, and the Spirit is number three. Or some have proposed that God is one, but depending on which face or mode he presents in a certain moment we see a different person."

"God has different hats."

"Yeah, but saying it like that is actually a heresy called *modalism*. It all gets complicated because people don't know what kind of analogy to start with. Is God sort of a government? Or is he like the human soul? Maybe God is like an egg or maybe like the sun."

"An egg?" I laugh. "This is definitely going in my article—the church who worships an egg."

"Now we're in trouble," he laughs with me. "You've not heard that one? It's an attempt to describe the Trinity by analogy. Yolk, white, and shell—three parts but one thing. Or God is like the sun with object, light, and warmth. Those are nice illustrations of how three different parts can be one. Only they're not quite right. Then we run into the problem of dealing with who God is by himself as opposed to who God is as he interacts with the world."

"This is where I usually change the channel," I laugh.

"Most people do. But another way of looking at God is sort of like a community. Three persons all one, so they have to have some sort of arrangement of living together like that, allowing their diversity to also be a unity, one might say."

"Do we really need to understand it? Maybe it's just something we're supposed to accept without bothering about the details."

"Well, I know that God doesn't seem too concerned if he doesn't make sense, but I do think God works and exists in a way that can make sense to us, if only on some level. One basic way of understanding God's interaction with himself is to think of his existence as a dance."

"A dance?"

"Yeah, a dance. What happens when people are dancing?"

I pause for a moment, not quite sure what he's asking. "Depends on the style I guess, but people move together following a specific rhythm."

"Take ballroom dancing," Nate says.

"I did, and lasted about half the class before falling too far behind."

"It's complicated," he laughs. "Two people have to act in a concerted way to the music. Moving their whole bodies in intricate patterns together, always acting and reacting to what the other person is doing, always moving with each other even if they aren't doing the same thing."

"God is a dancer?"

"God is all the dancers, and the music, and everything. Think of the Trinity as interacting in this complicated and amazingly intricate dance. They are all moving as one, together, even as they are not the same person and even if they are doing different things in different ways."

"God is not line dancing, is he?"

"No," Nate laughs. "That's everyone doing the same sort of thing together, all in a row. God is like a ballroom dancer, or even better, a ballet, with the whole show being this gathered collection of intricate steps and interactions. The dancers highlight each other, point to each other. They create this rhythmic flow out of their separate contributions."

"The Trinity is that sort of dance?"

"That's basically what the term *perichoresis* means. It's a swirling together dance of the Trinitarian persons."

"That's a mouthful," I say.

"And a mind full," Nate adds. "But I think it helps us understand. This is what the Spirit represents, you see. Where the Spirit comes from. This is what the Spirit knows and does. It's a dance, and when the Spirit comes on a community the Spirit naturally forms the separate pieces into a unity—a complex unity that reflects the Trinity itself."

"If we don't insist on our own steps."

"And our own music, and our own organization."

"You said there were two terms you liked. What's the second?"

"*Kenosis.*"

"I think my doctor tested me for that at my last physical."

Nate laughs. "Basically, the concept is about pouring."

"Pouring?"

"Yeah, pouring. Think of a waterfall pouring into a pond. Now, think of the persons of the Trinity as all being waterfalls pouring into each other. The community of the Trinity is not made up of one demanding from the other, but all of them pouring into each other, so there is a profound mutuality going on. Each is distinct, but requires the others. Each is individual yet because of the nature of their relationship they are all feeding into each other. Not as leeches or vampires, like Debbie talked about. Each *pours into* each other, not *pulls from* one another. The dependence isn't predatory."

"An M.C. Escher painting," I suggest. "You know the steps leading into more steps, all looking like it makes sense except you can't quite see a beginning or an end."

"That's a little like it, absolutely. Everything in Escher is pouring into everything else, making for this eye-twisting scene. God is like that. The Spirit is creating us to be the same sorts of people, never claiming or demanding or plundering each other's souls. Instead, if we're really walking with the Spirit we begin increasingly to live our lives so that we pour into other people, really seeking their fullness and best and fruition."

"Not our own."

"Our natural tendency is to be self-centered. That's what I fell into at my old church. It was about our ministry, our work, our efforts, our evangelism, how we were representing ourselves to the world, how we were spreading our vision and goals. Everything was about becoming a leader, which implies becoming more to someone else's less. When I stepped away I saw I should never have focused on myself. It's about helping other people find their lives, their visions, their fullness, their fruitfulness. If I am about that, then the Spirit will do a greater work in me."

"Becoming less you become more."

"That's the work of the Spirit, and what Debbie is talking about, and what Paul wrote about all through his letters to the churches. As long as the focus is on me, I am nothing. If I really begin to interact in the lives of others—not just in the typical religious ways, but in really helping them become who they are supposed to be—then the Spirit gets involved, spurring me onward, spurring them onward, building in us a unity that is amazing. The whole of the Spirit's work is much greater than the sum of the parts, Luke."

"So what does this sort of community look like? What does the Spirit do? In you? Through all of you?"

"What are we about? Is that what you're asking?"

"Or to put it in your terms, Nate: What is it that the Spirit is about in your community?"

Before Nate can answer another man comes up to our table and says, "Hello, Nate."

"Hey, Mike. How was the prayer time?"

"Very refreshing. Good small group of people this morning. Is this the reporter you mentioned?"

"Sure is. Luke, this is Mike. Mike, Luke. Mike has been with our church for about six or seven months."

"Nice to meet you, Mike."

"Same here, Luke. Nate has been filling your head with all our good qualities, I hope. Hate to have all our wickedness end up in print."

"Well, I am an investigative reporter," I laugh.

"Uh-oh," Mike replies as he takes a seat. "Now, we're in trouble."

"That's a great question you asked," Nate says to me. "Only I need to leave right now for a little bit. You're welcome to stay around here. It's a nice place to hang out. Maybe even Mike here could help you out. "

"Yeah, that would be fine," I say. "If you have a little time, I'd love to have as many voices as possible in my article."

Mike is wearing a pale yellow polo shirt and nicely pressed Dockers. Clean-shaven, and if I'm right he recently had a manicure. It wouldn't surprise me to hear he had been the quarterback of the football team and homecoming king twenty-five or thirty years ago when he was in high school.

"All the time you need," Mike says. "Have the day off."

I turn to Nate, "Can we hang out tomorrow? I feel like we just started. I still would like to know more about your story."

"Around ten?"

"Perfect," I say. "I'll see you then."

> " I focus not on the wrong and right, but on the goal.
> I focus on what the Spirit is doing in my life, bringing
> me hope, and life, and joy. That's what I learned.
> I learned that it is by walking with the Spirit—in all the
> ways this means—I will find real and thorough holiness.
> It's just something that will happen, because I will be
> increasingly thinking like the Spirit, listening to the
> Spirit, hoping with the Spirit, acting with the Spirit."

5

Empowering for Right Living

"What was the question I am helping out with?" Mike asks, after Nate gets up and walks into the kitchen.

"I asked Nate about the community. What that really means. Practically. What is it that the Spirit does in and with you all?

I am glad to talk to someone who doesn't have to give me the sell. Sometimes I get a more honest perspective with the lead pastor not around.

"Holiness," Mike replies after a moment. "Someone else may answer differently, but for me it comes down to holiness."

"Holiness?" I ask. "That doesn't sound quite as open as what Nate said, nor very practical."

"I think most people have wrong ideas of holiness," Mike answers. "I did. For a long time I did. Thank God I finally learned the real meaning. Though a little late, I suppose."

"Can I get the 'real meaning' of holiness and share it with my readers?" I ask with a smile.

Mike laughs. "It would be easier to answer your question if I could tell you my story. Do you have time?"

"Sure."

"Telling my story is a little bit of penance for me. I guess I'm a little like the sailor with the albatross around his neck. I tell anyone who will listen."

"The Mariner hath my will."

"Very nice," Mike answers. "You're well read. Does this English teacher's heart good."

"I had a season of Coleridge back in college. Always liked the Rime."

"Well, then 'the sun came up upon the left, out of the sea came he and he shone bright, and on the right went down into the sea.' Well, maybe not just like that. I wasn't a mariner. I was a pastor. I guess they're a lot alike really."

"A pastor?" I asked. "What happened that you are now an English teacher."

"Bad exegesis," he replied.

I laughed.

"No, I'm serious. I try to look back and see what happened—and a lot happened—but it all boiled down to bad exegesis. I didn't know Scripture as well as I thought I did."

"What kind of pastor were you?"

"That I didn't know Scripture?" he laughs.

"No, I mean where did you work?"

"At a church in Indiana. I'd rather not be more specific. I feel real comfortable with you, but I haven't forgotten you're a reporter."

"I was hoping you would forget that."

"Where was I? Oh, at the very beginning still. I was quite the fellow. Always the leader. Everything worked out for me.

God blessed me with a nice life growing up. My parents weren't rich, but they did okay, and we all had what we needed. Life was golden. Met my beautiful wife during my first week at college. Two good, holy, passionate young kids with strong morals who talked earnestly about our boundaries and wanted to get married as soon as possible."

"You did, I bet."

"I was a sophomore. She was a junior. Christian college, so it wasn't too shocking. She wanted to be an elementary school teacher. I knew God had called me to be a pastor. Everything was on track."

"What happened?"

"What happened? It all worked out wonderfully. She taught while I finished college and then seminary. We had two darling daughters. Quite a perfect life really. I had it all together and people knew it. There was a small bump finding the right church to work at after seminary, but we did. We moved to a nice little suburb and led a medium-sized church. I knew God had plans for me to go beyond medium-sized and so I worked, and worked, and worked. So did she. I'm not sure life was good, but it was certainly the life we wanted. In every way. I had pulled something off, and I was convinced that other people needed to learn what I had to teach."

"But?" I ask.

"Yeah, there's always that. Let me give you a sense of not only what I was, but how I thought. I was a firm believer in all the Protestant beliefs. Saved by God through grace. I said 'the prayer' when I was five or six years old. My parents were kind but firm. We were able to see only certain movies, and watch only certain television shows. There wasn't any drinking or smoking or any kind of modern music in my house. I never heard cussing until I went to school. Some people might chafe

against that. It felt comfortable to me. I didn't feel at all rebellious. I liked the discipline. All my energy was turned to sports
and leadership. It didn't make any sense for me to go out and do
things that were destructive. I kept myself clean. Kept myself
respectable."

"A good kid."

"Yeah, I was. And I grew up a good adult. More than doing
what is right, I just didn't understand people who went off and
did stupid things. Getting drunk, getting high, going to clubs,
sleeping around. It never had any appeal to me."

"You weren't tempted?"

"Yes and no. I was really active in school, and had all sorts
of invitations to do all sorts of things. But, I kept strong. I knew
that my faith, my testimony, depended on me keeping true. I
knew that God had called me to bigger and better things, and
that to soil myself with all the distractions would have been an
insult to my family and my faith. I was ambitious, you see.
Ambitious in life. Ambitious for God. For me this worked out in
two ways. I was always trying to get my friends to go to church
with me, and make friends with those who needed to go to
church. I was stoked by evangelism. Second, I sought holiness.
In high school—I remember this so clearly—I sat down one
Saturday and drew up a plan for my life. It was a chart that had
vertical and horizontal goals. I made it my mission to reach out
to people and to reach up to God."

"Evangelism and holiness?"

"Basically. This chart stayed with me. I was serious. I even
broke up with a girlfriend in high school because I thought she
wasn't serious enough. When MTV debuted she got totally into
it. I remember starting my senior year really confused about her.
It was new and I felt it was a tool of the devil. I mean she
seemed like such a great Christian to me, but I guessed I was
somehow deceived . I told her she needed to stop watching that

trash. I told her she was like Eve, that she needed to listen to my counsel and not eat the apple. She didn't see it that way. So I broke it off."

"You were intense."

"I was. That's likely why I fell for Missy so quickly. She never even had a television growing up. The only books she read were the Bible and books assigned for school. *That's the woman for me*, I thought. But, anyway, I was earnest about my chart and took it seriously. When I read Wesley for the first time in college it struck me that this was a guy I could follow. I even started a Holy Club like he did, where a group of us guys got together each week to talk about where we failed and how we could do better. Growing up I was a Baptist. But I began to feel Baptists were lax in their devotion. I wanted to grow. Grow close to God. Give up sinning. I wanted to be right in every way. Perfect. And I looked into myself and knew that I could do it. I could do it for God. God called me to do it."

"Works righteousness?"

"No. My salvation was from God. I didn't work to be saved, I worked because of it. Because I owed God, right? The holiness was my call as a Christian."

"How did that look for you?"

"I set boundaries for everything. I had a list of right and wrong, and made sure everyone around me followed this list. I loved the rules. I had little patience for those who strayed. At my college I was something. I campaigned for stricter rules, and served on a committee that addressed student discipline. I was ruthless. All with a smile and loving heart, of course. I knew that bad influences seep in, like yeast. Like mold. To be holy I had to set rules and stay disciplined. I had to keep my surroundings holy. I had to create and manage a whole world to preserve my identity and keep from stumbling. Much like I kept fit. I ate right. Exercised. Kept myself pure."

"I'll bet you didn't have any trouble getting into seminary?"

"I was ready. I studied the preachers—the good fundamentalists from the early twentieth century. Man, they knew how to hit sin. They called it like it was. They held up their Bibles and they spoke the truth about the pervasive perversions of popular culture. They were like honey to me. I loved it. Missy and I began a Bible study in seminary, where we pursued the depths of God in our lives. We read copies of those sermons. We got tapes. We did book studies. Learned apologetics. Everything came under a microscope. I mean it probably almost sounds like a cult, but it wasn't. I was a good leader. Firm and strong. Everything from the Bible."

"It sounds like the path toward becoming a television evangelist," I laughed.

"Now I can't imagine being like that; but I was. Well, we got hired to be the leaders of the church I mentioned, and we went with a lot of fire in our bellies. I was flying high. Everything was being confirmed. I was sharp. I was wise. I was ahead of the game. My denomination supervisor told me I was being watched with hopeful eyes. So I kept at it. I preached. I served. I was a brilliant pastor, if I may say so. It took a lot of work, but I was so disciplined. I felt like I was touching God. Holiness, Luke. I taught holiness, and knew that it was my holiness that kept me fresh and strong. I was doing so well I began to feel limited."

"Limited by having a medium-sized church?"

"Well, by that time it was growing by leaps and bounds, but yes, still limited. I began to start crusades in my town. My involvement with the Moral Majority had begun in seminary but really took off when I began to seek community changes. I pushed my members to get elected to the city council. I fought against all the right evils. I led teams to the state capital. I even gave a speech on the steps of the Lincoln Memorial. If I had any interest in doing television I likely could have become a national leader. 'Do what is right and God will work.' That was my motto. I made it my mission to change the world for Jesus, and to help shape communities that would expand across the nation. Holy communities—good for families and honorable to God."

"But, now you're here," I say.

"Now I'm here. Sitting in a pub. Can you believe it? Man, oh man, what my young self would have said to me! Righteous indignation wouldn't even begin to describe it. I guess my young self had some lessons yet to learn."

"What were the lessons and how did your young self learn them?"

"My young self wasn't perfect, you know, even if he wanted to be. But he had a persona, and that image needed to be kept up. For the sake of those who saw him as the model. And there were a lot of people who looked up to him. People needed a guide and a model. So everything wrong was kept hidden. Kept hidden from everyone."

"Even your accountability group?"

"Oh, I didn't need that anymore, Luke. I was fine. Just fine. Had it all under control. I was holy, you see. Sure, sometimes I did things that I wished I hadn't done. But, that's life, right? Romans 7 was really strong to me. I memorized it."

For we know that the law is spiritual: but I am carnal, sold under sin. For that which I do I allow not: for what I would, that do I not; but what I hate, that do I. If then I do that which I would not, I consent unto the law that it is good. Now then it is no more I that do it, but sin that dwelleth in me. For I know that in me (that is, in my flesh,) dwelleth no good thing: for to will is present with me; but how to perform that which is good I find not. For the good that I would I do not: but the evil which I would not, that I do. Now if I do that I would not, it is no more I that do it, but sin that dwelleth in me. I find then a law, that, when I would do good, evil is present with me. For I delight in the law of God after the inward man: But I see another law in my members, warring against the law of my mind, and bringing me into captivity to the law of sin which is in my members. O wretched man that I am! who shall deliver me from the body of this death? I thank God through Jesus Christ our Lord. So then with the mind I myself serve the law of God; but with the flesh the law of sin. *(Romans 7:14-25 KJV)*

There is passion in his eyes as he recites the verses. I hear the fire. His whole body is animated with the words. I bet he was a great preacher.

"That side of me existed," he continues. "But Christ in me made me holy, right? So even when I didn't do everything right, that was fine. I tried to do everything right, of course. Was embarrassed when I didn't, but knew that this wasn't an issue between me and others. I wasn't better than Paul, right?"

"Of course not."

"Well, I started taking this passage to heart. It was freeing in a way. I had my rules still but there was a new freedom. What was sin, really? It wasn't me. It wasn't my fault. I was exhausted trying to fight myself. All my life I kept these strict rules, and while they weren't oppressive to me, I started letting that discipline become an excuse. If I slipped I thought about how I had likely saved up holiness to earn a sin or two. What I did right so outweighed what I did wrong. So I did what I could do, and when that wasn't enough I didn't sweat it."

"How did this change your ministry?"

"Change it? It didn't. You see, I made it even more important to change the contexts. I fought the temptations because I thought that for my own sake, being unable to really fight, I had to take away all the influences. I had to fight those who made it sound like sinning is okay. I had to be firm in my congregation. For the sake of our weakness I had to make sure temptations were kept far away. Holiness was no longer an inner battle for me. I had to fight others, and fight for others. My causes expanded. People hated me for it. But people also loved me for it. Both the hate and the love fed into my identity. I was the pastor and the martyr. That is precisely what I thought true holiness would bring. I fed off of it, because at every turn, hated and loved, I thought my work was being affirmed as right and good. I was doing God's work."

"God's work. That's always a scary phrase to me."

"Ah, but Luke, it sounds so noble, doesn't it? Doing God's work. I was about God's work. Not my work, mind you. No, it's not about me at all. I'm a nice guy. But God is about his work and I'm doing it. So, sorry I have to be so firm and mean, right? Talk to God not me, I'm doing his work. I was totally convinced. I was totally convinced because it all meant so much. I had to get the message of Christ out there. I had to serve Christ. I was caught up in how noble it was."

"A crusade."

"A real crusade, not just the language. We dropped that word in the 1990s but I still had that attitude. Whether it was with Moral Majority, or the Christian Coalition, or any of the other organizations. It was a crusade, and I was a general for Jesus. We read about his commands in Scripture and then were asked to carry them out in this world. I loved the image of riding my horse, sword carried high, fighting the infidels. That's the life. For Christ and his kingdom, right?"

"Somehow, I'm thinking it didn't work out the way you expected."

"I was confident we were on target. Scripture denounced the things we were denouncing. It approved the things we were supporting. God had to be with us. It was a lot of work, but God was with us. And in every way he was with *me*. I had my outside work. I had my church work. I felt confident. God was using me to change lives. Because I was taking his holiness seriously. So seriously I began to expand my ministry to the hurt and the broken. They needed to hear what I had to teach. But there was a major problem."

"What?"

"Me. Do you know the story about the sons of Sceva?"

"No. Where's it from?"

"The book of Acts. Chapter 19."

> **And God** wrought special miracles by the hands of Paul: So that from his body were brought unto the sick handkerchiefs or aprons, and the diseases departed from them, and the evil spirits went out of them.
>
> Then certain of the vagabond Jews, exorcists, took upon them to call over them which had evil spirits the name of the Lord Jesus, saying, We adjure you by Jesus whom Paul preacheth.
>
> And there were seven sons of one Sceva, a Jew, and chief of the priests, which did so.
>
> And the evil spirit answered and said, Jesus I know, and Paul I know; but who are ye?
>
> And the man in whom the evil spirit was leaped on them, and overcame them, and prevailed against them, so that they fled out of that house naked and wounded. *(Acts 19:11-16 KJV)*

"I was the eighth son of Sceva, Luke. That's what my holiness was. I spoke the name of Jesus to people, and assumed that it was me who had the influence. It was a charm to me. It was always something outside of me. I used Jesus, but I didn't know Jesus. I didn't listen to Jesus. I worked for him. I told him what he needed me to do and I expected him to congratulate me. That's what I meant about bad exegesis."

"You'll need to explain that."

"Yeah, after I finish my story. Broken and hurting meant broken and hurting men and women. I had confidence I could help people confront what was binding them. I had confidence because some of my closest friends came out of difficult problems, and I had helped them. So, I thought I was strong. And wise."

"Uh-oh."

"Right. You can see it already. I was blind to it. Or at least I was deluded. My whole life was about discipline, and keeping within the lines, upholding what is true. So when a nice, pretty young woman came into my office I knew she would find help from me. I was happily married, right? Missy was homeschooling the kids at that point. I was gone and busy a lot, but there wasn't any tension. I don't know if we were happy, but I didn't think in those terms. Life was as it should be. We led marriage retreats together, and taught countless couples how to work out their issues. I was even writing a book on the subject at the time."

"So, you thought you were okay."

"I thought I was more than okay. My whole life told me so. Everything was so busy. Everything was so right. I didn't have time to stop even. We began to meet. For a few weeks she just told me her story. She had bad relationships. Some of them abusive. She didn't think God loved her anymore because of what she had done. Luke, she was this broken little flower. We talked about Scripture. We talked about God's love for her. About the call in her life. She told me all the stories she was ashamed to tell everyone else."

"What did Missy think?"

"Missy? She knew I met with all these people. I was very open to her. She saw me like I saw me. We were a team. I was the pastor. She was the pastor's wife. What we planned to be all our lives. She and I were committed to our laws, and she knew how seriously I took holiness, and she never had reason to distrust me. She never said anything was wrong, and even gave me advice on what to say to these people. She was very wise."

He pauses for a moment. I can see a lot churning inside. He blinks slowly. When he opens his eyes again whatever was churning has been pushed back again.

"Anyway," he continues. "I felt for this young woman. And, well, you likely know how the story goes. I was a good man. She had never had a long conversation with someone like me. My thoughts began to wander. I pushed them back. I rationalized them. Over the course of the next few months the rationalization continued. She didn't just need a helpful ear. She needed to be held by strong, loving arms. That's what Jesus would have done, right? He would have hugged her—a healing touch. I was a pastor, not a regular man. We began to meet more frequently. She slipped past all the defenses I had built up. Before I knew it we crossed line after line. No more boundaries. I felt fine with it. God was blessing my life, right? This was just a fluke. I was too important to be limited to the rules I demanded of everyone else. I was doing God's work. She was smiling, and happy. I had healed her."

I don't know what to say, so I remain silent.

"Each week I would get up and preach against the evils of this world in perfect sincerity. Each Wednesday we would meet. Sometimes in my office, sometimes at her apartment. I was so blind. Well, as the story had to go, it couldn't last. She was broken, not healed. I became her identity. And she wanted more and more. I couldn't give any more. I couldn't give anything. I got mad at her. Yelled at her. Called her a harlot or something like that. She had tempted me. She was of the devil. I threw her out of the church. My holiness was at stake, right? Who was she to ask more of me after all I had done? Two weeks after I told her she wasn't to come back, I came home after a long speaking trip to find her sitting on the couch with Missy. They were drinking tea. Drinking out of the small, delicate porcelain cups we bought during our anniversary trip to Scotland. They both smiled when I walked in the door. Very polite. Like old friends."

"Wow," I say.

"Missy was very calm. Didn't say a word to me even after the woman left. We had dinner with the kids—spaghetti. They helped clean up. Watched a video. Went to bed. I was sitting in my office, assuming the conversation wasn't what I thought it was. Then Missy came in. Stood behind me. Told me I was to leave the house by morning. She had called the elders and told them what I had been doing. There wasn't any anger. There weren't any tears. She just stood there, like she was asking the kids to clean up their room. In her eyes was something I couldn't immediately place. It was disappointment. But also something else: judgment. I had never had judgment turned toward me and it burned like boiling water. Missy knew right from wrong and never had a problem dealing with these. I wasn't a problem. I was a failure. I was judged to be unfit. Just like that."

"So that was it?"

"That was it. The rumors spread fast. The woman went to the local papers too. Told them things. What we had done. She exaggerated. She lied. But there was enough truth in what she said that I couldn't defend myself with any integrity. I had totally failed her. I was another man on her list of abusers. Maybe I had a kind word and a listening ear, but I still used her like she wasn't a real person. The elders put me on leave. Some wanted me to stay, but Missy took charge. She made it clear I was no longer welcome. She told me she would fight me at every point, that I would never see our kids again, unless I did exactly what she said. It was the Law, right? Just how things had to be done.

Banished outside the camp. I resigned and moved away. Long story short—or at least less long—I drifted out here after a couple of years. Lost everything. Everything had collapsed. I was completely soiled. My identity was gone. And I was extremely angry at how everyone judged me so quickly and so quickly rejected me. One mistake, Luke. One mistake my whole life! And it did me in."

He pauses, and we both think for a moment. Then, "Do you see your kids?" I ask softly.

"Yeah, we worked out a deal. I have them for a couple of months during the summer. Do you know why I told you this whole story?"

"Bad exegesis?" I asked.

"Bad exegesis. Luther and Wesley and the rest of them taught me about sin and holiness. Saved by grace, go out and be perfect then, but if you're not, God is. They didn't teach me the rest. Maybe they knew it, but I didn't see it. I didn't hear it from all those great fundamentalist preachers I loved and modeled. I didn't hear it from my friends or my colleagues."

"What is the rest?"

"When I got to California, I became a substitute teacher. I could barely pay rent. My faith was in total shambles. I was nothing. Not a single one of my old friends talked to me. I didn't blame them. I wouldn't have talked to me either. I was a complete embarrassment. But you know what? God didn't give up on me. Five years ago, he brought Rachel into my life. She was an angel. I have no idea what she saw in me. I told her everything. She stayed. She told me everything. I stayed. We both were a mess. I would have so looked down on her before. Now I so look up to her. Funny how God works. Man, I was blind."

"How did you get to the Upper Room?"

"Uh, Rachel was invited by someone she met at work. We didn't know what to think at first. I mean, I wouldn't have ever considered this even remotely Christian before. But God had opened me up. And she liked everyone here. I began to see how great this was, how it was tapping into the postmodern mindset. The more I got involved, the more I liked it. I began thinking about what I could do here, how I could lead them to the next step. I thought about the book I would write, taking advantage of the zeitgeist. Crazy stuff. I saw my big comeback."

"And?"

"And I had a talk with Nate about my plans. He knew my background. Never made a big deal about it. Treated us just like everyone else. Well, we talked and I was expecting him to get excited with me. I know churches, Luke. I know how the game works. We could be players. I could take them to a new stage. But he didn't get it. He wasn't impressed. Told me that what I was talking about wasn't the point. We bumped heads. I would have left, but Rachel refused. She told me I was being stupid. Can you believe it? Missy would have never actually said that to me. Not to the spiritual head of the household, right? Disrespectful. Took me off guard, especially at this stage of my comeback. I was getting it on all sides."

"But you didn't leave." I felt much more like a reporter again with Mike.

"I didn't. But I confronted Nate. And he confronted me back. We spent a whole weekend sorting it out. At the end of it I apologized. Apologized to Nate, apologized to God. With tears. Man, that was a day. I called Missy. She didn't care what I had to say and told me I was nothing. Once her mind was set that was it. But it wasn't about her. I still apologized to her. I wasn't the same man, but she wasn't able to see who I was now. To my lasting shame I ruined lives. But God can still work. God took everything that had happened, everything I was and shook it up. I was totally broken. But I hadn't been pieced back together again, and then when Nate and I were talking God just opened up my heart. It was like scales came off my eyes, Luke. I know what Paul felt like when God knocked him to the ground. I was seeing verses and passages like never before, and wow, God saved me. Saved me from myself."

"Good exegesis?" I asked.

"Good exegesis," he laughed. "Right. I learned to keep reading."

"Keep reading what?"

"Romans. I kept reading Romans. Romans chapter seven is a great chapter. But we seem to think Paul is making his main point in chapter seven. That's not it at all. Romans is a letter, not an outline. Paul didn't write the chapter headings. Paul didn't break it up into different chapters or different verses. He didn't have note cards that he pasted together. He was writing a letter with a pretty big argument behind it."

"What was the argument?"

"It's telling people what it means to be a Christian. Or, I should say, it is telling people what it means to see Jesus as the Messiah."

"What's the difference?"

"Paul was a Jewish Pharisee, Luke. That's huge. It means he was arguing out of that context. He was contrasting what he was with what he became, on the basis of who called him, and who empowered him. The whole letter is a contrast. Not a simple one either. He makes and remakes his points. He progresses through his points and then he stops, starts over and progresses through it again. All through Romans he is making a contrast of the Law versus the new work of Christ. Which is likely why I was really focused on chapter seven."

"You knew that you couldn't live up to it, so you needed Christ's salvation."

"Well, that's the common thought, isn't it? Grace makes up for what I can't do. But, that wasn't Paul's point. Paul isn't talking about the Christian life in chapter seven. He's talking about life before Christ, apart from Christ. Or rather, life apart from the Spirit."

"Really?"

"Absolutely. Look at the whole section. Not the chapter. The section. Most people start at verse seven, and they see the discussion about the Law as being a present reality."

"The Jewish Law?"

"That's a great point, Luke, and I'm glad you brought it up. It's an important one for me. Paul is talking about the Jewish Law here, and that's important for his readers. It's not as important for me. I was never tempted to follow the food laws, or offer the right sacrifices. But I was very much caught up in the Law. It was my own Law, the Law of my church. A Law that was just as binding to me. I had a Law for everything. Not just the big stuff. Everything. Everything had a right way and a wrong way. I judged people according to how they fit into my view of the right way."

"Good morality and ethics?"

"Yes. I judged people on their pride. I saw some of those young men who interned for us and knew they were wanting my job. So I preached on pride. I saw how people weren't content with the church and wanted to look elsewhere. So I preached on consumerism. All while keeping my eye out for the best leaders and potential leaders. I focused my time and energy on these people, and if someone didn't measure up, they drifted into the background for me. I hired good pastors from small churches so as to expand their ministry potential and the ministry potential of the church. I set myself apart, and became the judge of everyone, attacking their clearly sinful attitudes, while justifying my own because I had such holy motives."

"Your view of the Law made you the keeper of the Law."

"Right. The Law emphasizes sin. It defines life by the boundary. It assesses goodness by what is not good. The Law, whether Jewish or my own, exists to define sin. So that I live, and try to make others live, according to right rules. The trick is to stay away from sin, right? To stay away from sin I have to constantly determine the boundaries. I have to say this is sin, this is not sin. That is outside the Law, this is inside the Law. We were freed from the ceremonial laws of the Old Testament, but it's still a human need to know the boundaries. A Law-based mindset has to have a Law. My goal was to be holy and good. So I needed guidance on what that meant. How could I be holy and good if I didn't know what was bad, right?"

"Right. Which is what the passage is saying, I think."

"But notice what Paul does. He's a great teacher. Really creative. He knew his rhetoric. In verses four through seven he ends a section. Then he starts up again, making a spiral around his theme. What's he say in verse seven? We have been released from the Law. That's a key statement, because then in the rest of chapter seven he goes back to talking about the Law. But if by the work of Christ, 'in the new way of the Spirit' as he puts it, we've been released, what's all the talk in this chapter about being a slave to sin and not doing what we want to do?"

"What?"

"Life under the Law, Luke. Paul's not talking about the Christian life in chapter seven. He's not talking about his present self. He's writing in the first person throughout, but he's not talking about the present. He's speaking in the words of old Saul, the man under the Law."

"Paul isn't talking about the present struggle of sin?"

"No, that's a huge thing. I lived chapter seven, Luke. That was it for me. I defined all my holiness by chapter seven, basically. The Law was my guide and my curse. My whole focus was on it. All of my efforts were on it. I was unspiritual. Evil was always right there with me. That's why I had to constantly fight it. That's why I made it my life to fight it everywhere. It was always staring me in the face. It was my constant enemy. My constant fear. My whole identity, Luke, was defined by what I couldn't do, what others shouldn't do, by the rules. My salvation was in Christ, right? I was saved from my sin through God's grace. But I could never get past that. I guess I thought if I was saved then it was my duty to stay in line. It was my job to keep looking down. To keep looking back at what I was saved from. Which was always hard for me because I was mostly always a good kid. But I knew myself, and I knew my thoughts, and they frightened me so much I had to constantly reject them. I had to reject everything that would try to pull me down and back. That's why I fought so much, why I knew I had to be powerful, and lead with authority. People had to listen. Sin and death were so present to me, and they had me in their grasp, even though I was supposedly on the other side—the side of salvation. I was saved but I hadn't embraced the freedom. I didn't get the fact there was freedom. My focus was still on the sin and the death."

"What changed?"

"Romans 8, Luke. I had loved Romans 8 because it was the testimony of salvation. Romans 8:28 has always been one of my favorite verses. Only there was a huge problem. I never read Romans 7 and 8 together. The chapter divisions did me in. They were two completely different topics to me. The Spirit is great, right? Eternal life will be a blessing when we finally get there. But our present is difficult. I don't do what I want to do. Poor, poor me. I do what I don't want to do. Life is a constant struggle against it. Who will save me? That's what Paul asked too. Who will save me, Luke?"

"Christ saves you."

"Right! Christ saves me. Here's the biggest thing of all and when I realized it the scales fell off my eyes. Christ doesn't just save me when he brings me to heaven after I die. He saves me now. He is saving me now. 'So then with the mind I myself serve the law of God; but with the flesh the law of sin,' Paul writes at the end of chapter seven. But that's him talking about his old self. Why do I say this? Because of what he says next, Luke."

Because through Christ Jesus the law of the Spirit of life set me free from the law of sin and death. For what the law was powerless to do in that it was weakened by the sinful nature, God did by sending his own Son in the likeness of sinful man to be a sin offering. And so he condemned sin in sinful man, in order that the righteous requirements of the law might be fully met in us, who do not live according to the sinful nature but according to the Spirit. *(Romans 8:2-4)*

"Through Jesus, the law of the Spirit of life set me free from the law of sin and death. Chapter seven, Luke, is about the law of sin and death. So I can't use that chapter as an explanation of my Christian life. Not at all. That's not what Paul was talking about. He was making a contrast. With Christ comes the law of the Spirit, and what is the law of the Spirit characterized by?"

"What?"

"Hope, Luke. It is characterized by hope."

"Hope for Christ's return?"

"Hope for Christ's future and Christ's present. It is this hope, not the Law, that is the basis of real holiness. Because in this hope we really embrace the work of the Spirit, not our own work. That's what Romans 8 says. That's what Paul's own response to Romans 7 says. Read the next verses."

𝕿𝖍𝖔𝖘𝖊 𝖜𝖍𝖔 𝖑𝖎𝖛𝖊 according to the sinful nature have their minds set on what that nature desires; but those who live in accordance with the Spirit have their minds set on what the Spirit desires. The mind of sinful man is death, but the mind controlled by the Spirit is life and peace; the sinful mind is hostile to God. It does not submit to God's law, nor can it do so. Those controlled by the sinful nature cannot please God.

You, however, are controlled not by the sinful nature but by the Spirit, if the Spirit of God lives in you. And if anyone does not have the Spirit of Christ, he does not belong to Christ. But if Christ is in you, your body is dead because of sin, yet your spirit is alive because of righteousness. And if the Spirit of him who raised Jesus from the dead is living in you, he who raised Christ from the dead will also give life to your mortal bodies through his Spirit, who lives in you.

Therefore, brothers, we have an obligation—but it is not to the sinful nature, to live according to it. For if you live according to the sinful nature, you will die; but if by the Spirit you put to death the misdeeds of the body, you will live, because those who are led by the Spirit of God are sons of God. For you did not receive a spirit that makes you a slave again to fear, but you received the Spirit of sonship. And by him we cry, "Abba, Father." The Spirit himself testifies with our spirit that we are God's children. Now if we are children, then we are heirs—heirs of God and co-heirs with Christ, if indeed we share in his sufferings in order that we may also share in his glory. *(Romans 8:5-17)*

"All my life," Mike continued, "I was taught I was controlled by the sinful nature, and had to make it the chief focus of my life to fight what I just about couldn't fight. When I felt I had conquered myself, I turned the fight to other people. I made them my fight, included them in my fight, opposed them in my fight. I had an obligation to fight the sinful nature. But that's not what Paul wrote, Luke. We have an obligation to the Spirit."

"Which means?"

"Which means my whole focus was off. If you had asked me ten years ago if I was controlled by my sinful nature I would have laughed at you. Now, though, I see I was. Not in going out and constantly doing sinful things, not until the end, at least. No, it controlled me by taking all of my focus. I was controlled by it because it had all my attention. I couldn't get away from it, you see."

"The verses you read say, 'put to death the misdeeds of your body' so it seems there's something to fighting sin."

"Well, that's how I read it before. It fit my picture. Under the Law I focus on the Law. When I lived my life under my own law, I focused on my law. The Law emphasizes sin and death, right and wrong. My whole Christian life was a battle against sin. So I tried to put to death my own sin by sheer will and effort. Did a pretty good job of it for a long time too. But it was my whole effort. That's how I know I was controlled by it. I wasn't free. I wasn't free at all.

"The Spirit, Luke, is different. Freeing. I am called to put to death the misdeeds of my body, and in a very strong way called to be even more moral, even more whole, even more holy. But the key is that these aren't my emphases. I focus not on the wrong and right, but on the goal. I focus on what the Spirit is doing in my life, bringing me hope, and life, and joy. That's what I learned. I learned that it is by walking with the Spirit—in all the ways this means—I will find real and thorough holiness. It's just something that will happen, because I will be increasingly thinking like the Spirit, listening to the Spirit, hoping with the Spirit, acting with the Spirit."

"So you're saying holiness is a result, not a goal?"

"Right! Holiness is a result. You see, when we focus on the Law we focus on the things the Law is focused on: sin and death. When we focus on the Spirit we focus on the things the

Spirit is focused on: Jesus and community and giving and crea-tivity and participation. We focus on positives. We draw other people into these positives. The fruit of the Spirit plants seeds in others. We all grow. We all are nourished. We all become ma-ture and holy. With the Spirit our instincts change, so the thought of sinning comes to us less and less. That's why I'm such a different man now. An affair seems absurd to me. Not because I have more willpower or have a stronger sense of right and wrong, but because I would see that young woman so totally differently. I see my own goals so very differently. It's much less likely I will fall into that because I see there's so much more to life. I've tasted life with the Holy Spirit, Luke, and that means I've tasted heaven itself. What else compares to that?"

"You still have a lot of the preacher in you, don't you?"

Mike smiles, and keeps going. "I fell into sin because sin was always about power to me. I had power over sin. I wielded power over other people's sin. Sin became, in a perverse way, my identity. My power lied to me when I was talking with that young woman. It told me I was so powerful I wasn't held to the same standards as other people. Because I was so strong, boundaries weren't necessary. I asserted my power over her, and I actually thought I was righteous and wise. That's the lie. But now I have absolutely no power. It was all taken from me. Instead I now know real power. I know what it is like to take hold of God's power. No, I'm not perfect. The Holy Spirit is with all of us now, but we don't yet experience the fullness of power. We have a taste, though. And that taste brings us ever closer to God."

"So, how does this make a difference in your interactions?" I ask. "You say you still are interested in holiness. What about sin? What about, say, immorality on television or in music or in the club down the street? Doesn't that offend you?"

"Well, there's still a part of me that loves a crusade. I call that my temptation. Because it brought my downfall. Pride and vainglory. Two of the most deadly sins. But I'm not going to march into war anymore. It doesn't make sense to me. The Law tells me right and wrong. When I spoke from the Law I told people about right and wrong. I made sure everyone knew I stood for right and against wrong. Now? I realize the Spirit is the only way to move past sin. I realize the Spirit gives us a hope and a power and a life that gives us a reason to move past sin. Only with the Spirit can we put to death our misdeeds, Luke. So what am I doing telling people to do it on their own effort? I'm demanding they do what is almost impossible to do. I was the most disciplined person around, and I fell so far my whole life crumbled. So instead of going on a crusade, I want to live according to the Spirit. I want to share with people the Spirit in me so that they realize the work the Spirit is doing in them. I want to share the taste of heaven I have, not the fear of hell I had before. I want to tell them what is hopeful, what is peaceful, what is encouraging and rejuvenating. I want to tell people what Jesus did and what Jesus will do. I want to speak about possibilities and the glory of eternity. I want to tell people who they can become, not deride them for their struggles. People need to have the hope, the promise, to live according to the future, to keep their eyes focused upward. I thought it was right to look backward, downward, to the past where all my sins and temptations accused me. I thought that was the path to holiness. But it's not. It's a road that comes to an end. It doesn't go all the way through. Only the Spirit brings us to our destination, and the Spirit *is* bringing us to our destination. We can take hold of that in part even now, and what a part it is!"

"Hey," Nate says behind me, then takes a seat. "Looks like you were able to find someone else who's chatty."

"Yeah," I reply. "Mike's been sharing a little of his own story."

"The albatross?" Nate laughs.

"Right," Mike replies. "I only tell about the albatross because it is such a contrast to my life now."

"We've been talking about holiness, Nate," I say. "Do you have any thoughts?"

"Have you talked about Romans 8?"

"Mike did. I listened."

"Well, that's it right there. Holiness is about the Spirit, Luke. It's about our future, not about our past. It's about what Christ will do, and what Christ is doing. We keep our eye on the prize, and holiness happens. That's the power of the Spirit. The Spirit seems to get a lot of peripheral things done if we move in the directions we're supposed to move."

"It's all very interesting," I say. "Mike, thanks for sharing with me. I really appreciate it."

"My pleasure and my honor, Luke," Mike says. "Like I said, it's almost a penance for me. I just wish I could have learned this before I destroyed lives with my Law."

"The Spirit is good at redemption," Nate says. "Very good at his work. Even when we mess up."

"I really have to go now," I say. "That is, about fifteen minutes ago. Nate, we're still on for tomorrow?"

"Absolutely," he replies.

" *It was because the church of that era welcomed the strangers—strangers to them, not to God—that the church enjoyed a time of peace. It was strengthened because men and women held nothing back, even their own opinions. They took the evidence of the Spirit, even in people who didn't know Jesus at first, and let it shape what they believed. They let the Holy Spirit lead, as the Holy Spirit worked in a story much broader than they could realize. Nowadays we tend to do just the opposite. We tell the Holy Spirit who to work in and how to work. We say that can be a work of the Spirit, this can't. We say a person has to go through years of proving himself or herself in order to have a voice, and to make a substantial change that person has to go through years and years of climbing the ecclesial ladder to a place of authority. The Spirit—in Saul, in Cornelius, in countless stories—shows just the opposite. The Spirit pulls in people—sometimes foolish and ludicrous and wrong people—to make the most profound changes imaginable.*"

6

Welcoming Strangers

The next day I arrive late—a little after ten-thirty. I spent an hour in some inexplicable traffic. I hate traffic problems even when there's a reason I can explain. Everyone came to a stop, and then slowly moved forward, making me think there was an accident or lingering rush-hour delay. Nothing. We went around a broad curve and things began clearing up.

I was told once I should use traffic time in prayer or something meditative. Sometimes I turn on the radio, and that occasionally helps. But there are too many people, and too many people who are angry at all the other people. It doesn't make for a fruitful spiritual environment. I suspect that the person who mentioned that habit to me would suggest it's not up to all those other people to create a fruitful spiritual environment for me. I'm just not quite patient enough to listen. I think it shows.

"Long drive?" Nate asks when I arrive. I walk over to the booth where Nate has been reading. Nate stands up and shakes my hand. "How was the rest of your day?"

"Fine. The usual. Well, I guess that's not a nice thing to say."

Nate sits down again and pushes his books and papers off to the side. I join him at the table. "It's interesting to hear what churches are doing as they all face the same basic issues," I say.

"The same issues we've been facing for a long time."

"I guess."

"Of course, the problem as I see it is that there are issues and there are issues. Folks can get very caught up in addressing symptoms while avoiding the more important issues at the heart of it all."

"Such as what?" I ask.

"People."

"People? I ran into that problem just this morning."

"Hey," he says like he had a sudden realization, "you want to go next door? I feel like getting some coffee."

He gets up and gathers his books and papers into his bag while I also grab my stuff, and then we walk out to the coffee shop/bookstore next door called the Book Trail. He asks for a cup of coffee. The man behind the counter asks him if that's all he wants, laughing at him, even though he's already started filling a cup. Ordering just coffee isn't very common in coffee shops. I get a nonfat chai latte. We sit at a table near the window. At the two tables near us are a couple of harried men with notebook computers, papers, and assorted files.

"People are a problem," he continues after we're settled. "That's something we can't quite figure out, being people ourselves."

"What do you mean?" I ask, knowing what I would mean by this but not what he means.

"We honestly don't know what to do with them. We think we just need to find the right system or the right leadership models or the right principles of attraction. Only the problem is people."

"And what's that problem?"

"People are goofy," he says. "They never get around to doing or being anything that helps us do what we need to do. That's the big problem in churches, really. Except for the dozen or so folks who really do everything, most people are slackers, unable to lift a finger. Pastors do most of their work just trying to get people to see how things should be done, and a good bunch more work trying to get them to actually do it. It's a challenge to make any actual progress. What with people and all."

"I get the feeling you're being a little sarcastic."

"Maybe a little sarcastic, but people really are a problem. At least they're a problem to us. Were you stuck in traffic this morning?"

"Yeah."

"Bunches of people clogging up the freeway preventing you from getting here on time, stopping you from being where you wanted to be?"

"So it wasn't really my fault I was late? I can put the blame on *people?*"

Nate smiles and says, "While you were stuck in traffic, I had a really nice talk with a couple of guys who stopped by for breakfast. It worked out. That's the thing. We think irritations or frustrations are preventing us from moving forward. Instead they are all an opportunity to let go and see what the Spirit is in fact doing in each moment."

"God caused a traffic jam so you could talk to someone else?"

"Maybe," Nate laughs. "Did God cause the traffic jam or did he work with it, and redeem it? That's what I think. Troubles come, but it seems the Spirit somehow can redeem situations so there is fruit. Maybe that's where prayer comes in too. Using the time to pray can turn traffic into a blessing. The key is to see things and people not as bothersome, but to always look for the way of the Spirit in it all. Find the dance. That's a choice. We see that in the Gospels, and it makes for some of the better stories, I think."

"It would take a miracle for me to see traffic as a blessing."

"Jesus seemed to use every situation he encountered," Nate responded, "though he never had to deal with Southern California freeways. Jesus just didn't have a set mission strategy, other than meeting people and responding to them."

"There was the cross."

"Oh, of course, the end game was set. But the method of getting there was a different story, and it seems Jesus allowed his message to adapt to different contexts and situations, like a bed sheet draped over furniture. It pokes out and drops in different places, even though it is all the same sheet."

"The analogy doesn't do much for me," I admit.

"No? Hmmm. I was going to use that one for a talk next week. I guess I'll scrap it now. You know what I'm getting at, though, right?"

"Yeah," I say. "The message wasn't committed to a certain shape or style. It could fit whatever came because it didn't have a rigid shape that everything had to conform to."

"Yeah, isn't that what I said?" Nate asks and laughs. "Again, the key to it all is the Spirit."

"How so?"

"Jesus knew people. This wasn't just an understanding about how to manipulate or manage people. It's better to say he knew specific people. He knew what was going on in their lives, and he knew exactly the right way to listen and respond to them. It wasn't that he had a message to preach, or something he insisted people hear. He sort of did but that wasn't his main characteristic."

"Which was?"

"He welcomed people. Zacchaeus in a tree. The woman at the well. He met them, and he genuinely welcomed them by engaging who they were and who they needed to be. They weren't goals or targets. They were specific people, with specific needs, specific problems, specific hopes. He welcomed them—despite their sins and because of their potential. He knew them better than they even knew themselves. He welcomed them into his community for who they were and who they were meant to become. That's what we don't do. We want everyone to fit in with what we are doing, to feed into who we are, to justify our work and efforts, and give us validation. Jesus, not needing to work at being God, could let go of all of that and just reach out to people in whatever way they needed. He met them, and in the uniqueness of his reactions, they met him. He didn't always say what they wanted him to say, or end up being what they thought they wanted him to be. But he always engaged people—each individual—for their best even if they rejected that best."

"So we're supposed to be like that? How? I don't have the insight of Jesus. He knew things we can't know, like the background of the woman at the well. He knew people and used that knowledge in his conversations. We can't do that in the same way."

"Well, not in the same way...."

"Hey, Nate," a woman standing nearby says. She is thin and tall. Her furrowed brow makes me think she's a little frustrated or confused.

"Hi, Natasha, how are you doing?"

"Wishing a five-minute trip to the bookstore would at least once end up being just five minutes. You don't happen to know a good book on wildflowers, do you, Nate? There are so many, and I'm not quite sure which is the best."

"No, my field is more aquatic insects. Why do you need a book on wildflowers?"

"For a story I'm writing. I could probably just look online, but I like books too much."

"I have the same problem. I find not having very much money is a good answer. Natasha, this is Luke. He's trying to figure us out."

"Good luck with that, Luke," she laughs. "Nice to meet you."

"Great to meet you, Natasha," I reply. "Are you part of the Upper Room?"

"Absolutely. For about five months now, I think. Is that right?"

"About that, I guess," Nate answers.

"Luis and I came in for a drink one night after a long week, and I guess we've never left. I'd love to talk more, but I've already spent too much time in here and I've got more errands to run and then I need to pick Jessica up from kindergarten. Nice to meet you Luke."

"Are you all coming by tonight?" Nate asks.

"Yeah, unless an emergency comes up—which wouldn't surprise me these days—we'll be there."

"See you then," he replies. Natasha takes one last look at the stack of books then seems to force herself out the door.

"Great example," Nate says. "Natasha is trying to work as a writer, has a husband who is a rather successful psychologist, and they have two kids—two girls more specifically. So I know who she is. "

"But that's not really the same as the woman at the well," I say, and laugh. "You've had time."

"I suppose," Nate replies with a smile. "But, I guess you could say that five months ago when Luis and Natasha came in I didn't know them. Now they're part of the church, a really important part. We have to be about things a little differently than Jesus because we don't quite grasp what he did. So we talk with people, ask them questions, engage them more. It takes a little more investment but we get there, and that's really one of the key parts about what we do here."

"Bringing people in?"

"I don't quite like it put that way. That sounds more like we're recruiting for a club. I think the idea of evangelism is wonderful, but a lot of the language around it has mucked up the process, don't you think? People get to feeling they are a target."

"Which is a turnoff."

"Or worse. They get inoculated. So many of churches' typical marketing techniques give people just enough Jesus that they get turned off forever, never again interested and really difficult to reach with the big message of who Jesus is. That's the trouble. Everyone walking by thinks they know who Jesus is. Most folks don't have a clue, and I include church people in that. But they don't know that they don't know, so they don't know what they need to know."

"It sounds pretty bad when you imply even people in the church are clueless about Jesus."

"Well, yeah. But you can see it even in Scripture. The disciples themselves took a really long time figuring Jesus out, and they had Jesus in the flesh as a teacher. So it takes a while for the rest of us who have a less palpable presence to work with."

"But one of your points is that we have the Spirit."

"That's true. But I don't think any of us have a straight-line, no-interruption connection with the Spirit. George Fox, the guy who started the Quakers, always talked about people needing to read the Scriptures and trust the Spirit to teach them what they were reading. So it's not a new message. But a person has to be really spiritually mature to have a solid grasp on what the Spirit is saying."

"So what is the person who isn't spiritually mature supposed to do? You ignore new people who don't have it figured out?"

"Of course not," he responds.

"I don't mean to be rude, but what I hear doesn't seem to match what I see here. It seems you've set up the most seeker-friendly place possible. Totally in their environment and control. Aren't you selling Jesus here in an even more market-friendly way than a megachurch does?"

"Maybe that's the problem, Luke. You don't quite get what it is we are doing here. You think I hang out here so that I can meet people and sell them my religion."

"I wouldn't put it like that."

"Yeah, but that's what you're getting at. My goal isn't to sell anything to anyone, except maybe some food and beverages, I guess, but certainly not religion or faith."

"So, you're not doing evangelism? This whole thing isn't an evangelistic effort with urban décor and good food?"

"Not at all. I'm not here to tell people what to believe or how to think. That's arrogant and imposing. How should I know what people should think?"

"I see. So you're more of a universalist. Whatever someone believes is fine. All beliefs are equal?"

"Luke, that's totally not it. I absolutely don't believe that. I believe in the Nicene Creed, and I don't think it's just a few nice phrases to bolster my own beliefs. It's a statement of fact, and an expression of things which are true whether or not anyone believes them. I think Jesus is the way to God, and we need Christ's salvation in order to find any hope or fullness in this world, let alone the next. Don't confuse methods and theology."

"But you said you didn't know what people should think. Don't you want them to think Jesus is the son of God who died for their sins?"

"Was that Jesus' approach to everyone? That may be a truth, but Jesus knew that people are coming from all different backgrounds, with different questions and different vices and different virtues. How do I start off suggesting a person should ask for forgiveness—that they need forgiveness—when they don't feel a bit of guilt? Some folks may only realize their sin a long way down the road of discovering Christ. Maybe they're looking for wholeness, or direction, or something else, which if addressed can get them realizing the other parts of theology. Giving them answers to questions they are not asking—or worse, telling them they are asking these questions when they are not—only serves to bolster my own sense of being correct. It doesn't get anyone anywhere. My goal, Luke, isn't just to get through a script and get my evangelism count higher than everyone else. I really want to see people discover the light. I want to see transformation."

"Alright, I'll bite. What is it you all are doing here, if you're not doing evangelism?"

"We're here to listen. That's basically it. You think I'm here to meet people so I can tell them what they should think. I'm not. Instead, I'm here so I can meet people and they can tell me what they think. I'm here to be evangelized."

"You're here to be evangelized?"

"Absolutely. Here's the thing. Bringing people to Christ isn't my job. I'm not the one who would ever make that happen. The Spirit is already doing a work in people's lives. If I don't listen to people, if I don't hear what they have to say and how they say it and what they care about, then there's no way I'm going to be able to find out what the Spirit has been doing, and how the Spirit is leading them along. Then I miss out."

"You mean they miss out."

"No, I miss out. Because, like I said before, I can't understand the fullness of God. I'm not enough of a person yet. The Spirit hasn't given me full disclosure. So I have to meet people. The Spirit is doing a work in your life, Luke, and expressing something through your gifts and your perspectives. The Spirit is working in a different way in you than in me. I've never walked along the path you've walked. So you've seen things, experienced things, learned things that I might never come across if I don't listen to you and hear what it is you have to teach me."

"You need to hear my lessons?"

"In as much as you are a stranger to me, Luke, the part of God that you know is a stranger to me. As much as I get to know you, I can get to know that part of God, that unique work and character of the Spirit, as well. It's not that I'm using you, or anyone. It's that God has designed us so that we have to be in a community, have to engage with and listen to each other."

"So how do you see evangelism?"

"Because God has worked in me, too, you see, I need to meet you, and listen to you. But you don't have the full picture either. You don't have the story I know, and you need to learn the lessons I've learned. As a pastor I've been trained in a certain way that adds to what else I've learned through life experiences. So I can teach Scripture, or theology, or spirituality. But that doesn't mean I have ownership of even those things. The Spirit inspires each person, and so any person can say something brilliant on any given subject.

"We're not given the Spirit as a membership card. The Spirit is not just working inside the clubhouse to make sure we follow all the rules. We're called to speak. We're called to listen."

"I ask about evangelism and you start talking about how we need each other and the Spirit."

"I easily get ahead of myself. Let me try to be more sequential. Have you ever heard of Saul?" Nate asks.

"The first king of Israel?"

"No, the guy who killed Christians."

"Paul?"

"Later on, yes. First we know him as Saul. Saul was a rather disagreeable guy. He was at the execution of Stephen. He's not the sort who would be welcome in a church. This isn't a guy who most pastors would be eager to greet. If he showed up at your church on a Sunday, people were going to die."

𝔄𝔫𝔡 𝔖𝔞𝔲𝔩 was there, giving approval to his death.

> On that day a great persecution broke out against the church at Jerusalem, and all except the apostles were scattered throughout Judea and Samaria. Godly men buried Stephen and mourned deeply for him. But Saul began to destroy the church. Going from house to house, he dragged off men and women and put them in prison. *(Acts 8:1-3)*

"Saul was a guy who not only didn't believe in Jesus," Nate continues, "he actively tried to make sure no one else believed. We're not told this, but it's my guess he had a whole apologetics ministry, too, arguing against Christians. When that didn't seem to work he brought down the hammer."

"He was the persecutor."

"He was on his way to Damascus to do just that when everything changed. Jesus convinced him things were quite exactly what Peter and the rest were saying. Even if they were yokels, they were right yokels."

"What does this have to do with welcoming people? Paul received that nice gift of a specific invitation from Jesus, a mission, and everything spelled out for him. He didn't seem to have a choice, and didn't have doubt anymore."

"Because Paul himself tells the story a lot, and because we tend to identify with Paul's strengths and weaknesses, we always see things from his perspective. He was blinded and still ended up in Damascus. What was the church in Damascus supposed to think? No one saw what Saul saw. All they knew was that Saul killed Christians. Ananias had a vision, and that's the only thing they could go by. They had to trust God knew what he was doing. We're not in Paul's position. That's the thing. The Spirit brings people and we have to figure out what to do with them. Like the church in Damascus did."

> **In Damascus** there was a disciple named Ananias. The Lord called to him in a vision, "Ananias!"
>
> "Yes, Lord," he answered.
>
> The Lord told him, "Go to the house of Judas on Straight Street and ask for a man from Tarsus named Saul, for he is praying. In a vision he has seen a man named Ananias come and place his hands on him to restore his sight."

"Lord," Ananias answered, "I have heard many reports about this man and all the harm he has done to your saints in Jerusalem. And he has come here with authority from the chief priests to arrest all who call on your name."

But the Lord said to Ananias, "Go! This man is my chosen instrument to carry my name before the Gentiles and their kings and before the people of Israel. I will show him how much he must suffer for my name."

Then Ananias went to the house and entered it. Placing his hands on Saul, he said, "Brother Saul, the Lord—Jesus, who appeared to you on the road as you were coming here—has sent me so that you may see again and be filled with the Holy Spirit." Immediately, something like scales fell from Saul's eyes, and he could see again. He got up and was baptized, and after taking some food, he regained his strength.

Saul spent several days with the disciples in Damascus. At once he began to preach in the synagogues that Jesus is the Son of God. All those who heard him were astonished and asked, "Isn't he the man who raised havoc in Jerusalem among those who call on this name? And hasn't he come here to take them as prisoners to the chief priests?" Yet Saul grew more and more powerful and baffled the Jews living in Damascus by proving that Jesus is the Christ.

After many days had gone by, the Jews conspired to kill him, but Saul learned of their plan. Day and night they kept close watch on the city gates in order to kill him. But his followers took him by night and lowered him in a basket through an opening in the wall.

When he came to Jerusalem, he tried to join the disciples, but they were all afraid of him, not believing that he really was a disciple. But Barnabas took him and brought him to the apostles. He told them how Saul on his journey had seen the Lord and that the Lord had spoken to him, and how in Damascus he had preached fearlessly in the name of Jesus. So Saul stayed with them and moved about freely in Jerusalem, speaking boldly in the name of the Lord. He talked and debated with the Grecian Jews, but they tried to kill him. When the brothers learned of this, they took him down to Caesarea and sent him off to Tarsus.

Then the church throughout Judea, Galilee and Samaria enjoyed a time of peace. It was strengthened; and encouraged by the Holy Spirit, it grew in numbers, living in the fear of the Lord. *(Acts 9:10-31)*

"Saul saw the risen Christ," Nate continues. "He was put into a place of absolute weakness, absolute brokenness, and told to seek help from the people he would have persecuted had he arrived without incident. God knew there would be trouble, so he mentioned Saul to Ananias. I love Ananias's response. 'Well that's all well and good, God,' he said, 'but I've heard about this guy and he doesn't like us. He makes us nervous.'"

"And God replied, 'Do what I say.'"

"That's it," Nate agrees. "God told Ananias he had chosen Saul, and God was sending Ananias to Saul, so Ananias had better do what God told him to do. But you know what was in Ananias's mind, and everyone else's, right? Deceit and deception were Roman art forms. People would hide while Saul the persecutor was in town, but if Saul could make himself appear as one of them then he could get a much bigger list of names. But how could he make it seem like he had a change of mind? What would make someone like him turn in a completely different direction?"

"Act like you had a vision," I answer. "Perhaps the Romans knew ways to cause temporary blindness."

"Likely. So God stepped in and told Ananias what was up, and Ananias, even then, doubted. I hear God tell me something and I say, 'Yes, sir.' Ananias heard God, and the fear and doubt were so strong he said, 'But God, do you realize....'"

"I think I tend to be a lot more like Ananias."

"That's true. You know, I think I do as well," Nate admits. "I often say 'But God, have you thought about this point....'"

"And he has," I add, "but hasn't given us all the details. He gives an order, like the centurion, and expects it to be obeyed."

"That is what Jesus called real faith, the likes of which he had never seen. It seems those in the church didn't quite have all that faith."

"Except Ananias did what he was told, after his hemming and hawing."

"Yeah, he did. He chose to follow God. God didn't take control of him and make him into a robot. God asks us to trust and act in faith, and being a robot doesn't require faith. Ananias was a man who listened when God spoke to him. And because he listened, the church in Damascus had someone special join them."

"What if he hadn't listened?"

"That's a good question," Nate answers. "I don't know. It seems like God uses us to answer prayers and uses us to further his plans. In this case my guess is God knew he was talking to someone who would listen. But if Ananias didn't listen? Maybe God would have asked someone else. Sometimes, though, I think things just don't happen, even if God finds another way. He leaves us choices, and our choices have an impact. That's why we need to always listen for the Spirit. Even if what the Spirit says seems crazy, like it did to Ananias."

"It sure worked out for them in Damascus. The relationship went from persecution to friendship."

"But the church in Jerusalem was still nervous. And maybe they're a better example of who we are today. No one there had a vision about God's call on Saul's life. No one even saw blind

Saul being carried into town. They all certainly saw Saul standing there over Stephen's dead body. Saul of Tarsus had a reputation and it was not a good one—not as far as Christians were concerned. Acts tells us he tried to join the disciples. I love that we don't get the details of how that worked out. It's like a bad comedy. He's goes up to people and they walk away. He tries to get an invite and they give him the wrong phone number. They tell him they're meeting in one place, and are really meeting in another.

"Here's a guy who had become one of the most influential Christians in history. He preached in the synagogues and had been seriously threatened with martyrdom for his testimony. But he was locked out of the church in Jerusalem. He was a stranger to them. They didn't want him. Wouldn't have him. He couldn't get connected. Then one day, maybe in the temple courts, he happened to talk to the right person. Barnabas. This was a guy with discernment, and he argued Saul's cause. Those in Jerusalem accepted Saul, and he began to preach boldly about Christ."

"Too boldly, some might say," I suggest.

"Yeah, he had to be shipped off somewhere safer. The really interesting part of this, however, is in the last verse of that section on Saul's introduction to the church. Luke writes, 'Then the church...' and talks about it having peace, strength, and encouragement. I am absolutely convinced there is more to that *then*. It's not just this happened, that happened. It's this stuff with Paul happened, and because it happened in that way— because he was pulled into the ranks—*then* the Spirit came and brought the church to a new stage of existence. Just like at the end of Acts 2. Because the church prayed, the Spirit came, then they had real community. Because they welcomed Saul, because he was brought into the ranks despite their fears and worries, the church had peace and encouragement and it grew."

"Paul was a very important person. How does that relate to what we are doing today? Do we wait for someone to have this vision from Jesus?"

"No, even Paul knew his entry was somewhat unique. That makes our roles even more important and maybe a little more difficult. We have no expectation that Jesus will knock people to the ground, blind them, and call them to be world-class evangelists. Now, we look for the Spirit's work. It is the Spirit who is doing the work of bringing people to Jesus, working in people's lives, working in their existence and whispering to them. It's the Spirit who calls, and shapes people's lives so they seek out the fullness of Jesus in their lives."

I jump in, "So while not everyone encounters Jesus like Saul did on the way to Jerusalem, everyone does encounter Jesus in a way?"

"The Spirit is broadly active, much more broadly active than we would want to admit."

"Why wouldn't we want to admit it?"

"Because if we admit it, suddenly it's not our thing anymore. That upsets our plans and our power structures and our authority. Think of Paul. No one, not a single soul, would have ever suggested Saul of Tarsus would become the leading Christian of his era—the one most responsible for passing on the broader message of Jesus to even our generation. But he was chosen. The Spirit empowered him. James seems to be the head of the church—as we see in Acts 15—but we forget about him. We think of Paul whenever we think about what to do in our churches. We think of Paul whenever we think of our theology. Paul has even become for many of us the only lens through which we see Jesus."

"I hadn't thought of it that way," I say. "Saul's calling upset the whole church. This guy who hadn't earned anything—any right to be up on a stage—suddenly was called to preach and become more important than just about everyone."

"Just like with Cornelius the centurion," Nate replies. "All these Jewish Christians had—in many cases—was the pride of knowing they were a chosen people, and Gentiles had to join that club to be a part of the Jesus club. Then the Spirit does a work. Peter gets a vision. The whole order is upset—something that apparently never was quite accepted, as the presence of the Judaizers even after the New Testament era suggests. What more could the Spirit have done? Still these people refused to admit the Gentiles as Gentiles.

"So, now, in our era the Spirit is still working, still pulling people in and through ludicrous circumstances to become something for Christ and the church. But we don't have visions like Ananias did when he was told to welcome Paul. Even when visions came, the early church had trouble accepting people. What do we expect now? People upset our plans, sometimes because of sin. But often it's because of the Spirit doing a work that is entirely different from what we've invested in. That's why we have to see the Spirit working in everyone."

"The work of the church is never really ours then?"

"Never. I keep an eye out for people. I look to see who God is bringing through our doors. I cannot be the Holy Spirit for these people, telling them what to say, or where to stand, or how to act, or what to be concerned about. I listen to people. I listen to the folks who have made commitments to the Upper Room community and to the folks who come by—folks I've never met but need to meet, for them and for me."

"You both benefit by following the lead of the Spirit."

"Like Peter did in the Cornelius story. Men stopped by and the Spirit told Peter to have no hesitation in following them. He had to hear what they experienced, and they had to hear the fullness of the message behind what they experienced. They were called by the Spirit to join the church, but Peter had the specifics. He knew the story. He knew the right words to put to their experiences. He knew how they should pray. But he didn't know their experiences and thus didn't know a major part of the work of the Spirit."

"Like pieces of a puzzle coming together," I say.

"Exactly, and that's exactly how we all encounter the Spirit in this present world. We all have a piece. We all represent a part of the picture—a shard of the mirror, so to speak. The danger comes if we deny that our piece represents anything at all, or on the other side, proclaim the piece we represent is itself a picture of the whole. We can't know the whole picture on our own. We've been designed—the church has been designed—to need everyone in order to have a picture of the fullness of Christ in our lives. The scary thing is it's been designed to need folks we've never met and who we wouldn't even want in our club."

"So we will never know what the Spirit is doing for us through the strangers we meet unless we make a point of finding out?"

"That's a great way of putting it. The Spirit, like Aslan in the Narnia stories, never tells us more of the story than our part. We are not given a full picture of everyone's worth or value or experiences or potential. Going back to your question of evangelism, we never quite know what it is these strangers need from us. People may need something more than what is apparent on the surface and they definitely need a lot more than a cookie-cutter explanation of the work of Christ. Four clear points of God's promises may very well influence someone. For another that list of points is entirely meaningless. Lots of people don't think in terms of lists so another list is meaningless. We have to stop blaming people for not fitting into our plans or methods. Everyone is an individual who the Spirit has uniquely designed for a unique work and unique gifts."

"People have different gifts," I say, "so of course we will have different interests and passions and perspectives."

"Right, and we try to create unity by making everyone like us. But with God, unity comes from diversity. The unity of Christ is built by the diversity of the Spirit. The unity of the Spirit is built by all of us having a diversity of experiences with Christ. That's the four Gospels, and why these Gospels offer different testimonies. These testimonies aren't settled statements of systematic theology. They are not contracts demanding agreement and a signature on the dotted line, to make sure our theology on every bit of minutiae is exactly right and in order. No. If Jesus wanted lists he would have written down lists. Jesus is a story; he lived a story; and the Spirit is still writing that story in you, in me, in that guy walking by outside, in that woman ordering coffee, in the person you love, in the person you hate. The key—the real key—is to learn how to listen to this story so that it becomes a fulfilled story, as Jesus had a fulfilled story. We can offer the message of fullness. Specific people can offer a context in which to pour that fullness so God is glorified in a unique way, as he was glorified in Cornelius; as he was glorified in the Ethiopian; as he was glorified in Saul of Tarsus, that persecutor of Jesus."

"We just never know who is coming through a door, or walking next to us on the sidewalk?"

"That's my whole philosophy with the Upper Room and the Columba Pub. We're not going to be shaped by what I think is important or affect people by what I'm interested in. Each person who walks through the door, who tells me they want to be a part or hear more or share what is going on, will shape the church according to the plan of the Holy Spirit. We are always changing because we are always dependent on the work of the Holy Spirit. That's why we're not following food laws now, feasting on certain days, or being committed to a plot of land in the Middle East. It's not because of some insight or plan the church leaders came up with. It's because God called in strangers to make changes. Because the church leaders were willing to embrace the work of the Spirit, the church became something world-changing."

"Let's back up just a little. You're saying the church is shaped by who comes, and this becomes the plan of the Holy Spirit. Isn't it possible that people would come with their own agenda that is self-serving instead of spiritual?"

"Oh, yeah. That's a danger isn't it? That's where the spiritual gift of discernment comes in. Where honesty becomes important."

"Honesty?"

"Yeah, I'm pretty straightforward. I ask questions and try to probe. But there are going to be people, like Simon in Acts 8, who want a piece of the power."

"So not everyone who comes to the Columba comes because the Holy Spirit brought them?"

Nate pauses for a moment to think, then says, "No, I think everyone who comes is drawn by the Holy Spirit. But just as the people the Holy Spirit brings aren't necessarily fully in touch with their gifts already, likewise not every person is fully in touch with the goals of the Spirit. It's a different challenge, because instead of trying to lift them up, I think the Spirit is trying to get them straight, so their wrong motives become right motives. I don't think Mike would mind me telling you that when he first came, he had all sorts of different motives. We had some pretty tough talks."

"Yeah, he shared some of that."

"But God worked. God worked even though Mike at first expected something different. I believe the Spirit brought him and Rachel here. But they each had to discover why. We had to discover why. Even self-serving people are not outside the work of the Spirit; the Spirit may in fact use their false motives to bring them to where they need to be in order to find right motives. What's important to me is not to expect false motives but to see each person who comes as important, even if that person doesn't realize it or wants to be important in ways that may not be how the Spirit wants to use them. Whether a person comes with hurts, or with inexperience, or with false motives, I think the Spirit is calling that person here to discover who they are supposed to really be."

I say, "Okay. I think I'm getting it. When the church fails to recognize that the Spirit is bringing people, or when the church puts limits on or makes firm decisions about people for whatever reason, the church may miss the fuller work of the Holy Spirit who changes the world."

"I put Acts 9:31 and 11:17 together because of that. In Acts 11, Peter tells the story of Cornelius and says, 'So if God gave them the same gift as he gave us, who believed in the Lord Jesus Christ, who was I to think that I could oppose God?' In Acts 9 the story of Saul's conversion ends with, "Then the church throughout Judea, Galilee and Samaria, enjoyed a time of peace. It was strengthened; and encouraged by the Holy Spirit, it grew in numbers, living in the fear of the Lord."

"So how do you put them together?"

"It was because the church of that era welcomed the strangers—strangers to them, not to God—that the church enjoyed a time of peace. It was strengthened because men and women held nothing back, even their own opinions. They took the evidence of the Spirit, even in people who didn't know Jesus at first, and let it shape what they believed. They let the Holy Spirit lead, as the Holy Spirit worked in a story much broader than they could realize. Nowadays we tend to do just the opposite. We tell the Holy Spirit who to work in and how to work. We say *that* can be a work of the Spirit, *this* can't. We say a person has to go through years of proving himself or herself in order to have a voice, and to make a substantial change that person has to go through years and years of climbing the ecclesial ladder to a place of authority. The Spirit—in Saul, in Cornelius, in countless stories—shows just the opposite. The Spirit pulls in people—sometimes foolish and ludicrous and wrong people—to make the most profound changes imaginable."

"That's why you're interested?

"That is why I welcome strangers—so that they won't be strangers, so that I can learn what the Holy Spirit is doing in them and they can learn what the Holy Spirit has and is doing in me. We both learn what the Spirit has done in Scripture and history. Put these stories together and we can really become something, just like the early church became something."

"That reminds me, Nate, you never did tell me the 'long and complicated' story about the Columba. You told me why you left your old church, not how you ended up here. Since you say this is a continuing story, I think I really need to hear the beginning."

"It was a miracle really," Nate says. "Can I say that?"

"It's your story," I laugh.

"I mean," Nate continues, "it wasn't like lightning flashed from heaven, or someone rose from the dead. But when something happens that seems impossible, I call that a miracle."

"So what happened?"

" *When we read about the Spirit in the Prophets, we always read that God cares about people in need, and that the person of God will have this same care. This is the most basic sign of the Spirit among us: that we will let go of what we have—sometimes even what we want—whether time, resources, skills, or whatever. We will willingly withdraw our demands and instead give to others.*"

7

Spurring Us to Give

"How did we come to the Columba?" Nate begins. "Well, my brother had a friend in college—a good guy, really strong Christian. He got killed the year after graduating. Drunk driver hit him when he was crossing the street. He got thrown twenty feet into another car. Died a week later in the hospital; never regained consciousness. My brother was devastated by Nick's death. They had known each other since junior high. The family was devastated. No one had answers. Their shared questions brought them close. "

"When was this?"

"Oh, about fifteen years ago. Well, Nick's father owned a restaurant here in town—nice place, California cuisine, pretty successful. I mean he had owned it for thirty years, so that's something. Most restaurants in Pasadena don't last for more than a few years."

"That's not a positive statistic for the Columba."

Nate is not distracted from his story. "I guess Carlos— that's Nick's dad—got tired of working seven days a week with hardly any vacations. He wanted to retire. But he couldn't let go of the restaurant. It meant too much to him, all that work, all his life. He had always planned to pass it on to Nick. But that changed. So for a long time he refused to think about letting go of it."

"What changed?"

"Mild heart attack. Jay—my brother—and his wife were at his house at the time. It was a lot more worry than anything. They got him to the hospital. He was fine. But that was it. He knew it was time to make plans about the future of the restaurant."

"So your brother is the link."

"Yeah. A few months prior, when I was really butting heads with my senior pastor, I mentioned how cool it would be to have a church somewhere other than a church. I didn't think Jay was paying much attention."

"Why not?"

"Oh, he gave up church and Christianity not long after Nick died. I never thought he took me all that seriously when I decided to go to seminary and then work in a church. He was angry. But I guess he was still interested."

"Why did he think of you?"

"You know, I have no idea. It had to be the Holy Spirit—a miracle. I never mentioned a restaurant, let alone this. Didn't even occur to me. I thought about having a church in a gym or in a storefront in the suburbs. Something like that."

"Too trendy," I say. "Very hip in a 1980s, avant-garde sort of way. I like this better."

"Me too," Nate laughs. "Me too. That's why it seems like a miracle. Goes way past anything I knew to pray about. Jay told Carlos about my thoughts on church. Somehow they assumed I meant a place like this. They started talking about it; made plans for me. A week later they let me know what we would be doing. Well they asked me, but they had already planned it out. Carlos would retire, but first he would invest in a new venture. It's still his property. We pay him rent. But he did all the remodeling and helped out for the first few months getting us started."

"Is he a Christian?"

"I think so. He doesn't talk about his faith much. Tends to shy away from conversations, but I think there's something there. Otherwise why would he have pushed for this?"

"Why would he step in, and basically give you a place and then help you turn it into a church? A church with an Irish-style pub on the first floor."

"Well, the whole building is the church; that's how we think of it. Why would Carlos do this? It's more than what we ever thought to pray for. It's a miracle."

"A miracle of community."

"Yeah, it's the Holy Spirit at work."

A large group of students comes into the coffee shop and covers the remaining tables with books and papers. Their conversations and laughter fill the room. They are having a fun day. But the noise makes it difficult for me to hear Nate. I think he sees the disturbed look on my face.

"Want to go back into the Columba?"

"Sure," I reply, gathering my own notebook and standing up. "That story wasn't long at all. A little complicated maybe. Definitely a miracle."

"Yeah, I think it was. Still is, for that matter."

We start walking toward the door.

"I know what your philosophy is, I think; or at least I'm getting closer to understanding," I say. "How do you express this in action?"

"Do we ever do more than sit and talk in a pub?" Nate replies and laughs. "Our plan for action loops us back into that story. It's about giving. We were given to so that we might give."

"Okay. Carlos gave something to you, so now describe what you are giving."

"Carlos could have made a lot of money selling his business—enough to provide for his family for generations. Talking to him I saw something deeper going on. I realized his work was never for the money. He was working for Nick, giving part of himself, letting go of his own leisure or interests, so this place would be here for Nick. By handing it over to me—knowing what I had in mind—I knew Carlos was wanting me to do something deeper with it."

"Deeper?"

Nate stops, looks at me and says, "Yeah. He didn't assert all of his rights and didn't try to milk the last drop of profit from this place. Still doesn't. He willingly lets go and gives us space to become ourselves. He gave, but it wasn't just giving in the normal sense. It wasn't his excess he handed over—it was his dream and vision. He opened the door to his house, so to speak, giving us a place to live and dream. We want to be about the same kind of giving. Embracing and stepping back, taking and handing over. Giving in a full sense."

I pause in thought for a second as he continues walking, then ask, "So this is about more than good tithing."

"Well, yes. So many churches expect little more than people putting money in a bucket on a Sunday morning. A professor I had once said most people in a congregation exist only to support the church budget. Too often people don't even meet this expectation, which often causes pastors to think their congregation is inconsiderate or caught in the trap of consumerism."

"It sounds to me like giving can become a source of resentment."

Nate stops near the door of the Columba. "Think of morale. People have higher morale the more they are invested in something. Giving money is really a very passive sort of investment. Passive investments express and build low morale."

"Why is that?"

"Because giving money hands off responsibility. We want people to give of their own gifts, whatever those gifts are. They let go a part of themselves—their firstfruits—and participate in the context with more freedom. I'm not talking just about money. At the Upper Room we are trying to give ourselves—to each other, to the community."

"What about costs?" I ask.

"Because the restaurant and coffee shop are self-sustaining we don't have much overhead. What normally goes toward all the overhead in a typical church is directed outward here. So we would rather have someone give of themselves than give money. We value tithing, but we don't set that as the primary expression. Tithing has to come out of an attitude of self-withdrawal, you see. Like how Carlos let go of his rights in order to help us land here. Giving only money may look like giving, but it's not done with that attitude of self-withdrawal."

"How is giving not self-withdrawal?"

"Sadly, in many churches a person can buy leadership. People who tithe a lot to begin with get more access, no matter how well-meaning or holy their motives may be. Money has too strong a connection with buying. That connection is too hard to overcome if there isn't already an established concept of self-giving—giving without obligation and without expectation."

"How about within the community?"

"Our giving to each other? It's what we read in 1 John. If we see a need and don't give to each other, then we're not loving. In fact if we're not willing to give to each other, help each other, be there for each other, I don't even think we're a church, no matter what some official definition might be."

Nate opens the door and we walk in, heading over to an empty booth. The place is getting to be a little busy, and all the staff, including Debbie, are hurrying around taking everyone's orders.

"You said before that the Holy Spirit would inspire people to serve," I continue. "Where does that come from?"

"How did Peter, and Paul, and the rest of the earliest church get their information about the Holy Spirit?"

"From Jesus?"

"Yeah, that's true. But when Jesus left they had a lot of time on their hands. So they read."

"The Old Testament?"

"What we call the Old Testament they called the Scriptures. Funny how we don't pay attention to it. Yet, to understand the early church—why they did what they did—we have to look at the books that came before Matthew because those books and Jesus were all they had to go with. If fact, we're told Jesus explained what was happening by going through the Scriptures."*

"What does the Old Testament have to say?"

"You've missed a good bit of the Bible and a good bit of Christian theology as well if you think what happened in the New Testament was altogether new. God is a trinity, right?"

---

*Luke 24:27

"Right."

"So the God who is a trinity now was a trinity before, right?"

"Right."

"Then the Spirit must have been doing something. That something is all through the Old Testament. The Spirit told people what God's anointing would be like, what they would do, who they would become, how they would hope, and so on."

"In the Prophets?"

"Exactly."

"What do the Prophets say?"

"We need to be giving. Be really, really giving. We need to let go of our rights and what we are owed. Let go of our demands and expectations. Hand over what we have that someone else needs. We tend to think of giving or service or helping people as something those without the 'real' spiritual gifts are supposed to do. Whereas really spiritual people pray. Or they are prophets. Or they preach. Or teach. Or whatever. Going back to the story about the waiting on tables, we find that the disciples acted according to what they had been reading. They knew the Prophets, so when it came time to appoint seven people to do the more practical acts of communal care, they chose seven men who were known to be full of the Spirit and full of wisdom."

"In Acts 6, right?" I say, trying to show how well I was listening yesterday.

"Yeah. These guys were appointed to these duties, and yet the only thing we hear of them afterward is how they were extremely effective evangelists. And that shows another point we believe here."

"Which is what?"

"That by embracing the work of the Spirit we open up more work of the Spirit. The Spirit isn't our tool to use. Instead the Spirit is more alive than we are, working more, doing more, and a lot more sensitive to the contexts. By letting ourselves embrace the full work of the Spirit we discover the Spirit working more and more. By limiting how we will let the Spirit work in our midst—because of greed, sexism, racism, theology, or whatever—we end up grieving the Spirit. The Spirit never forces us, but works in and through us when we allow a context for that work and when we keep from trying to be lords over the Spirit."

"Giving says we're willing to let go a little bit," I say.

"Right," Nate replies. "When we read about the Spirit in the Prophets, we always read that God cares about people in need, and that the person of God will have this same care. This is the most basic sign of the Spirit among us: that we will let go of what we have—sometimes even what we want—whether time, resources, skills, or whatever. We will willingly withdraw our demands and instead give to others."

"This makes me think of forgiveness taken a step further."

"That's right. We want the Spirit to work and we have to work with the Spirit. Because the Spirit fills us and works to our benefit, we have to work for the benefit of others. This isn't trying to earn our salvation; it's a reflection of our salvation. It is an embrace of our salvation. An investment in our salvation."

"Can you give me some specifics?"

"I think Isaiah 61 says it well."

The Spirit of the Sovereign Lord is on me,
    because the Lord has anointed me
    to preach good news to the poor.
He has sent me to bind up the brokenhearted,
    to proclaim freedom for the captives
    and release from darkness for the prisoners,

to proclaim the year of the Lord's favor
and the day of vengeance of our God,
to comfort all who mourn,

and provide for those who grieve in Zion—
to bestow on them a crown of beauty
instead of ashes,
the oil of gladness
instead of mourning,
and a garment of praise
instead of a spirit of despair.
They will be called oaks of righteousness,
a planting of the Lord
for the display of his splendor.

They will rebuild the ancient ruins
and restore the places long devastated;
they will renew the ruined cities
that have been devastated for generations.

Aliens will shepherd your flocks;
foreigners will work your fields and vineyards.

And you will be called priests of the Lord,
you will be named ministers of our God.
You will feed on the wealth of nations,
and in their riches you will boast.

Instead of their shame
my people will receive a double portion,
and instead of disgrace
they will rejoice in their inheritance;
and so they will inherit a double portion in their land,
and everlasting joy will be theirs.

"For I, the Lord, love justice;
I hate robbery and iniquity.
In my faithfulness I will reward them
and make an everlasting covenant with them.

Their descendants will be known among the nations
and their offspring among the peoples.
All who see them will acknowledge
that they are a people the Lord has blessed."

I delight greatly in the Lord;
my soul rejoices in my God.
For he has clothed me with garments of salvation
and arrayed me in a robe of righteousness,
as a bridegroom adorns his head like a priest,
and as a bride adorns herself with her jewels.

For as the soil makes the sprout come up
and a garden causes seeds to grow,
so the Sovereign Lord will make righteousness and
praise spring up before all nations. *(Isaiah 61:1-11)*

"This is a chapter we usually think of as referring to Jesus," Nate continues. "And it does. But the key is in the first verse: 'The Spirit of the Sovereign Lord is upon me.' Then what? The ten verses that follow say what it means when the Spirit of the Sovereign Lord is upon Jesus and on the rest of us as a gathered body."

"As the body of Christ," I add.

"His church. This chapter does what a few other chapters in Isaiah do. It is a framework, revealing the gospel for what it is. It provides a model. This is the measure of whether we are walking with the Spirit, you see. That's why Jesus answered John in the way he did."

"You're losing me. Which John and when?"

"The Baptist, in Matthew 11."

When John heard in prison what Christ was doing, he
sent his disciples to ask him, "Are you the one who
was to come, or should we expect someone else?"

Jesus replied, "Go back and report to John what you
hear and see: The blind receive sight, the lame walk,
those who have leprosy are cured, the deaf hear,
the dead are raised, and the good news is preached
to the poor." *(Matthew 11:2-5)*

"John wanted to know if Jesus really was the Messiah. Jesus answered John, saying he was indeed fulfilling the prophecy. Isaiah gave the description, telling us what it is like when the Spirit comes. What's the first thing Isaiah mentions?"

"Telling the good news to the poor. Evangelism."

"It depends on how you define *evangelism*. Have you ever been poor, Luke?"

"My family struggled for a few years when I was growing up."

"What was good news to you? Was good news hearing religious doctrine?"

I laugh. "Not really. Good news was payday, or anything that would have made us—well—less poor."

"Right. I've learned recently the Spirit isn't really interested in the vague spirituality we so often expect. When the Spirit comes, Luke, something happens. Usually not something ethereal or emotional. Those are the things we often look for, and they're sometimes a part of it, but often they're our attempts to see the Spirit apart from the Spirit."

"See the Spirit apart from the Spirit?"

"Yeah, we are embarrassed if we don't see what we should see, and so often we don't see it. Rather than doing those things which would lead us to the Spirit, we decide the anemic things we do see are in fact the evidence of the Spirit."

"Even if no lives are really being changed."

"Even if there is not a bit of good news in our so-called 'good news.'"

"So if I hear you right, you see this all more in terms of a social gospel?"

"No."

"Oh, I don't mean like the early twentieth-century liberal version. I mean, you see the good news connects with the physical world. The gospel is about helping the poor and the needy."

"Yes, in a way," Nate replies. "That's partially it. The problem with the split between liberal and conservative is neither had the whole picture. What I'm saying by telling you we express our faith through giving is not that we do nice things for people, and leave it at that. We see theology and action as being inseparable. Giving is not just handing someone a loaf of bread, because that can be done with a really wicked heart. Just look at the workhouses in Dickens's books."

"Fairly awful places, right?"

"Yeah, and Jack London wrote a really good book called *The People of the Abyss*. He went undercover for a few weeks in East London and lived among the poorest of the poor of British society. It is a very eye-opening read, and sadly, still very real. He and Dickens both talk about these workhouses, and how a chapel service was held during part of each work day. The people in charge were more often than not Christian ministers or workers. Bible verses were quoted and posted, often to remind the poor of their failings."

"Things have changed though."

"We've learned—don't get me wrong—but charity itself can still be a form of sin if it carries that quality of judgment or even hatred."

"Hatred?"

"Yeah. Love isn't always the reason you show charity to people. You might help them because your hatred for them drives you to try to change them, or put them in their place, or otherwise manage their lives. Sometimes we might help others only to help ourselves—so things don't get so bad for them that we lose what we have, too, through riots or societal collapse or something like that."

"What does the Upper Room do?"

"I know you are asking *what,* but finishing *why* is more important than the specifics right now. I don't mean to dodge your question, but let me go back to Isaiah. The gospel is good news if it really is *good* news. The Spirit not only evokes religious thoughts but also brings power to change people. Actually, it's more than just power to change—a lottery can do that for people. The Spirit brings a renewal of soul. Hope. Courage."

"Love, hope, and joy."

"Yeah. I think of love, joy, peace, patience, kindness, goodness, faithfulness, gentleness, self-control. All the fruit. Underneath this is where the real problems can be found. People without these are the most lost. What people don't realize is that poverty, crushing needs, or even annoyances infect the soul, and cause people to lose hope and lose life. They literally cannot think of higher things anymore. So they are poor, and in a sad way they wallow in that. This is the affliction of the inner city. People can live in poverty. People cannot live without hope. That's the brilliance of this passage in Isaiah. The good news is hope, a very real hope, a very palpable hope. It's change and transformation. Not only do circumstances change, the whole picture changes. We receive justice and so expect justice. We are fed and expect food. We become productive and worthwhile, and expect our value to continue. That is the evidence of the Spirit: power and hope. This is the good news for one's life and one's soul so there can be faith. So that faith in something means something."

I jump in, "People think of poverty as a situation, is that what you're saying? But it's more than that. A person can be poor—not have a lot—but be rich because of hope and faith. I think Mother Theresa said this—people in the West seemed so much poorer to her than the men and women she worked with. Maybe that's the reason."

"That's exactly right. Which is why to really discover the Spirit we have to let go, engage in self-withdrawal rather than self-assertion. In doing that we realize life is not about possessions or power. Real peace doesn't come from having a luxury car or diamond jewelry or name-brand clothes. Contentment doesn't come from our investment strategies or our really nice house in a beautiful suburb. Hope doesn't come from impressing our neighbors, squeezing out the better deal, or asserting our rights in every possible area of life.

"When the fruits of the Spirit are absent we are poor. If we do not have love, joy, and peace then we are utterly destitute. People need an investment. They need a context of discovery and a pathway toward that discovery. Knowing they can come to a soup kitchen or get a shirt from a bin is sustenance, it isn't hope. Such things make for an animal-like attitude toward life. We're about more than just working to provide sustenance."

"Aren't most churches involved in charity work? What makes your approach distinctive?" I ask.

"Don't get me wrong. When I talk about charity work, it's not a criticism of everyone else. There are people in the trenches doing amazing things, which is precisely why we don't run our own charity work. Every day we learn from what people are doing. The Spirit works everywhere, in all sorts of people, toward good things. The Spirit is working, has been working."

"Alright, I accept your caveat," I say and laugh. "So, again, how would you characterize it?"

"When I was leaving my old church there was the potential for me to leave with a lot of judgment. I felt hurt. I felt my rights were violated and that I was ill-used. I felt others weren't living up to their responsibilities. I had to let that go. There would always be people and situations that didn't measure up to what I thought was an ideal. It could be a never-ending obsession, as it is for many people. Being right becomes a distraction and it leads us away from the peace of the Spirit. I had to learn how to do what was right without expectation. Do my part and trust the Spirit to fill in other parts."

"So in a way you gave to them. You gave them grace."

"To be who they are. I had to withdraw from asserting myself and what I thought was right. Yeah, in a way I gave to them. We think of giving as something we do for someone who has less than us. We don't often think in terms of giving as something we do for someone who has different perspectives or opinions. That very much requires the attitude of self-withdrawal. Giving grace is at the heart of giving anything generously. If you can give to someone who doesn't seem to need it, or seems to be the oppressor, then maybe you've truly learned what it means to give. Then you won't be giving with hidden judgment or expectation."

"That's the difference, it seems," I say, "from the work-house people Dickens and London wrote about, and Jesus. Jesus gave to the poor and healed the sick, but he also gave to the rich and healed the powerful. He saw real needs, not circumstances."

"Which is the trick, isn't it? That's why we depend on discernment more than any other spiritual dynamic. We cannot be fluid in anything we do without that. This scares people because discernment isn't some list of right things to do and check off. It's reacting to each situation on its own terms, always scanning and assessing the Spirit in each moment. It's a constant work, no matter where we are."

"Lists and rules make things a lot easier."

"And require a lot less thinking. Giving is not something we do because it is the right thing. It really is something we do because in doing this—in allowing ourselves to be freed from our attachments to our resources, or time, or even our judgments—we participate with the work the Spirit is already doing around us, and in us."

"In us?"

"The Spirit does not work merely so that we can be happy and fulfilled individuals. The Spirit is doing a work—a broad work—and has empowered us to join in that work. Too often we want to arrange how it is we express this participation—putting together just the right services or programs or whatever so that the Spirit fits into our schedule, like going to the gym or taking the kids to soccer practice. Giving is a way of recreating our perspective on this. Giving always involves someone else, and it is rare that someone else matches up with our own values and perspectives."

"So we have to choose whether we shape them or allow them to shape us?"

"Right. One of the biggest problems in the spiritual life is our own will. We want what we want, and we've been told—especially here in the Western world—that what we want is ours for the taking. It's not just in the West, though. All countries believe that, even if pop anthropology will tell you differently. The West did not invent the despot. It merely popularized and spread out roles, so that we all become despots of our little kingdoms, seeking to manage and control and manipulate for our little advantage."

"Society is based on that in a way."

"Yeah, mutual manipulation becomes a dance of sorts. Everyone seeks the advantage, never quite getting it because in our society we have equality, and so everyone joins in the fray rather than getting squashed beneath. Giving—when we give in whatever way the Spirit provokes in us—is a statement that we don't join in this fray. We are saying we listen to a different music that requires a dance of a different sort."

"What was the word you used yesterday to describe that? Kenesis?"

"Kenosis—that's pouring into each other. Perichoresis is the dance. Yeah, that's the dance we participate in. Only the Spirit never forces us. There's always inspiration and then choice. We are tempted—in a manner of speaking—to give in certain ways but then we have to decide which music to listen to, and that shapes our dance. In giving we have the most stark choice. Everything except giving can be done while retaining ownership over our own souls. We can go to church, read the Bible, pray—all according to the patterns we determine, doing what may seem right to religion but never giving up those core parts of ourselves that reveal the fullness of our inner religion."

"Inner religion?"

"Who we really are in relationship with God. Get rid of all the ceremony, all the statements, all the assertions, all the posturing. Leave only our real hopes, real fears, real faith, and real love. That's our inner religion. People can hide that from other people."

"People can hide that from themselves," I say.

"Totally. But not from God. How we give, like James said, shows who we really are."

"And if we don't give?"

"Then we don't become. We don't find who we are meant to be, all because we want to hold to some supposed value or ownership. We don't give, and in essence we tell the Spirit we will be in charge and we will choose how we relate to people and God. But the brilliance of the Spirit is that we only give to God by giving to others, just as Jesus said."

"Are you talking about the 'when you give to the least of these' passages?"*

---

* Matthew 25:31-46

"Yeah. The Spirit inspires us and leads us. As we embrace this reality we are more inspired and more led. Surprisingly, as Jesus said in that passage and as the verse in Isaiah reveals, the Spirit isn't about inspiring us to do lofty, religious things. The Spirit is quite practical and quite wide-ranging, knowing that people need us and we need people. So to embrace the fullness he is offering, we have to take it together, only together."

"So where's the problem?"

"We get in the way of ourselves. We convince ourselves or distract ourselves—we do it or let it happen. Giving requires something of us, and since most of us feel like we are required to do so many other things, we don't like going out of our way for things that seem to have no direct benefit. So we ignore the whispers of the Spirit, sometimes so well we begin to not even realize the Spirit is whispering."

"We drown out the voice."

"That's right, and it's not hard to do because the Spirit never yells. It is the quieted soul who hears the whisper, and it is the willing soul who responds to the soft call. In our frenzied life that never stops for us to assist those around us, we fail others and we fail ourselves. This causes a reverberation that extends significantly farther than we can imagine."

"How so?"

"I like what Hebrews 12:15 says, 'See to it that no one misses the grace of God and that no bitter root grows up to cause trouble and defile many.' We don't think in these terms— that we have a responsibility going past preaching the initial good news. But here the writer exhorts people to make sure they do their part, because if they don't, some people might actually miss the grace of God and their souls will fester. The Spirit doesn't need us, but the Spirit sure does use us—in ways that may be more practical than spiritual."

"To visit the prisoners. To feed the hungry. Clothe the poor."

"If we do those things we do them for Jesus. If we don't do those things, you know what happens?"

"Jesus rejects us."

"Well yes. But also, more immediately, those things don't get done. People go hungry. Prisoners become lonely. The poor walk around in shameful rags. God does not inspire us to do things so that he can assert his control over us and make us uncomfortable. The Spirit whispers and asks us to help others because they really need help. They do not need the words of grace as much as the actions of grace—the doing of grace, the experience of God's grace in which he uses our hands because we are supposedly his children and his servants. He asks us to help because his grace is a holistic grace, not a grace limited to a church building and words."

"When people don't get help, then they get bitter?"

"Yes. In their souls they know there was help available but it wasn't given. They prayed, or maybe they didn't, and God began to work, drawing together his people so as to alleviate the burden. I know the bitterness of not getting help from those I trusted to help me. I've felt it myself, only I knew enough to get past it and see it for what it was and cry out to God. Not everyone realizes the root of their bitterness."

"But God is the God of salvation, so how can we be responsible for that?"

"He is the God of salvation, and those who trust in him will not be disappointed. But the path to that salvation—the path through the trials and difficulties and injustice—is not as settled. By banding together, by giving and by receiving, we can alleviate the struggles and trials, making for rejoicing. Or we can ignore other people and make what could have been a lighter burden into something immensely heavier. Other people will be led and taught and God will work through them if not through us. But in particular circumstances if we do not give, people simply go without. The same goes for us. There are seasons in which we need people to be there for us, in whatever way. If people are not there, then God will work things out, but that doesn't dismiss the fact we needed those people, and feel the loss. I felt that loss. Stacy and that guy were wrong. I know that for a fact. Stacy would not give, he would not give. They stole and broke and shattered. Others in the church weren't involved and kept out of it. God did work. He still is working with them. But in their selfishness there is a reverberation. You know what is one of the most difficult things to overcome in our spiritual growth?"

"Pride."

"That's one of the worst sins, and maybe the source of what I'm getting at, but that's not it. I'm talking something more specific."

"What is it?"

"Like I said before, it's the need to assert our will on everything. We want to assert our will in our whole lives. This is anti-Spirit. That is our spirit, not the Holy Spirit. That's why we pray, 'Your will be done' in the Lord's prayer."

"So, our need to assert our own will is the big hurdle for spiritual growth."

"We want *our* will to be done. Our whole society encourages this, and churches are not outside the bounds. That's why power struggles are so potent and common in churches. That's why head pastors will step in on—or just step on—successful ministries in order to make sure the ministries do not go outside the pastor's bounds of control. A lot of young leaders I've met in the last couple years have talked about being stepped on or pushed aside, and this is the reason they couldn't stay at their churches."

"Isn't that an assertion of their own will?"

"That's the question isn't it?" Nate replies. "Sometimes it is brutally hard to figure out the difference between our will and the will of the Spirit. Not that they are similar, but because the Spirit whispers and our wills yell. Which brings us back to giving."

"How so?"

"Giving is a release of my will. We can give to people what we have in an attempt to assert our will over them. This might be money. It might be teaching, wisdom, or power. We can give in order to assert our self. Or we can freely withdraw, let go of our will, and give. In freely withdrawing we give according to the need, the situation. Being neighbors even if—especially if—it goes against what we want to do. That's the heart of spirituality, and something we often miss."

"Going against what we want to do?"

"Not that. We think that we do things for other people. We give so they can be blessed. We judge so that they can be corrected. We think of ourselves as their Holy Spirit. In fact, when we give we are opening ourselves up more to the Holy Spirit. We are doing the most direct act in letting go of our own will and finding the will of the real Holy Spirit in our lives. If we are sued for our tunic, we are called to also give our coat. We are told to go two miles if ordered to go one mile. In doing that, we are pursuing the work of the Spirit in our own lives and, more importantly, in the broader community."

"How does that work out practically? Here, I mean?"

"Like I said, we don't insist on running our own show—in anything. We work with people, giving time or money or whatever as we can. I'm not the point person on this, however. I tend to be a little unpractical at times, and need this part of me to be encouraged by others. Giving is not a spiritual gift for me. It is something I need to do. Fortunately, we have someone who really is passionate about charitable work. So Larry is in charge of this area and helps direct our efforts."

"Larry?"

"Dr. Lawrence Nguyen. He's an associate professor of Poli Sci. I should get you in touch with him. He has a good story to tell. After a few rough years, in which he got a divorce, he found something in his life, and God began to really use him. Somehow he felt drawn to us. Now I don't know what we would be without him. He's such a great push for all of us."

"What does he do, if Upper Room doesn't run programs?"

"Part of being committed to our community, part of joining in with who we are in a more formal sense, is being willing to commit time to giving. We don't say what kind of giving, mostly because we want each person to determine how the Spirit is leading in his or her life. We just say, 'Do something.' Or rather, Larry is the guy who says that. He is the pastor of these things; encouraging, exhorting, and advising. He's also the point person if any one of us has a pressing need that could use help. This keeps me focused on what I am good at, and allows him to really pour into things he's good at."

"Like Stephen and Philip, in a way."

"Yes! That's exactly it, though we didn't do it intentionally. We weren't trying to follow a model. There was a need in our community. He stepped up. I stepped back. The Spirit works more fluidly through us all."

"What kinds of things do people do?"

"Well, a small group works with a homeless shelter. One woman volunteers at a center that works with battered women. A few people are working with Big Brothers and Big Sisters. Our assistant manager here, Melissa Choi, is doing some really great work with an AIDS clinic. When anyone has an event or something that could use more people, we're all willing to jump in. In this we seem to have point people for different causes."

"What do you do? Or is this it?"

"That's the temptation, isn't it? Because I'm a pastor I already spend my life in ministry. But for me this is also a place of power and authority. Even with our setup my will is important and people listen to it. That's a problem for me, and it can be a problem for the community. So to reset myself for my work here I realized I had to get into a place where I could really be a servant. Not a so-called servant leader in a position where everyone does what I say and I choose what to do for them. Instead I have to let go that which is so natural for me, for the sake of my soul. Which means I get out like everyone else, outside of my vocation and experience and area of leadership to just give of myself."

"Doing what?"

"Well, it's a little embarrassing really. I talked with Larry about this, and he says it's worthwhile, but it's not quite as acceptable in some circles."

"Now I'm really curious."

"I work with the Sierra Club and environment groups. I help out with cleaning wilderness areas and with some other volunteer activities."

"That *is* surprising."

"I realized that whatever my setting, I'm always a pastor. It's just who I am, and so of course I want to assert myself. So now I work on environmental causes that require time and effort, but not my leadership. To be honest, I'm like Melissa— I'm working with people who often have a really poor opinion of the church. So there's that too."

"Why did you choose this? It doesn't seem like giving. You seem to be asserting your will by rejecting it."

"Yeah, that can be true. The fact is I do it because that's the area I'm drawn toward. I get passionate about God's creation. I think I appreciate Jesus' desire to go off into the wilderness, and got to thinking about our own need for those kinds of spaces to remain whole. The Christian Church has for far too long fallen into a trap of thinking that because God made it we are called to abuse it. We have a reputation now not as gardeners—like Adam was made to be—but as despoilers. We've taken up the role of the serpent, who encourages destruction and waste and arrogance. So rather than do what maybe I 'should' do, like everyone else, I'm trying to listen to the Spirit in my life in an area I can't have control, and just leap into it."

"Sounds like you might be doing more than you can imagine."

"Maybe so. Are you hungry? All this talking makes me hungry."

"I am. But first I really need to use the bathroom. I don't want to become vulnerable to a control issue."

I get up and walk toward the labeled door in the back.

" Listening to the Spirit, watching for the Spirit, trying to align ourselves with what the Spirit is already doing in our lives and in our community. If it's important to watch for what the Spirit is doing in the broader community, it's just as important to constantly discover what the Spirit is doing within our smaller community. The Spirit is not passive. If the Spirit comes on a person then that person must participate. If a person isn't participating then either the Spirit is not in them or those of us in leadership are rejecting the Spirit who is in them, either saying the person is not filled at all or not filled in the way we want."

8

Provoking Participation

"What do you want?" Nate asks when I return.

"Do you have fish and chips?"

"We do. I highly recommend them. One second."

Nate walks over to the bar and talks with the man there. Their laughter suggests it's not only about our order. Then he comes back.

"Shouldn't be long. Sorry if you've been hungry all this time. I get to talking and don't think about it."

"No problem. I'm curious how it is you function here. We've talked about the motives. But what do you actually do? How do you lead, for instance? What specific ministries do you have? I've enjoyed the depth of our conversations, but my readers want more *who* and *what* and not as much *why*."

"Well, Luke, I have nine principles of efficacious ministry which help guide us in everything we do. We repeat these principles each week in our service."

"Efficacious?" I laugh. "I'm writing a newspaper article, not preparing a theology lecture."

Nate laughs too. "Hey, if we're doing ministry, it might as well be efficacious. You might want to write these nine things down."

I poise my pen on my notepad.

"The first one is study. The second principle is insight."

"That's a logical sequence."

"The third is love, and the fourth is laughter."

"Laughter? You must have picked up that one from the Holy Spirit. I don't remember reading about that in the Bible."

Nate replies. "I think a sense of humor—a good sense of humor—is important in keeping a healthy perspective on the silliness of everything. Life is funny—but not crude funny or ludicrous funny. There are even some good bits of humor in the Bible if you look closely."

"Okay, I won't argue it," I laugh. "Because I want you to be right. What's next?"

"The fifth is inspiration."

"From the Spirit."

"Sure. The sixth is nothing."

"Nothing?"

"There is no sixth thing. No, that's not it. It's holding onto nothing," Nate says. "Let go of everything that binds. Then we have excellence."

"Wow! You go from nothing to excellence. That's a fast journey."

"What number are we on?"

"That was seven."

"This is why I had you write them down. Number eight is...I forget," he pauses, lost in thought. He turns toward the bar and yells, "Chris, what is number eight?"

"Smoked turkey wrap with sliced avocado and salsa," Chris yells back.

"Never mind," Nate responds, then turns to me. "It's silence."

"Being quiet."

"In voice and soul. Then finally, number nine. Service."

"So all the first eight things lead into service, which you mentioned is at the heart of all you do. That makes sense."

"Does it? I suppose it does. That's a good catch. Interesting."

"Why?"

"Read me the list again."

"Study. Insight. Love. Laughter. Inspiration. Nothing. Excellence. Silence. Service."

I stare down at the list and it hits me.

"You just made this up, didn't you?" I ask, then laugh. "SILLINESS. That's the heart of your ministry?"

"Yeah, well it's in my heart at least. It was a pretty good list. Must be the fine training I had for coming up with lists. I can draw you a chart too, with circles and arrows and rectangles all flowing together into a nice pattern of ministry."

"No thanks," I say and laugh. "This is fine. I take it you don't quite follow the usual trends of leadership discussions then."

"I guess I laugh at it too much to try to incorporate it. There's a quality about such ministry styles which are dangerous and would be amusing if they weren't destructive. So no, we don't see silliness at the heart of what we do, but I do see a lot of silliness in many attempts to manage ministries according to some detailed plan or order. Personally I hate these kinds of lists because I tend to get lost and have to start at the first letter again. I never get to where I'm supposed to be."

"What did you mean when you said a more serious conception of order is potentially dangerous?"

"Did I say that? Sounds ominous," he says and laughs.

"I think you used *dangerous* and *destructive* in the same sentence as *ministry.*"

"You caught me with a slip."

"You didn't mean it?"

"I did. But this opens up a whole can of worms, and on some issues I can be a bit more prickly. Really, what it all comes down to is participation."

"I hope you're not going to turn that into an acrostic."

"No," he says and laughs. "That would be far too many principles for any one group of people to keep. The key to what we're doing here basically boils down to participation. Each person participates. Each person produces and contributes and helps shape what it is we are doing."

"This goes back to what you said about the importance of strangers then. They are important because they help shape how you think."

"Totally. This becomes even more important once a person has entered into our community with more dedication."

"You keep listening."

"That's the heart of it, Luke. I—we—listen. But this isn't just about listening to each other."

"What's it about?"

"Listening to the Spirit, watching for the Spirit, trying to align ourselves with what the Spirit is already doing in our lives and in our community. If it's important to watch for what the

Spirit is doing in the broader community, it's just as important to constantly discover what the Spirit is doing within our smaller community. The Spirit is not passive. If the Spirit comes on a person then that person must participate. If a person isn't participating then either the Spirit is not in them or those of us in leadership are rejecting the Spirit who is in them, either saying the person is not filled at all or not filled in the way we want."

"Back to the Spirit, then."

"Back to the Spirit, always. Having worked in and attended a variety of churches in my life, I'm convinced a great many churches have their understanding of the Spirit entirely backward."

"That's a pretty arrogant thing to say."

"Look at how most churches function. They have theology and ministry styles that encourage the Spirit, in a way. But only in certain ways. They create a strict context in which they'll let the Spirit work. They have their particular ministries, particular ways of doing things, particular styles of worship. Each church has a jar of sorts, made of their own design, which they carry to the well each week to fill."

"And what do you do?"

"We look for the stream that is passing by. Living water."

"Christ."

"Yes, Christ. He brings life. But living water is also a way of expressing water that is moving. Like a stream or a river. A pool of water can become stale and bad if it sits too long without new water refreshing it. Having staid, impenetrable patterns of doing ministry can become the same way. If we require that the Spirit only work according to certain patterns or methods or contexts, then we risk missing out on the freshness of the Creator Spirit, who is often leading us in totally new directions and opening up the doors for something fresh."

"Like the Spirit did with Cornelius and the Gentiles."

"Exactly. And with Philip and the Ethiopian. This creativity doesn't stop with conversion, which is often how people view it. We think there are a lot of different ways of coming to Christ, but we insist on people fitting into certain roles and losing a lot of their independent drive once they do come to Christ. We encourage people to stop listening and stop creating in their lives."

"What do you mean?"

"Once they join our churches we tell them, 'Here are the five ways you can express your faith.' We try to get people to feed into us, to give more validation to our present ministries. They have to fit into a mold just when they should be finding their true selves for the very first time."

"Isn't that part of joining a community?" I ask. "Aren't they drawn to a church because of the ministries going on?"

"Listening is a two-way street. They are drawn to us because of what we're doing, but they are also drawn to us to help reshape what we are doing. They are bearers of the Spirit, Luke, and so each person has in them this new perspective, a new piece of the puzzle, with which we all will become fuller. Without this we will only be shadows of what we should be. Unfortunately, staying incomplete is also a way of power for people. The incompleteness highlights the passions and perspectives of those who are good at what is being done and alienates those— keeps those down—who would be good at so-called unacceptable things. They are only unacceptable because they aren't what those in power appreciate or prefer or can lead."

"People who stand out for doing something want to keep standing out," I add. "Is that what you're saying? I see that. Then they make all sorts of rules and theology in order to emphasize what they do, and what people like them do. But how do you know someone is listening to the Holy Spirit and can contribute something? There's a great risk in letting everyone contribute and shape."

"There's a huge risk. This can get out of our control, and leaders can become less while the whole becomes more. That scares pastors. So instead of using spiritual discernment they go by all the obvious signs. Only so many of those signs aren't spiritual but natural. They go by what the rest of the world sees as validation. In doing that they may pick out the seeming best and brightest, but they may miss those who really have been called, and they may encourage those who aren't close to God at all. I look for the signs of the Spirit, not the validations of the world."

"Sounds like John the Baptist had it right."

"It does, doesn't it? That's why he was such a good prophet. He had this brilliant ministry. But when he saw the Spirit descending he had to step back. Not give up, but step back and let the Spirit work in and through this other man Jesus, and another group of men. Some of his own disciples even left his work and joined with Jesus. John was able to encourage this because he had the right perspective."

"His ministry was good because he was committed to the goal of his ministry, not the ministry itself."

"He had his eye on the prize, so to speak. He knew the streams of living water did not come from him. He was only a part. He was a link in a long chain of people who said what was going to happen when God came down. Too many pastors these days see themselves as a conduit of this water—the spring from which the water flows into other people. That's not it at all."

"But even Jesus went to John, so there must have been something to the idea of spiritual representative."

"Sure, John had his part, his role. But when his role had been accomplished he diminished. He was in the line of God's work of salvation. He did his calling; then it was time to pass the torch. Or rather, it was time to let go of the torch that had already been passed."

"We think of the streams of living water in terms of preaching, I suppose," I add. "I tell you, and you listen, and you get inspired. Like Jesus talking at the well."

"But that's the thing. Jesus wasn't talking about the words being the living water. The living water was that which gives real life, Spirit and truth. What was it he said in John 7?"

"I think I need to start bringing my Bible to these interviews."

"Might not be a bad idea," Nate replies. "You never know when it might be needed. I have mine memorized."

"You do?"

"Well only in the original languages, and I have so much trouble translating on the fly I still need to keep a translation handy," Nate says, and laughs. He pulls out his Bible from his bag and turns to what I am assuming is John. "Okay, here it is— 7:37 through verse 39.

> On the last and greatest day of the Feast, Jesus stood
> and said in a loud voice, "If anyone is thirsty, let him
> come to me and drink. Whoever believes in me, as the
> Scripture has said, streams of living water will flow
> from within him." By this he meant the Spirit, whom
> those who believed in him were later to receive. Up to
> that time the Spirit had not been given, since Jesus had
> not yet been glorified. *(John 7:37-39)*

"I like this," Nate continues. "Whoever believes in Jesus will have streams of living water flowing from them. Now that's a really curious statement. What does it mean? Well, explanations of statements like this are rare, but John tells us what it means, maybe because it is so important. Jesus meant the Holy Spirit."

"I haven't heard that before."

"Think of the imagery. The Jewish writings were full of imagery our boring and dry approach rarely matches. Streams of living water will flow from each person. Not just from the leaders, not just from those we approve, not just from those who we say can work in certain ways. No, living water will flow from whoever believes in Jesus. This means I, as a pastor, am completely out of the picture in deciding who can and cannot be used by the Holy Spirit. A theologian is out of the picture in deciding. None of us has the authority to decide."

"Well, there are passages about sin and judging."

"Oh, yeah, that's definitely the case. We do have an obligation to make sure the Spirit isn't grieved and we have to be aware if there's something bad going on that could cause problems, but outside of that—outside of sin—I'm not to pick and choose, in anything. Have you ever tried to dam up a creek?"

"No."

"When I was young my family went up and stayed in a mountain cabin for a week. On the land there was a creek, and I spent a good part of the week trying to dam it up in order to have a pond to play in. I piled rocks and sticks, but the creek kept going around what I tried to do. I imagine if I was a five-year-old who knew how to work with concrete I could have done it. But even if I did finish it I wouldn't have done anything worthwhile. I would have ruined the creek."

"Plus, water that sits can become stagnant."

"Never drink from a sitting pond, that's right. But that's what I was trying to do. A good pastor, in my estimation, isn't in the business of controlling the water, but following it—discovering how it is already flowing. Really, he's in the business of navigating the living water. I watched a documentary on

Mark Twain the other evening and it discussed Twain's job as a steamboat pilot. There was a lot of romance to that job, but as Twain learned it he realized it was a lot of work too. The pilot wasn't responsible for choosing the cargo or setting up the schedule. Instead, the pilot helped navigate the boat along the river, memorizing over a thousand miles of twists, turns, shallows, and other dangers. He had to know how to move along without crashing. Because the Mississippi is a living river, the job always changed. The weather was always changing. The flow of the river itself changed, which meant even in the same exact spot on the river the pilot had to keep his wits about him."

"A pastor is supposed to know the terrain and know how to keep out of danger, while still moving along at a good clip," I add to the metaphor.

"It's a lot safer to stay in port. The dock is very safe and free from danger. At the dock a person can still play at being on a steamboat without risking a thing. But cargo is not delivered and people don't get to their destinations if the ship always stays at the dock. Oh! Here's the food. Luke, this is Chris. The Columba manager."

"It's a full-time job keeping an eye on this guy," Chris says. "Enjoy the food."

"Thanks," I say. "Nice to meet you, Chris."

"Sorry I can't stay to chat. Some of us have to work for a living," he says, then walks back.

"Some of us have to work without expecting any tips in return," Nate says to him as he walks away. They both laugh. Nate puts his napkin on his lap and puts some vinegar on his fish and fries.

"Sometimes," Nate continues the conversation as we begin to eat, "I think church leaders are a lot like strict camp counselors. Sure, mom and dad may have sent the care package, but the counselor has to go through it to make sure there's no contraband. Everything in and out has to be managed because these are kids, and kids are apt to be a little too goofy and get into trouble."

"Or get hurt," I say.

"Right. So it's all for their own good. But I'm not the counselor, Luke. That job has already been taken. Jesus promised us a counselor to help lead us in this camp of ours, and I'm not that counselor. The Holy Spirit is the one who delivers the gifts from our Father. The Holy Spirit is the one who sets the schedule, chooses the teams, plans the activities, and takes us out for nature hikes."

"Puts us on the bus and ships us back home," I add.

"Well, we've done that analogy in," he laughs. "But it's true. Luke 11:13 tells me that the Father gives to those who ask. What does he give?"

"The Holy Spirit."

"Exactly! The Father gives the Holy Spirit to those who ask. Now, the Father doesn't give the Holy Spirit to just those people I prefer, or the people I would choose. He doesn't let me be the captain of the team, choosing who to pick and who to leave out. Jesus said—this is Scripture—the Spirit is given to those who ask. That's fierce."

"Why?"

"Because then we have to look at all it means for the Holy Spirit to be given. We have to also look at all those who confess Christ, to help them see what the Spirit is doing in and with their lives."

"And what does it mean for the Holy Spirit to be given?"

"Well, I've read my Bible once or twice—some parts more than others. I can't seem to find the verse that talks about the Spirit coming onto a person and that person being content sitting in a pew, staring forward, reciting words as commanded."

"When the Spirit comes something happens."

"The person on whom the Spirit comes does something, is something, becomes something. It's not my job to say what. It's my job to *see* what and help create a context in which that can be affirmed, developed, and utilized."

"Otherwise you would—I suppose—be denying the work of the Holy Spirit."

"We have a tendency to be addicted to words. Words mean a lot, and that's all we go by, forgetting that actions mean a lot more. I can heartily affirm the presence of the Holy Spirit in my church while at the same time actively deny the work of the Holy Spirit in my church. God watches what we do, not what we say, which means there's a lot of danger in being a pastor. More than just coming up with an interesting thing to say on a Sunday morning."

"You have to navigate the river."

"We are not the river. We don't control the river. The river doesn't really even listen to us. We go with the river. When the rain comes, when the streams of living water start flowing into those who ask, my responsibility is to keep everything moving steadily while the floodwaters come, or when the drought comes."

"What about levees? Levees are built to control the flow, to keep it from flooding and causing terrible damage."

"We've seen what happens to levees when the rain really comes. There are good reasons for levees, and I think maybe there are some good reasons for rules and structures within church—to help provide guidance, for example. Heresy can be destructive. Misguided or misdirected enthusiasm can cause problems. But a lot of times the merits are outweighed by the problems. The rules and structures set up a false confidence when the river really gets moving. It's often much better to get to know the rhythms and live with it as it naturally flows.

"So what does that mean? I mean practically. Everyone is important, right. How does that work itself out here?"

"Sorry. I assume the practical bits and get to talking about the philosophy bits, since I think if someone gets the philosophy first they will understand a little better that what we're doing isn't just random chaos and whim. Of course there has to be some kind of order, but the question is whether it is a simple order that I can manage or control, or something more fluid."

"More fluid? Like a river."

"Which means it's always a bit difficult to describe what it is we do because what we do isn't always the same. I mean we go through different seasons. We see different patterns. What we're doing this week may or may not completely change next week. The important thing for us is not the static commitment to something but the established commitment to each other as Spirit-filled people. So my role isn't to do all the things a lot of pastors do. I don't always preach. I don't lead the weekly staff meeting."

"What is your role?"

"My primary role is to foster an understanding of the Spirit in each person. My real goal—and how I shape my week—is to develop people. I want to really see people, get to know them so I can help them hear the whispers of the Spirit in their heart and follow the Spirit's lead in their life, and in our lives together."

"Where do you get this from?"

"I listen to what Acts has to say—Acts 2:4, for instance. Let me look it up here to get the words right."

"From the English translation, right?"

Nate laughs, then reads from his Bible, "All of them were filled with the Holy Spirit and began to speak in other tongues as the Spirit enabled them." All of them were filled, Luke. All of them began to speak. As the Spirit enabled them—it seems to me that's the only bit left open for discovery. All of them are filled—that's assumed."

"Does this happen with you all?"

"The Spirit works, but doesn't work in the same way in any context. That's the whole point about the word *living*. Life changes. Life adapts and grows and shapes and responds to the context. The Spirit doesn't have to learn or grow but the Spirit does adapt to each situation and each generation. The fullness of Christ can be reflected through one to another and back again."

"Everyone has an important role to each other."

"Paul says this in 1 Corinthians 12. We in the church have become so interested in what particular list we want to use, which gifts we'll accept and which we don't think are around anymore, we forget that the emphasis isn't on a particular list."

"I'm following. The emphasis is on the people."

"Always. Paul is always trying to get the focus away from the vague theology and tell his readers that their mistake is they de-emphasize people. It's almost funny, really. Paul is saying everyone has a part and not everyone is the same so we should value each person's contribution. Some people can do this thing, he writes, others can do that thing. He gives us examples. Then we take these examples of God's creative variety in his people and make it into a firm list. 'Okay, now we have these six things people have to do,' we say. We are so into the rules and lists. Paul was into the people—what the people could do, what the Spirit was doing through the people."

"Do you think the lists are designed for organization or control?" I ask.

"Both. Lists make for easy management. Everyone can be grouped without too much bother. Also, with the lists leaders can play favorites or highlight some things more than others. What the verses seem to emphasize however is the *all* aspect. A lot of churches emphasize the *how* or *what* aspect. We've lost the *all.* Again in Acts 10 we read the same thing, 'While Peter was still speaking these words, the Holy Spirit came on all who heard the message. The circumcised believers who had come with Peter were astonished that the gift of the Holy Spirit had been poured out even on the Gentiles.' These folks who the early Christians didn't even want were already being included by the Spirit. Including them wasn't a decision the early Christians could make. The Gentiles were already included by the Spirit, and if Peter, James, the rest of them chose to reject the Gentiles and not let them speak in tongues, they would have been denying Christ in a way."

"But doesn't this lead to chaos?" I ask. "I mean how can any church function with a group of people doing whatever it is they want, however they want, when they want? Forgive me for saying this, but it seems a little naïve to suggest a freeform community."

"Well, it can be. It is complicated. It is difficult. Everything that goes on in a church is for a reason. Churches have learned human tendencies and weaknesses, so over the years different patterns and styles and rules have built up. At first they were correctives or cautions. Then they became settled habits. After a while theology came that makes these early choices into mandates."

"We've overcompensated."

"Yeah. For good reasons. Some problems still may pop up. In trying to face real issues, good people came up with ways to manage, ways to keep order, ways to make sure everyone understood what Christianity was about, and what it wasn't about. Hey, have you ever seen the Sistine Chapel?"

"Not in person, but I've seen pictures."

"It's not just the Sistine Chapel, I guess, but any old work of art, and seeing pictures is just as good, really, for understanding my point. Basically, Michelangelo got up on his scaffolding in the early sixteenth century and chose certain colors, slapping them on wet plaster in certain patterns. He created creation and a lot that came after in a brilliant way."

"Right."

"But this world is a messy place. There's dirt in the air. There are chemicals and—especially after the industrial age started—there are all kinds of pollutants. This makes things dirty. Even though they were in a church, the paintings that Michelangelo made got grimy, got dirty, with the dust of the centuries becoming a layer of filth on top of the beauty."

"They restored it recently, didn't they? I think I saw a story in some magazine a while back."

"There was a controversy with that," Nate says. "Some folks—artists and historians or whatever—thought that the ravages of time added to the character."

"But that's not what Michelangelo intended."

"If he wanted dingy colors he would have chosen them. He mixed his paints, he threw it up on the ceiling, all with a specific purpose and image in mind. We get used to dirt. We think the layers that build up because of a dirty world are inherent to the original. Some people were horrified by the idea Michelangelo painted in much brighter colors—'Disney colors' one person called them—instead of the dull and subdued tones they had seen all their lives. They were used to the dull and didn't want the original bright."

"So you see your work as restoring the original intent of the artist."

"Yes. That's it. I see people—all the people who are brought by the Spirit into our community—as being the colors. The Spirit mixes and chooses the palate and the scenes and everything. I'm not the painter. I apply a little solvent here and there, tidy things up. I help discover the colors as the Spirit intends them."

"If I can continue this analogy," I say, "I think some of the problem comes in the fact that not all restoration is helpful. I've heard of attempts—especially in previous centuries—which sought to clean things up but instead destroyed the work of art. The solvent corroded the colors."

"Totally. That's why I'm really cautious and respectful of those who aren't taking the leaps we are. But the fact remains that the artist intended something specific, and used specific colors and painted in and for a specific context. Pasadena is the canvas. The Columba is the canvas. The Upper Room is the canvas. There are canvases everywhere, all over the world, each a different scene, each different scene contributing to an even larger unified display of God's Spirit in this world. To reject the colors the artist brings for duller, dirtier, less brilliant colors because that is what we prefer and what we are used to seeing seems a particular sin of sorts. It is a sin of arrogance. As if we had a better understanding than the genius who did the original. Who are we? Who am I to say this person can do this thing, or that person cannot do that thing? I better have a very good reason if I'm going to say that. Neither personal preference nor my own hold on power are good reasons. Not at all."

"So you try to include everyone because everyone has been filled with the Spirit and therefore has something to say. Is that what I'm hearing?"

"Yeah, but let me make sure you understand the way I mean it. We have a weekly service in the Upper Room in which we all, at least once a week, gather together. Most of what we do goes on outside of that. We don't see the gathered meetings as being the church, but they are important, and a variety of people are involved in putting them together, including me. But we don't insist everyone do a stand-out thing during those couple of hours. Instead, I encourage participation by seeing people as already being called by the Spirit for something. When people want to step up and join with us, then I meet with them individually as we figure out who they are and how the Spirit is leading."

"How do you figure that out?"

"Well, I think one of the mistakes of the church is to generalize a calling. Just because I am passionate about something doesn't mean everyone has to be passionate about it. That's part of being the body. In fact, some things we may be passionate about could be in direct contrast to someone else's calling. So I want to let go and listen."

"How can you have direct contrast when you have a single mission?"

"It is a big mission and a deep mission and a very lengthy mission. The most stark contrast I can think of is between evangelism and formation. You can have a person who is totally excited about bringing new people to Christ, fired up and getting everyone else to join with him. But he's always looking for the next person. He's a salesman, inspired to talk to people and help them discover a path to Christ. He is very careful about not getting too deep because people might get turned off.

"On the other side is a woman, let's say, who is shy and really struggles talking to new people. But she is wise, and she has wrestled with a lot in her life, and she loves prayer and the deep things of God. When people struggle with their faith she can always help them grow more deeply and stick with it even in their struggles.

"He is outward; she is inward. Both fight internally against what the other is doing because they don't feel that same call. So often we are willing to alienate one or the other of these people and make our churches unbalanced. The challenge is to find ways to encourage both. To help people learn to carry out their individual calling and mature in their faith so they become their particular color."

"So how do you do that? You know you're really tricky to nail down on the specifics."

"Ha! I've been told that. Well, you can always visit our Web site," he says and laughs. "My buddy Simon generally keeps it updated with our goings-on. You know I think I swing away from saying the practical things because I'm such a child of the church-growth movement. Everything is done according to a model. What one successful church does, other less successful churches want to mimic no matter who attends their church. So they try to be like the successful church and attract the same kind of people. And, in a way, they give up on the people who are already there."

"Sounds like a bad sitcom episode. Marcy and Tammy are nerds, but Marcy gets invited to the party the popular girls are having, and Tammy doesn't."

"Then," Nate continues, "all the popular girls make fun of Tammy, and Marcy starts to join with them."

"Until Marcy insults Tammy herself, and Marcy realizes—"

"Usually with the help of a wise and wisecracking adult—"

"That Tammy has been her best friend and she needs to reject the popular girls to be herself."

"Yeah," Nate says. "It's kind of like that. I suppose. Maybe."

"Or maybe not," I say and laugh.

"My point is, especially in conversations like this, I swing away from saying the practical things because I don't want anyone to do what we do. I don't want you to write down our conversation and share it with others so they think opening a pub in the middle of the city is what they have to do, and so they then do all the other things we are doing. It is all about the Spirit, Luke, and while our particulars are fun and exciting—to me at least—they are not for everyone. But the Spirit is for everyone. Even new approaches like what we're doing can become a set of rules. Sort of like a group of teenagers who rebel by gathering in a group and then dress and talk like each other. They reject one conformity for another, and never really discover themselves."

"Paul says something like what you're saying, I think, in 2 Corinthians."

"Do you remember which verse? I'd love to get that."

"In English, of course," I laugh.

"Right, in English. Greek wouldn't be a problem, except they didn't have the verses and chapters in the earliest manuscripts and that's all I read," he says and laughs.

He pulls out his Bible again, then adds, "I'm probably letting you down by not knowing that verse."

"Something about the letter kills, but God gives life."

Nate turns the pages as he scans quickly over the text.

"Here it is," Nate says, "2 Corinthians 3:4-6."

> **Such confidence** as this is ours through Christ before God. Not that we are competent in ourselves to claim anything for ourselves, but our competence comes from God. He has made us competent as ministers of a new covenant—not of the letter but of the Spirit; for the letter kills, but the Spirit gives life.
> *(2 Corinthians 3:4-6)*

"Yeah," he says after a moment. "That's it exactly. Thanks. It's really true, and just what I am saying. So much of leadership training is developing confidence in ourselves, in our gifts, in our abilities to lead and do what is right for the organization. That's why there are certain types who rise to the top—people who have in themselves a measure of their own leadership, in which the Spirit really is an extraneous part. They would be leaders in any situation and act almost entirely the same way in any leadership context, often with a great deal of success. But, even if it's amazing, it's still a limited success. It doesn't change communities, it doesn't hold back the tide of evil. Those who need Christ the most—those who are most in debt—remain in debt while those who merely have a five-dollar charge against them come in droves."

"Paul says God has made us competent," I say. "I like that. So much of what I've seen in my own experience and as I talk with others does refer to the letter, the rules, the traditions, the 'way things are done.' I think I'm getting what you're saying now. Having the set patterns becomes the letter of the law. We start to believe the Spirit has to work during a sermon on a Sunday morning, or at the prayer meeting on Wednesday, or through this approved person but not that squirrelly one. You're reticent about details because you are wary of the letter. Is that it?"

"That is it totally. Even a fluid community like what we're doing can become fixed in a certain form. The church is a lot like concrete, you know. Each movement is fluid at first. Look around at all the mainline and established churches. They were all raging rivers in their day. Then they hardened into certain forms. Concrete seems like a good building material, but it makes for a terrible drink. Concrete doesn't flow. It isn't flexible. There's nothing that seems to indicate the Spirit is comparable to concrete. Concrete is not living. Jesus didn't say the Spirit is immobile. He said the Spirit is the stream of living water that flows through us. Rivers keep going even though they change course over the centuries. Rivers break down barriers, dig deeper, form new patterns."

"You want to be a church that is a river."

"Just that. I think to be a river we have to always be very attuned to the work of the Spirit. Watch the rain that comes and the streams that pour into us. There are seasons of flooding and seasons of drought. Our community is the river—it's not me. Neither am I a dam. I am not the locks that regulate anyone's passage down the river. Instead, I'm one of the creeks that pours into this community. Maybe because I'm doing this full time and have some level of formal training I am a bigger creek than others, but no single creek makes the river. I saw that in my old church. People were these little rivulets pouring into the creek that was our head pastor. He was a big creek indeed, but nothing could grow past him. His gifts, his interests, even his schedule dictated what went on. That limited us, even as it seemed to make us brighter because he was so talented and gifted. Our identity became him, and he was the identity of the church. We could never be more than him, and yet the Spirit is significantly more than any one person. If a flood came, there would be destruction, not renewal."

"You all participated in the head pastor's work rather than everyone participating in the broader work of the Spirit, right? That made his work seem especially powerful, and likely fed into more and more of it."

"Not to say he is a bad person, or arrogant or domineering. That's just church culture and part of the culture of leadership that afflicts so many of our churches."

"Afflicts?"

"Yeah," Nate says. "Because the call is always on being a leader, everyone wants to be a leader, and the unspiritual way of becoming a leader is by asserting one's own rights and pushing down others. Everyone has this Spirit-given drive to participate. But if real participation and contribution can come only from approved leaders, then everyone wants that approval. Political alliances of a sort are made and bolstered while standards are set up that create an institutional wall to keep particular people from ever moving to their potential. It's a lot like racism in that way. A lot of it comes not from an inherent rejection of a color, but very deep fear of competition. Cut out the competition with a potent philosophy and you have a much better chance of rising yourself."

"Even if you are small, you can at least see yourself as big compared to others."

"Right, and while we don't alienate according to race, we do according to gifts, or gender, or temperament. But my goal is to break through that. If someone is here, in my estimation that person is here for a reason, called to produce something with our community that only that person can produce. What makes a distinction, however, is that since we don't limit our definition of church to a service, neither do we limit our understanding of contribution to that service. Maybe someone is called to preach or teach or sing or decorate or do repairs here. Maybe, however, the Spirit has planted that person here as a point of reference as they use their gifts in other contexts such as work or in another organization. Because we are helping to bolster this person, we extend into a realm we would have never reached otherwise and this person is helping us to spread the message beyond our borders. My goal is to see everyone as part of the production— everyone producing, everyone using their gifts. I'm a lot more flexible on what that means, because what it means is often quite flexible."

"I guess I'm not going to get a copy of your organizational flowchart to include in the article," I laugh. "I am left wondering then about the New Testament. It seems there are particular superstars—people like Paul or Peter or Barnabus. Aren't there leaders, and then the people to support them, as we see in the New Testament? Why should things be different? I mean, of course, everyone has gifts like you suppose. But it doesn't seem that things can be as egalitarian as you suggest."

"What do you think about Agabus?"

"Who?"

"Right. That's my point."

"What is?"

"You have no idea who Agabus is."

"Should I?"

"He's a featured and important part of the early church who prophesied over Paul."

"What does that mean?"

"It means there are a lot of details left out of the New Testament. It means we can't just look at the featured characters, but we have to read closely and realize that throughout the New Testament there are men and women—some named only once, some not at all—who are really the key folks doing key things in these churches. We model ourselves on some perceived model of Christian heroes. But there are heroes at all levels, and we need to realize that it is precisely because these unnamed people were praying, serving, creating, and participating in all sorts of ways that we even hear of the people we usually think of as the heroes. Participation by everyone the Spirit brings is not simply a nice leadership option. It's at the very heart of seeing Christ in our midst. The Spirit reveals Christ, not just through us individually, but to us all together. That's why we need to meet together, Luke. It's not because of some rule that insists on our attendance. By seeing the work of the Spirit in and through others we realize Christ more deeply and broadly. The church is a reflection of Christ to this world. The more participation, the more accurate a reflection. That's how the Spirit works. That's how Jesus told us it would work, and Paul insisted this is the way it has to work."

As he was finishing his last sentence my phone rang. I forgot to turn it off like I usually do. Nate waits while I pull it out and look at who is calling. Heather.

"Nate, I really need to take this," I say, standing up. "Back in a minute."

" Creativity is at the heart of the Spirit, from the beginning to the end. If the Spirit has been given to you then you are creative. Maybe you don't paint or sculpt or sing all that well. But the spiritual gifts are our particular areas of creativity."

9

Inciting Creativity

After standing outside and talking to Heather for fifteen minutes, I come in and visit the restroom once more; mostly to settle things in my mind and make sure my eyes aren't too red. When I get back there is someone else at the table. I can see her long, straight black hair, but little else as she is facing away from me. Before I sit down, even before she turns, Nate introduces us.

"Luke, this is Melissa Choi. Melissa, this is Luke, my inquisitor this week."

"Getting you to talk is a tough assignment," she says to Nate and turns my way.

She holds out her hand. I shake it and sit down.

"Everything okay?" he asks.

"Yeah," I reply. "Well, maybe not, but that's a long story."

"Want to talk about it?"

"No, not really. Personal stuff."

"Alright," he replies. "Let me know if you change your mind."

"How was the bathroom?" Melissa asks me.

"Um, well, clean and useful," I reply, a little flustered at the question.

"It should be. We're paying Nate a lot of money and he really should be doing something useful, or he's totally fired."

"I clean the bathrooms," Nate adds as an explanation. "Being a janitor technically pays for my room, board, and just enough salary to occasionally buy a muffin next door."

"Thus supporting our competition. We should pay you less," she says and laughs.

"Plus, very few things keep a person as humble as having to clean public restrooms on a regular basis. Melissa is the assistant manager here so what you just heard is not an empty threat. I was going to ask you for a wee raise, actually."

Melissa rolls her eyes with a little dramatic flare and says nothing.

"Melissa is a talented artist," Nate says. "She would make an interesting article when you are done with this church series."

"What do you paint?"

"Sculpt. I mostly sculpt. Though I do paint occasionally. I'm the Asian Michelangelo currently looking for a rich patron who recognizes my utter genius and investment potential. Some of the works in here are mine. I won't tell you which ones. You just have to guess."

"I don't even know where to begin. Everything in here blends so well together."

"I think that's a compliment," she says and laughs. "Or a dodge. Anyway, Nate says you are asking what we're doing here—what gets us up in the morning."

"Besides cleaning the bathrooms," Nate says.

"What has he said so far?" she asks. "Something about community and helping people I suppose. He's big into that."

"Um, yeah, he talked about community, um, generosity, and, uh...."

"We were just talking about participation. Getting everyone involved."

She asks me, "Do you know why I'm here?"

"Well...."

"Of course not. That would be freaky if you knew why I am here. Then I'd have to ask how you knew, and more likely than not I would have to put a restraining order out on you because you have been stalking me. I better just tell you, before you incriminate yourself."

"I...."

"Creativity, Luke. That's why I stopped attending church for five years and why I'm back here. I gotta have a bit of creativity. I became exhausted with clip art and bored suburbanites who think they are poets without ever once, in their whole lives, doing anything poetic. Creativity is at the heart of everything church should be about. But from what I've seen the heart has been torn out and put on some museum pedestal so we all have to stare at what used to be but can't be anymore. The heart is a relic to adore, not to live anymore. You know why?"

"Control?"

"I can tell Nate has been talking to you," she says and laughs. "He looks meek and mild but he has a revolutionary fervor underneath his conservative exterior."

Nate asks, "Is that a good thing?"

"Depends on which side you're on, Nate," Melissa answers.

"Sometimes I feel more like the church leader who gets shot while holding an olive branch."

"Ah, how sad," she says. "Poor Nate is attacked from all sides. Nobody understands all that you're going through."

"Sarcasm makes no friends," Nate replies.

"Now, see, I think you're totally wrong about that. Whole communities are formed with sarcasm. Maybe not happy communities…but let's get back to creativity."

"How did creativity bring you here?" I ask.

"Nate, who's the guy in the Old Testament you like?" Melissa asks.

"Joseph? David? Uh, Jeremiah?" Nate guesses.

"No. It's Oholiab. That's it. And his friend. What's his friend's name? You talked about the two of them a while back."

"Bezalel," Nate replies.

"Oholiab and Bezalel, Luke. Those are my heroes. I might even say they are the reasons I'm still a follower of Christ."

"I have no idea who they are."

"Your loss. Really. They are these two guys who peek their heads into the story, do this amazing thing that reveals something extraordinary about God that goes against everything I was taught growing up, and then they drift away again."

"Is that your goal, Melissa?" Nate asks.

"Drift away? No, drift along," she says. "Drift with the wind, right?"

"With the wind," Nate says.

"Why are these guys your—"

"Why are Bezalel and Oholiab my heroes," Melissa charges ahead, "and what do they have to do with the experiences of growing up as the somewhat rebellious daughter of a rather proper, very successful, and well-respected pastor, right? Everyone always asks me that."

"Um...."

"Yeah, how did I know that's what you're thinking? I guess it's a gift of mine. Let me tell you, Luke, it's really simple. I'm an artist. I've always been an artist. That means I want to express. I have to think outside the box. I was told I should be a good little girl, sit in my pew, and find a nice husband to pay all my bills and give me security in life. He could work and become an elder in the church while I gossip with the gals and make brownies for the bake sale supporting little Cameron's T-ball team. I hated the thought, even when I was young. Then I got rebellious, was kicked out of my house, and wandered around for a while doing all sorts of things I shouldn't have done. But you know, God never let me go."

"You sound like the prodigal."

"Not really. I never returned. The prodigal went back home to daddy. I always believed in God, and that kept me from doing a lot worse things I could have done—like my new friends were doing. I was the holy one in that group, if you can believe it. But, I still haven't returned to my home. I didn't leave because I was sinful. I left, then became sinful, because I was so alienated. I mean there was more to it. I'm not blaming anyone, that's just how I see it. I was an alien, living on a whole different planet where everyone talked a different language and threw bananas at me. What I threw back was a lot worse than bananas."

"Tell him why you like Bezalel so much," Nate suggests.

"Beyond how the name just rolls around my tongue? Go ahead, say it, Luke. It's a fun name to say out loud."

"Bezalel."

"No," she responds. "Say it. Don't rush it. Savor the letters. Bezalel. It's a meadowy sort of word, don't you think? Oholiab, however, is a very round name. Oho... liab. Like a mountain."

"I...."

"No? Okay. Thought I'd try it. Words are like little sculptures don't you think? When we write we fill pages and pages with a transformative sculpture garden. But you don't care about that. Bezalel. Let's see, Bezalel shows up in the book of Exodus. Toward the end."

"Exodus 31 and 35," Nate adds. "But those chapters are pretty much the same. The first is God telling them to do something. The second is them getting to it."

"I like the getting-to-it chapter," she says. "It has those extra little bits about how well everything worked out."

> Then Moses said to the Israelites, "See, the Lord has chosen Bezalel son of Uri, the son of Hur, of the tribe of Judah, and he has filled him with the Spirit of God, with skill, ability and knowledge in all kinds of crafts— to make artistic designs for work in gold, silver and bronze, to cut and set stones, to work in wood and to engage in all kinds of artistic craftsmanship. And he has given both him and Oholiab son of Ahisamach, of the tribe of Dan, the ability to teach others. He has filled them with skill to do all kinds of work as craftsmen, designers, embroiderers in blue, purple and scarlet yarn and fine linen, and weavers—all of them master craftsmen and designers.
>
> So Bezalel, Oholiab and every skilled person to whom the Lord has given skill and ability to know how to carry out all the work of constructing the sanctuary are to do the work just as the Lord has commanded."
>
> Then Moses summoned Bezalel and Oholiab and every skilled person to whom the Lord had given ability and who was willing to come and do the work. They

received from Moses all the offerings the Israelites had brought to carry out the work of constructing the sanctuary. And the people continued to bring freewill offerings morning after morning. So all the skilled craftsmen who were doing all the work on the sanctuary left their work and said to Moses, "The people are bringing more than enough for doing the work the Lord commanded to be done."

Then Moses gave an order and they sent this word throughout the camp: "No man or woman is to make anything else as an offering for the sanctuary." And so the people were restrained from bringing more, because what they already had was more than enough to do all the work. *(Exodus 35:30—36:7)*

"What's the Hebrew phrase you said is so important?" Melissa asked.

"*Ruach elohim*," Nate replies. "The Spirit of God. Used in other places to describe how the Spirit came down on someone. When Balaam spoke his prophecies, or when Saul was first king and was empowered to lead the people. The way it's phrased always seems to mean the Spirit coming down on someone for a work of divine empowerment."

She asks Nate, "Didn't you say this passage is the first place we're told the Spirit came down on someone?"

"Yeah. I'm pretty certain that's the case. I mean, Joseph and Moses seem to have been blessed, but the Spirit language wasn't used in the text."

"So, Luke," Melissa continues, "this is the first time the Spirit of the Lord comes down on a person and what happens? Healing? Prophecy? Flashes of lightning? Nope. Nothing like that. Nothing like anything my dad would say are acceptable spiritual gifts in the church. The Spirit came down and they started sewing, and sculpting, and carving. Doing all sorts of other works of art."

"Creativity," I say.

"Yes!" she replies. "Very good. God is an artist. I mean look around. Well, not here, this is all people work. But go to a forest and look around. Take a hike. God is totally an artist. I always felt so alien compared to the people in my church. But I wasn't far away from God at all. My dad still doesn't get that. I had to choose who was my guide. The Spirit is a creative Spirit, and when the Spirit works—here in the first time the Spirit comes down on a person and ever since—the Spirit provokes creativity. Insists on it really. I mean, some churches get so excited about tongues and the wild stuff. But this first time, Luke, it's about art. Art for God. Art commissioned by God. He's the great patron, the one who inspires and pays, all because he seems to like meaningful things. We think of God as totally pragmatic, like some executive businessman keeping his eye on the bottom line or whatever. God is this Lord. Sometimes practical, oftentimes lavish. He's God, not a CEO looking for salvation profits."

"So they're your heroes because they are artists?"

"Because they show up and are these men chosen by God to do something few pastors now would see as important. But here, here they are. This building of the tabernacle is a central story, and we're all still a part of it. We're all the tabernacle now, and our creations can be inspired by the Spirit, for spiritual reasons. These bland warehouse-style churches that look like hotel conference rooms but without even the interesting carpets show that there's this major part of the Spirit that everyone has left out. The Spirit is creative. I'm creative. I'll bet even you are creative. Are you creative?"

"I suppose I can be."

"Well, I suppose you are and you need that side of you to be mined in order to really get a taste of the Spirit. This is the thing. Pastors preach. That's creative. They think this is so important but then don't let anyone else play. They have to have this spotlight on their creativity but don't ever understand why others don't feel the same passion and excitement. I mean, I like going to museums and all, but it's not nearly like getting my hands in clay or carving into marble like it's this wonderful, thick dough, and bringing out something new. Feeling like this doesn't mean I'm rebellious. I can't stand bad singing, ugly paint, terrible decorations. The disregard for aesthetics bothered me to no end. I knew who I was and I thought the church didn't have a place for me, so I left it. I still believed, but I thought somehow I couldn't track right. But then I got to thinking that it's not me at all. I started to feel I was hearing and everyone else was deaf. Then I stopped by here, chatted with Nate a while, and kept coming back. Then he talked about Bezalel and Oholiab and everything came into focus. That's it you see. I am given gifts by the Spirit. The original gifts. The ones that came first. Only no one I ever knew gave me space or freedom or even acceptance to be who God made me to be. That's what the church should be about, don't you think?"

"Yes."

"What I love about that passage," Nate says, "is how all that creativity poured back into everyone. For most of their wandering so far the people had been grumblers and complainers, always seeing the glass half empty and always letting Moses know how much better things were in Egypt. But in building the sanctuary, they are really given a chance to respond, to use their gifts, talents, and resources. Unfortunately, that same urge earlier sparked their sin while Moses was on the mountain."

"They got all their gold," Melissa adds, "and made themselves a stupid gold calf, thinking if they weren't allowed to see God, well, they'd make a god they can see and participate with. That's the yearning isn't it? To participate with God. We hate being spectators. Most of us do, at least. We want to get into something. Proclaim something. Be something. I couldn't stand the thought of being this passive wife who only existed for someone else's life. I wanted a life of my own. I had to have it."

Nate continues, "That's the beauty of this Exodus passage. Early on with the golden calf God punished the people. But now, here, he called out two men specifically so they could lead all the people. God redeemed that urge—which earlier prompted the golden calf—by inspiring them to build him a tabernacle."

Melissa jumps in, "Something a lot more grand than what they had dreamed up. It's like God saw the calf and said, 'That's it? Here, let me show you what creativity is like. I want beams and embroidery and gold and silver and carvings and color. You all don't know what creativity means. Let me give you my Spirit, and then you'll see what it is.' That's God. We're so content doing this little stuff. He wants us to be bigger and better. More creative, not less. More free, not more constrained. He wants to hone us, and when I learned that, I was able to bring my art to this new level, for me at least."

"For all of us," Nate adds.

"You're so kind," she replies. "But I'm still going to have you clean the bathrooms."

"But cleaning toilets doesn't give me the creative opportunity I need to participate with God," Nate mockingly complains.

"Get over it!" Melissa says, then turns to me. "You say you suppose you can be creative. That's a cop-out. Creativity is at the heart of the Spirit, from the beginning to the end. If the Spirit has been given to you then you are creative. Maybe you don't paint or sculpt or sing all that well. But the spiritual gifts are our particular areas of creativity. A woman with the gift of evangelism is going to be characterized by her creativity in telling other people about Jesus. Those not given that gift aren't let off the hook, they have to work at it. A gifted teacher will feed on creative ways to teach. Someone gifted in giving will find all sorts of ways to give and be energized. Creativity is who we are, Luke. It tells us who we are and it feeds into who we are. If we are not creative, in whatever way we're given to be creative, then we are not ourselves. Do you get that? We don't know who we are. So are you creative?"

"I suppose I must be. I like to write."

"If you don't know, then you don't know who you are. If you aren't being creative, then you have no idea who God has made you to be. That's why having a context of discovery and exploration and honing is so right. I ended up going to art school, but it was only when I really embraced God again—when I realized he had made me into an artist because he is an artist—that I went from becoming someone who sculpted to becoming a real sculptor. That's what church should be, don't you see? It should be a place where you go from being someone who has fond thoughts for Jesus into becoming someone empowered by the Spirit for Jesus."

"That takes a lot more than sitting around passively waiting for someone else to do his or her thing," Nate adds.

"A lot more," Melissa responds. "The Spirit has been poured out on all people and if the Spirit has been poured out then you have to start walking. You have to get in and get your hands dirty doing your thing. You have to get your feet dusty and your mind working, your whole self engaged. Otherwise you're going to go rotten."

"That's what Nate said earlier," I reply.

"I've taught him well," she says and laughs. "When I was growing up in my dad's church everyone knew me. But I didn't know hardly anyone. They were faces, hands, legs, bodies. They weren't people to me. They were totally anonymous, even as I knew a lot of them were really dedicated to my dad—a lot more than I was at a certain point. When I ran away I felt a lot of anger toward all these faces who didn't have names. A lot of anger. At first I blamed it on all the usual crap. Suburban malaise. Religious hypocrisy. Rich bank accounts and poor lives. You know, the stuff that gives people like me an excuse to leave and hate all the people who I think aren't like me."

"You said *at first*," I say. "What came later?"

"I realized I hated them—and I mean really hated them—not because they weren't like me, but because we were exactly the same. They were these images of who I was becoming, who I was. Maybe we played different games and had different tastes in music, but we were the same people. I hated them because I hated myself, and I hated myself because I was so totally anonymous."

Nate asks, "What do you mean by anonymous?"

"I was this other person. I didn't know who I was, but when I left I was so sure I knew who I was. But that was some other person. I went from role to role, always playing a part. First the good little daughter then the smoking, messed-up teenage rebel. I hated those anonymous faces from my dad's church more and more. I didn't realize why, but it was because I saw so much of myself in them. I was hating myself through them. I wasn't a person. I wasn't anybody. All that time I thought I was this special little girl, the daughter of a great pastor, but really I was no different. I was there to sit quietly in my pew. Be an inspiration to others in the youth group. Do all the things nice little Christian girls are supposed to do. But I never showed up. All that time I never showed up. Have you shown up, Luke?"

Melissa is turning out to be a better reporter than I am. It's uncomfortable being on this side of the questions.

"Sorry, that's a terrible question to ask." She continues. "So I got kicked out. I knew I was going to, and I kept breaking every rule until I broke my dad. That was my goal. He played a part, too, and it became my goal to break him, to see what was there, to ruin him if I could, all because I hated myself so much and had no idea what to do. Someone had to be real, and I made it my goal to see that reality in the one person who seemed to have it all together. It worked."

"You broke him."

"I made him cry. Up to that point I thought this would be my best moment ever. I saw his real self. But I hated myself more because of it, because it made me feel something. He had enough. I had enough. I was gone. I broke him, and I was sure I broke everything about him—all the religious stupidity, all the spiritual lies, all the church sham. I wanted to break it all."

"Did you?"

"No. But it took me eight years to learn that. I was anonymous the whole time. I was nobody. I thought I was this person, among all these other people—my new artist friends. But we were no different than the faces I grew up with. We had different parts, different costumes, different lines. But we were all extras on the set."

"In case you're wondering," Nate interrupts. "She's dating an actor. This has led to a lot more analogies about acting over the last two months."

Melissa laughs, then says, "Yeah. I guess that's true. Tommy has gotten into my vocabulary."

"Is your boyfriend part of the community here?"

"Yeah, we met here, actually. Tom has been showing up for—what, six months longer than I have?"

"Something like that," Nate answers.

"So what was I saying? What was I saying, Nate? You interrupted me just when I got going!"

"You were all extras on the set," Nate says.

"Thank you."

"You're welcome. Tangents are my specialty."

"None of us were real people," she continues. "That's what I didn't get. I just switched costumes. But I was still a nobody."

"What changed?"

"It was when I realized how much I was a nobody. I don't mean that in a depressed sort of way. It was like one morning I woke up and saw myself in the mirror. It was just like that. I stared at myself like I was someone I had never met. Because I had never met me. I had no idea who I was. I was totally anonymous to myself. I think the Spirit was doing a work that morning by opening my eyes to who I wasn't."

"Because you left the church?"

"Well, sort of. At church I was this one character. When I left I threw all that away and embraced this other character. But, I was both. That's what I didn't get. My dad was wrong. He didn't let me be who God had made me to be. But he was also right. Absolutely and totally right. He was right and he was wrong, but at the time I could only see the wrong and it blinded me to everything else."

"What was he right about?"

"Jesus. He was right about Jesus, Luke. And I knew it. That's why I stayed a nobody. It was the Spirit who was calling me to be creative—to dance and paint and sculpt and respond to God in wonderful ways. I thought it was the creativity calling me away from the Spirit. So when I left I lost that innocent drive that had pushed me for so long. I wanted the results so much I abandoned the cause. But it's the cause that brings the results, right?"

"Yeah."

"Yeah? Yes! Yes! Yes! Of course it is."

Nate interrupts, "I like what Paul says in the beginning of 1 Corinthians. 'My message and my preaching were not with wise and persuasive words, but with a demonstration of the Spirit's power, so that your faith might not rest on men's wisdom, but on God's power.' We make it all about wise and persuasive words now. That's what I learned in seminary. That's what I did as a pastor on staff. That's all I saw. Wise and persuasive words define the ministry now. Paul said it was about something else. About power. You know what power is?"

"What?" I ask, knowing Nate's description of power will be different from mine.

"Power is the creativity of the Spirit being exploded onto the scene. That's why I want to invest in everyone and get them to participate. But participation isn't enough. It's not enough to have people get up and do any old thing."

Melissa adds, "Because they will get no closer to who they are."

"Right. The Spirit calls us to be who we are. For others to become who they are. Melissa said she felt anonymous and saw the people in her church like that. Well, I'm sure that's not because she wasn't doing something, or they weren't doing something. Have I talked about this yet?"

"You touched on it," I answer. "But I don't mind hearing more."

Melissa continues, "Things felt wrong because we weren't doing what we were created to do."

"You didn't know how to do that," Nate says, "and you weren't given a context of discovery for that. So much of the perspective on Christianity accuses it of making people into automatons. Claiming it stops thought, stops individuality. People claim that faith compresses everyone into a mold, crushing them and drying them out. It's not like that. Well maybe in some places it has been. Yeah, it may happen, but that's a sure sign the Spirit is long gone. The Spirit and Jesus are not in the business of crushing or making everyone the same. One of the great phrases I have come across in studying the Holy Spirit is 'diversity in unity.'"

"We are one but not the same one," Melissa says.

"Right. We have a unity through Christ but the Spirit makes us all different. We have all been made different and becoming the same will not reveal the brilliance of Christ's work. Instead, the brilliance of Christ's work is revealed by us becoming who we were created to be. It is by being creative in whatever ways we are inspired. A church with everyone alike is a shadow church. The real church is where everyone is in this dance of creative participation. Here a giver, there a teacher; here an evangelist, there a pastor. Prophets, artists, singers, leaders, healers, people with wisdom, people with discernment, those with faith, those who like to get into the dirt and do things, those who like to rise up and have a look into heaven through worship—they all join the dance, playing the part they were born to play, becoming who they are in their creativity."

"Perichorosis," I say, proud I remembered the word.

"It's pronounced perichoresis," Nate says, "but yeah, that's exactly it."

"Because it is the Spirit who has created us," Melissa says. "The Spirit comes alive in us when we respond with our creativity. That's what I didn't understand. I ran away and ran away from myself. When I finally realized this—when I realized I had never really let God go and he had certainly never let me go—I was able to begin the process of becoming a real person. It wasn't until I had this realization that I began to lose my anonymity. Fortunately, I found the Upper Room and I didn't have to choose which role to play. Instead, I could really figure out who I was as a whole person with the Spirit guiding me in wisdom and creativity. It's a package deal you know. I learn more about God, become more in tune with the Spirit, and my creativity takes off. I should show you the work I was doing then compared to what I'm working on now."

"Is it better?"

"Technically, not all that different. But now it's real. It's like before my art was as anonymous as I was—negative, brutal, harsh, dark. Now, I'm actually saying something, becoming something in my sculpting as I become someone through the Spirit."

"That's why Paul got so upset sometimes," Nate says. "It wasn't that they were breaking the rules or not following his severe leadership. He got mad because they weren't getting this was all for them. They didn't get they could rise up and rise out. He wanted the people to give up all the things that tied them down. He wanted all the leaders to give up all the ways of tying the people down. There is order, but that order has to have freedom, creativity, life. The Spirit is fire, wind, water— elements of freedom and change."

"My dad's church had a little water, but no wind or fire. I need my wind and fire."

I ask, "Why is that?"

"Why do I need wind and fire? Do I have to start from the beginning again?"

"No, why did—or does—your dad's church only have a little water but nothing else?"

"I think he's afraid. I think that's at the heart of it. That's what surprised me when I left—when I broke him finally. I thought I would see shame. I saw fear. That scared me and has stuck with me. My dad was afraid."

"Afraid of what?"

"I don't know."

"Losing control," Nate suggests. "That doesn't mean quite what you think it might. This isn't about being some power-hungry person. It's about being settled in life. That's what you saw in all those people, Melissa. That's definitely what I saw in myself when Stacy left me. I mean, I told you about how pride was there, and all sorts of other sins were there. But it took me a long time to realize—not until recently really—that her leaving made me afraid."

"Afraid of what?" Melissa asks.

"All my life I had lived according to plan. Then everything fell apart. That's why the house was such a big decision for me. It was that last thing, you know. This one last part that I could build on again. I lost the woman who was going to be my wife and I felt dissatisfied in my work. Everything in my life was suddenly uncertain except for that house. That was something to hold onto. It was grounding. But holding on meant not leaping into the river of the Spirit. I could have started this, but all that fear about control over my life would have undermined absolutely everything."

"I don't get it," I say. "How does that affect creativity?"

"Because if we get too addicted to control, if we are so attached to the fear of losing the control and we don't even realize we feel afraid, then we will begin to make decisions which are less about following the Spirit and more about making sure the Spirit stays within the bounds of our control."

"Control over our lives?"

"Yes, in part. But also control over everyone's life. If one person gets out of control then that person reminds me it's all a lot more fleeting than I want to think. That's the hallmark of fundamentalists, you know."

"What?"

"People think fundamentalists are defined by their zeal and faith. That's not it at all. Not at all. They are defined by their fear and lack of faith. They don't really believe so they have to go out and make sure everything they see, everyone they meet, fits into what they want to believe. They don't want to see themselves. Seeing themselves in other people makes them ravenous in their fear."

"Like me," Melissa says. "I never thought of myself as a fundamentalist."

"For art, maybe you were," Nate replies. "I think we all have a tendency of being like Elijah or like Obadiah."

"What does that mean?" Melissa asks. "Who's Obadiah?"

"Oh, I love this passage. I haven't talked on it before?"

"You love every passage," she jokes.

"I do, don't I? Maybe that's why I've missed talking about this one."

"I'll expect to hear more about it in coming weeks."

"And you likely will. So in 1 Kings, Israel is having this huge famine. No rain at all, for something like three years. Then God tells Elijah to go to King Ahab and tell him rain is coming. Elijah meets Obadiah on the way there and tells him to announce his arrival to Ahab. Obadiah was Ahab's palace administrator and a devout believer. He had already saved a bunch of prophets from being killed. So he had proven himself to be a good servant of God. But he got afraid. I love this part."

> **As Obadiah** was walking along, Elijah met him. Obadiah recognized him, bowed down to the ground, and said, "Is it really you, my lord Elijah?"
>
> "Yes," he replied. "Go tell your master, 'Elijah is here.'"

"What have I done wrong," asked Obadiah, "that you are handing your servant over to Ahab to be put to death? As surely as the Lord your God lives, there is not a nation or kingdom where my master has not sent someone to look for you. And whenever a nation or kingdom claimed you were not there, he made them swear they could not find you. But now you tell me to go to my master and say, 'Elijah is here.' I don't know where the Spirit of the Lord may carry you when I leave you. If I go and tell Ahab and he doesn't find you, he will kill me. Yet I your servant have worshiped the Lord since my youth. Haven't you heard, my lord, what I did while Jezebel was killing the prophets of the Lord ? I hid a hundred of the Lord's prophets in two caves, fifty in each, and supplied them with food and water. And now you tell me to go to my master and say, 'Elijah is here.' He will kill me!"

Elijah said, "As the Lord Almighty lives, whom I serve, I will surely present myself to Ahab today."

So Obadiah went to meet Ahab and told him, and Ahab went to meet Elijah. *(1 Kings 18:7-16)*

"Obadiah knows Elijah and knows how the Spirit works," Nate continues. "So he doesn't want to tell Ahab anything because he's worried the Spirit is going to whisk Elijah away."

"The wind blows where it will," Melissa adds.

"It blows Elijah all sorts of places," Nate says. "So Obadiah won't do it. Not because the Spirit isn't working but because he is totally afraid of losing control of the situation and being left holding the bag. He doesn't want to be the one responsible when Elijah disappears again."

"He believes in God," I say, "but he doesn't know quite what God will do."

"Right," Nate responds. "He doesn't know. All he knows is the Spirit does crazy stuff. You get the sense things like this have happened before. Obadiah is worrying about real dangers. Elijah doesn't rebuke him. It's like he, too, knows how the Spirit works and he wants to reassure Obadiah that he's going to stick around this time."

"Obadiah is afraid," Melissa says, "because things can get out of control. But that's exactly what you have to risk—things getting out of control. If you don't, then the Spirit doesn't get space to really work. Creativity demands a certain loss of control. That's what happened in the trial too, I bet, with Peter and Jesus. Peter was totally afraid because it was all spinning out of control. 'I don't know him,' he said. Three times. Wow."

"What?" I ask.

"That's what my dad said about me, and I said I don't know me either. That's when I left. I haven't talked to him since. We were both so afraid. Neither one of us could see Jesus. I couldn't see Jesus in him, and he couldn't see Jesus in me, so we both got trapped in total fear and couldn't handle it anymore. I broke. He broke. Our relationship broke. It's still broken. We were so afraid the Holy Spirit was going to leave us hanging. I would have to be an average nobody. He was afraid I was going to be someone who broke his boundaries. We were both too afraid to trust the Spirit so we created a rupture."

"That's what happens," Nate says. "We break apart community. We sever it into pieces because of our fears. Some of which are well-founded. But we are so controlling—so worried about everything working out—we step in and manhandle it all. We build a fence around our lives and ministries so there's not even a worry that something might go wrong."

"Then nothing really goes right either," Melissa suggests.

"It all stays in a vague mediocrity," Nate says. "We no longer allow ourselves to see the real work of the Spirit. We are so afraid. Creativity breaks that fear. It forces us outside of the fear. That's why it's not an option here for me. I have to be creative. I have to see Melissa's creativity, and Tom's, and Debbie's. Everyone's. That's how we see the Spirit working among us. That's how we know we will stay lithe and free for the Spirit to do even better works among us. Peter tells those in Jerusalem the Spirit will pour out on all people. The Spirit was poured out and we have to see that. We have to make a context that encourages that. A setting that fosters that, and brings it out of people who may have never realized they had any creativity."

"And," Melissa interrupts, "have never really known themselves, or who God has made them to be."

"Yes," Nate continues, "and may not have tasted the power of what it means to be a follower of Christ. Creativity is the expression of the Spirit's power, Luke. That's the beauty of it. That's the brilliance of the Spirit among us."

❝ True Christian leadership demands discernment and that means listening to the broader work of the Spirit in the community. With the Holy Spirit everyone will have an area of leadership of some sort or another. The more a person matures in Christ the more this leadership increases. The church, however, tends toward a corporate model in which there are limited positions. People are picked and chosen to rise up. People are raised up according to the track of promotions, not according to fit or purpose. Everyone else exists on a lower plane. The Spirit, however, could care less about our organizational models. I have to always be aware that a brand-new Christian, never before in church, can be inspired by the Spirit to give us a radically new direction."

10

Leading as a Body

There is a crash in the kitchen, followed instantly by the sound of rolling plates. Everyone in the pub stops talking and looks up. At a few tables, diners burst out into applause.

"Ah, the dulcet tones calling me to the joys of gainful employment," Melissa says and stands up. I expected her to be taller. "Nice to meet you Luke. I'm sure we'll be seeing you around these parts some more."

"Sure. Nice to meet you," I say as she walks off. I should have stood.

"She seems nice," I add after a moment.

"She is. Usually. Melissa is one of those people who is great to have around and at the same time irritating."

"What do you mean?"

"Most people have filters. She tells you exactly what she's thinking. You always know where you stand with her. You know even if you'd rather be hidden in a cocoon of self-delusion. Most people go through life striking a balance between honesty and artifice. Melissa had all the artifice burned out of her. She considers her honesty her real art. But, really, I don't know what we'd do without her."

"Having an artist like her does seem extraordinary."

"Well, yeah, but it's not just about her creativity. We churchy people can get caught up in our own worlds, you know. Everyone wants to be seen as thinking right—according to the accepted template. So plans go forward when the majority, or even a vocal minority, are enthusiastic about something. You know: 'the best thing ever,' 'world-changing,' all that. The funny thing is how often no one actually likes the plans that much. I've seen this over and over, especially after programs or approaches fall flat. Leaders start saying how they felt uneasy or disagreed but didn't share their thoughts. They wanted to be on the team."

"Not really leaders then."

"Well, that's harsh, because they did do a lot. But in a way you're right. I don't blame them because that's the way our culture is set up. Those who disagree, in my experience, get pushed aside for anyone who plays along with whatever is happening, right or wrong."

"People want to dislike yes-men, but the yes-men are always so comforting to have around," I say. "Reminds me of Micaiah."

"Micaiah?" Nate says, looking more than a little surprised. "The prophet?"

"Yes. A few weeks ago one of the churches I visited had a preacher going through 1 Kings."

"Good choice."

"I thought so. I had been on a streak of visiting topical preachers, hearing all sorts of stuff about marriage and kids, which for a lot of reasons was frustrating right now. So it was nice to hear a good exegetical sermon."

"It's a fine balance," Nate says.

"Anyway, he was in the last chapter of 1 Kings—I forget what number that is—and he was talking about false prophecy. The king wonders if he should go to war. All the court prophets tell him one thing—what they think he wants to hear—but he doesn't trust them with something really important so he calls in Micaiah."

"Who, at first, also tells him exactly what he wants to hear. I think I remember this one."

"The king—"

"Ahab, I think."

"Ahab insists Micaiah tell him what's what, even if it's bad news and goes against what all the other prophets are saying."

Then Micaiah answered, "I saw all Israel scattered on the hills like sheep without a shepherd, and the Lord said, 'These people have no master. Let each one go home in peace.' "

The king of Israel said to Jehoshaphat, "Didn't I tell you that he never prophesies anything good about me, but only bad?"

Micaiah continued, "Therefore hear the word of the Lord: I saw the Lord sitting on his throne with all the host of heaven standing around him on his right and on his left. And the Lord said, 'Who will entice Ahab into attacking Ramoth Gilead and going to his death there?'

"One suggested this, and another that. Finally, a spirit came forward, stood before the Lord and said, 'I will entice him.'

"'By what means?' the Lord asked.

"'I will go out and be a lying spirit in the mouths of all his prophets,' he said.

"'You will succeed in enticing him,' said the Lord. 'Go and do it.'

"So now the Lord has put a lying spirit in the mouths of all these prophets of yours. The Lord has decreed disaster for you."

Then Zedekiah son of Kenaanah went up and slapped Micaiah in the face. "Which way did the Spirit of the Lord go when he went from me to speak to you?" he asked.

Micaiah replied, "You will find out on the day you go to hide in an inner room."

The king of Israel then ordered, "Take Micaiah and send him back to Amon the ruler of the city and to Joash the king's son and say, 'This is what the king says: Put this fellow in prison and give him nothing but bread and water until I return safely.'"

Micaiah declared, "If you ever return safely, the Lord has not spoken through me." Then he added, "Mark my words, all you people!" *(1 Kings 22:17-28)*

"Melissa sounds like your Micaiah," I comment.

"Hopefully I'm not Ahab," Nate says and laughs.

"Hopefully not," I say, "but my guess is you've known a few Ahabs in your time."

"Maybe not quite as bad, but I could give you the names of some I've worked with who have engaged their inner Ahabery."

"We all have," I say, laughing.

"What you're saying really opens up another part of what I want to be doing here."

"Which is what?"

"Our view of leadership has to change. The Spirit makes a difference, Luke. This story is a great illustration of that. Ahab is not illustrating a problem of leadership. The man was a leader. He was king. But he didn't listen to the right people. He listened to Jezebel, his wife. He listened to prophets who weren't speaking God's words. All the while ignoring everyone else, ignoring the real prophets, ignoring the people. He was isolated. His leading became isolated and blocked off from the Spirit. The scary thing is that leadership does not assure discernment. Leadership can mean leading people into disaster. The ability to lead people doesn't mean we can discern God's leading in our midst. Leadership is a tricky issue, Luke. Not long after I graduated I really wanted to get a sense of leadership in the Bible, and so I actually spent a good long while rereading and going through the text."

"The whole thing?"

"Yeah, well most of it at least. I gave myself some freedom to skim parts. It was cleansing for me."

"What did you find out?"

"Being a leader is a good way to bring the judgment of God down on oneself. Yeah, some leaders did great things, but wow, most every disaster we read about was also caused by a leader. We read that being a teacher is dangerous. Being a leader is even more dangerous. Walk wrong and it can get people killed. Literally."

"So what do you do? How do you respond to that? Back away from leadership?"

"No, not at all. I had to take what I was learning and see how it changed my leadership principles. When I started getting really interested in the work of the Spirit, those lessons came back to mind and really took off. Yet another thing I didn't expect from the Spirit."

"The Spirit changed your view of leadership?"

"Totally. I realized I had to make sure there were many voices involved, and everyone could have a voice if they wanted to say something. Like you said, Micaiah wasn't part of the elite here. He was the one who had something to say. Leadership is about decisions but it is also about conversation. True Christian leadership demands discernment and that means listening to the broader work of the Spirit in the community. With the Holy Spirit everyone will have an area of leadership of some sort or another. The more a person matures in Christ the more this leadership increases. The church, however, tends toward a corporate model in which there are limited positions. People are picked and chosen to rise up. People are raised up according to the track of promotions, not according to fit or purpose. Everyone else exists on a lower plane. The Spirit, however, could care less about our organizational models. I have to always be aware that a brand-new Christian, never before in church, can be inspired by the Spirit to give us a radically new direction."

"How do you do that?"

"Well, it keeps me on my toes, that's for sure. There has to be a balance, and we read that in Paul's letters. Just because someone wants to say something doesn't mean that person should, and at the same time a person who wants to say something cannot be wholesale prevented because there's a good chance that person's words will help."

"This still seems like confusion to me."

"We've run into that," he says and laughs. "That's why I really try to make it a point not to be critical when people stick to the standard approaches of the church."

"You sound critical."

"Well, I do offer a critique. The Spirit is pulling me toward something different, and I have to see what I'm being pulled toward."

"And out of."

"And out of, right. But, there's a certain point at which critiques can become judgments. I'm supposed to follow the Spirit in my own life, not determine how people have or have not followed the Spirit in their contexts. That means I might disagree with decisions, but wisdom doesn't come from the juvenile 'I'm-right-they're-wrong' point of view. Wisdom comes from trying to see it all through their perspectives, to get a sense of why they did what they did, so I can grasp why we're doing what we're doing. It comes from listening to the story the Spirit is teaching. A lot of this, Luke, is pure instinct. If you talked to me seven months ago our conversation may have lasted an hour. I would have told you to just show up and participate because I wouldn't know how to express in words what we are doing. Maybe you would have appreciated that more."

We both laugh.

"Yeah, maybe," I say. "No, I'm enjoying the conversation. But I would like to show up for something more purposeful. Maybe your Sunday night meeting. Do you call it a service? What is it?"

"Well, it is a service, I guess, but we don't call it that. More of a gathering. I had a great name for it. Perfect, but it was shot down by the rest."

"What?"

"Love Feast."

"That doesn't sound very Christian."

"Oh, it's quite Christian. That's the original term for a church service. A translation actually. The earliest Christians spoke in Greek. And some of them spoke in Aramaic, too, I guess, and I think those people called their gatherings synagogues, which I wouldn't use because then people wouldn't know where we stand on a lot of key issues."

"I can see why they shot you down on that one. You obviously don't get to make all the decisions, but how are decisions made?"

"Depends on the decision. Leadership is where the rubber meets the road, Luke. I can say 'welcome, welcome' all I want. I can tell people they are valuable and needed and important. I can send them cards, visit them, affirm their salvation. I can give them hugs, and mention them in sermons. I can give them a job to do that seems really important, like praying in our service or organizing a meeting. I can even—like we talked about—encourage their participation in some important way."

"The usual church involvement stuff," I add.

"Exactly. I can do all that and really make it look like I believe everything I've told you about the Spirit. But if I'm not opening room for leadership—for people to make real decisions, have real authority, and risk making real mistakes—then everything I've said is just words. My view on the Spirit doesn't come from what I say, but from what I do. This means I have to take risks on people and voluntarily let go of my drive to do everything my way. This means, in my view, everyone is a leader in something. Everyone can and should step up to the next level, and everyone needs to be encouraged to do that. This goes back to what we talked about at first. Doing what Jesus did. He chose Peter, John, all the rest—not because they were the cream of the Galilean crop."

"What about the gift of leadership?" I ask. "It seems clear Paul talks about a spiritual gift for that role and there being organizational needs. The leadership model is found in Scripture, Nate. It's not something people made up to secure their own power."

"Yes and no. There is a functional leadership model in Scripture. Elders, deacons, and so on. But we've institutionalized this a lot more than anything we find in Scripture."

"Because of the fear?"

"Well, yes, but most of it was a good fear. I mean how do you really deal with all the issues that come up when a guy comes saying he is God, then he dies, and then he rises, all while having to balance thousands of years of traditions which insist on the fact God is one? It takes a lot of wrestling. And when something like this happens, people want to run their own way with it, so boundaries are set up. Boundaries mean referees and referees mean judges and judges mean strict rules, and well, you get the point."

"I'm surprised you would worry about that."

"Why?" he asks.

"Because you seem to have jumped the bounds of everything so it seems odd for you to think about the importance of boundaries."

"We've changed appearances but we haven't changed the core values. That's the trouble right there, Luke. People see changes in appearances and assume everything has changed. Such people then attack any suggestion or threat of change in tactics or style or approach or setting because they think they are defending the core values. But they're not. They're building a fence around their law. Then they think their fence is the same as the original. Attack the fence and you're attacking their understanding of the law. People forget that their fence isn't the same as their core values; their fence is built of the customs and conveniences that may, in many cases, be distortions of the original intent. People confuse the barriers for the law itself, and build a fence around the fence. Centuries later, there's quite a barricade built up. People forget what the law itself looked like."

"So what do you do?"

"I watch the core. And we risk. Really risk. Not risk by saying something bold. I risk by letting someone else do a task I might be better at. Or I risk by letting someone take charge of something really important that reflects on me or on all of us. I risk by letting go of my authority at times and giving into some-one even when I disagree with that person, if it's on a matter outside the core. It's amazing how much I've learned by letting go of my need to always be right. Not just in humility. About God and the Spirit. Now I can't imagine insisting on my way all the time. I'd be the worst off for it."

"How does this work practically? If you throw out func-tional leadership, I mean. How do you get anything done?"

"Well, we don't throw out functional leadership, we just see it as more of a fluid thing depending on the situation. Every-one who has been filled by the Spirit is a leader, Luke. That's just the way of things. I don't look for leaders from among the people. I look for leadership in all the people. It's my job as the captain here to bring that out, train it up, and ship it out."

"What?" I ask, laughing.

"Oh, just an analogy I'm playing around with. The modern military doesn't look for leaders, it makes leaders. That's the secret of its success, many say. We have an amazing non-commissioned officer corps in all the branches. When someone enlists, they don't enlist with the expectation they will always do the bare minimum and be the lowest on the totem pole. Well, maybe they think that, but once they meet a sergeant they realize there are expectations. They have to learn to lead. The longer they are in, the more they will be taught—in classes and on the field—how to lead. It's a constant process. People rise up and new people come in. It's not enough to have motivated and skilled officers. It's definitely not enough to pick officers because of their initial qualities of birth or personality."

"Your point is that instead of looking for leaders, the church should create them?" I ask.

"There are gifted leaders, that's for sure, and that's the gift of leadership given by the Spirit. I don't deny that. But there's also a gift of evangelism, but that doesn't mean everyone else is off the hook. I'm not doing my job if I am not bringing out leadership in others, helping them develop their particular gifts and equipping them to lead. If I weren't helping everyone become a leader, I would not be a pastor. I'd be a lecturer. This is precisely what many leaders have become. They look at the competitive corporate models where the central mission looms large, but is always secondary to individual drive for success. The church is often like that. It limits promotions, keeps a hierarchy, establishes CEOs and vice presidents. The military, however, is a cooperative organization, with the mission and the people inherently unified. There is no mission possible apart from the specific skills and leadership of the specific people. So the specific people have to be invested in and developed."

"The mission and the people are unified in the military, but not in the church?"

"Maybe what I'm thinking and trying to communicate really has more to do with expectation. Everyone in the military is expected to improve, develop. Everyone is given an opportunity. They see the need because life and death are so vivid. It's not that way in the church."

"I think I understand what you're getting at."

"Churches I've been a part of have given a lot of importance to the number of new members or converts. But what is really important for the mission is not just new converts. We have to retain the old ones. People who are maturing become stifled because the church has a limited understanding of participation and leadership. People feel stifled and they wander. They feel the tug of the Spirit to embrace more, but they hit a wall."

"Which would then make more of the same within the church," I suggest, "because if maturing Christians are leaving, you have no sergeants to train the privates. There are fewer people able to step up, more people on the lower ranks, and thus more emphasis on the leaders already active in the church."

"Exactly, and that means more habits and traditions develop to solidify what's going on. It's always easier to theologize a problem than fix it."

"Theologize?"

"That's what I call coming up with big words and fancy philosophy—sometimes even Scripture—to justify what is going on, even when it's not what is supposed to be going on. We're all very good at that."

"Your leadership-development model seems very universal or inclusive, but Jesus seemed to pick and choose."

"But who did he pick and choose? That's the question. Did he pick these amazing and dynamic leaders who stormed the countryside with dashing good looks, overwhelming charisma, and unimpeachable logic? Nah, he picked Peter. And two Sons of Thunder, a name that to me says they had attitude problems. And a tax collector no one liked. He even picked someone he knew would let him down eventually. Jesus took a chance on Judas."

"It got him crucified."

"Now that's risk," Nate responds. "To see real freedom you have to take risks. There's no getting around it. Playing it safe may ensure you don't fall into error, but playing it safe will also ensure you never discover fullness. Not too long ago I was out camping with some friends out on the Channel Islands not too far off the coast. These aren't Caribbean-style islands with nice sloping beaches. They jut out of the water like big rocky warts."

"Sounds appealing."

"It's a national park. Really a beautiful place. These islands are so close to one of the biggest metropolitan areas in the world, but they are totally isolated and peaceful. All around are cliffs. Very steep cliffs that drop a hundred feet to a rocky, sea-lion filled beach. There are no fences or barriers, so you have to watch your step. One of my friends is a lot more cautious than the rest of us. He's afraid of heights and wouldn't even come close to one of those cliffs. I walked to the edge and looked out. I saw sea gulls flying fifty feet below me. I watched sea lions jockeying for position on a preferred boulder. I even saw a manta ray swimming underwater twenty feet off shore."

"Wow."

"Yeah. But even better was what we saw in the evening. The sun sets in the west, and on these islands you can sit on the edge of a cliff and watch the sun set, watching it illuminate the ocean with dazzling colors before it finally disappears behind the great blue sea. My friend who wouldn't look over the cliff missed those last moments. He was safe, that's for sure. He was not going to fall. But he also missed some spectacular beauty. He didn't see what the rest of us saw. He can't share our wonder and our memory. There are a lot of other beautiful things to see out there, so it's not like he was isolated and sad, but he missed that beauty. Do you get that?"

"Because he wasn't willing to go up to the edge."

"On the mainland such cliffs would be fenced off, blocked from access. You could look out but not over."

"Kids might fall off."

"Exactly. You have fences so those without sense or balance aren't tempted to do what they really shouldn't. No one should fall off a cliff, so authorities figure it's better to fence it off, make a law, whatever, so there's no risk of injury."

"Or lawsuit."

"Right," he laughs. "What's the verse in Romans? 'By dying to what has bound us, we have been released from the law so that we serve in the new way of the Spirit, and not in the old way of the written code.' This is generally just applied to issues of salvation, but I don't see God drawing the line that sharply. Paul was arguing against Jewish influences here—not just about salvation. They were interested in the continuous relationship with God. The Law was how they knew to serve God. The Law provided the assurance they were right with God and doing God's work. This was a lifestyle, not a method of salvation."

"He's talking about how to live, not just how to find life."

"That's a good way of putting it. The Law mandated how to live. The Spirit gives freedom to live. When the entire community is filled with the Spirit, then we have to apply all the freedom the Spirit brings to all the people. It's not up to me to pick and choose. I don't anoint people. The Spirit anoints people and I respond to that anointing. I like what God told Samuel when he was looking for a new king, 'I will show you what to do, anoint the one I indicate.'* Samuel goes to Jesse and has a look at all his sons—each a fine specimen. None of them was chosen, until they hunted down little David. God chooses whom he will choose."

"But that's for a single leader, which I get. You are saying everyone is that leader."

"When Samuel poured the oil over David's head 'the Spirit of the Lord came upon David in power.' It also says that Saul's loss of kingship was defined by the Spirit being removed from him. On the day of Pentecost the Spirit came upon the whole church in power. That means neither you nor I nor anyone has a priority. None of us can be defined as having something that stands out more than the rest. The only thing that can distinguish us is our maturity and faith. Our inherent positions, however, always remain fluid."

"That helps, but I still don't totally get your *everyone-a-leader* thing."

"I think I see the problem with what I'm saying. You're thinking I'm telling you everyone is the same kind of leader, which would lead to some kind of mass bureaucracy in which everyone had to agree for anything to happen. That's not it at

---

* *1 Samuel 16:3*

all. Organizationally we have to have decision makers and people in front, so I'm not saying it's a leadership free-for-all. My goal is to understand the potentiality."

"The what?"

"The idea that at any moment any one of us can be, and may be, pressed into leadership. We have organization but it has to remain fluid. I even have to be willing to step aside if someone else begins to really step up as the overall pastor of this community. I serve in a role, but that's the key word. I serve. I serve God, and I serve the Spirit in this community. The Spirit does not serve me, and does not follow my commands or approvals. This means I have to serve anyone the Spirit raises up. I have to do that using discernment."

"Which is the standing on the edge of the cliff."

"Exactly that. In the book of Hebrews we see this. The author interrupts himself and tells his readers they should all be teachers by now.* He has to keep covering the basics because they aren't getting it. But the mature get it. Because they get it they teach it. Because they understand the foundations they have trained themselves to distinguish between good and evil. This means they are leaders. They are able to provide counsel and make decisions, as the decisions are led by the work of the Spirit in them."

"So you have a normal structure but remain open to intrusion. Is that what you're saying?"

"Well, I wouldn't say *normal,* even if what we're doing matches what I see in Scripture. They had organization to deal with all sorts of issues, as do we. Paul Evans takes charge of everything related to our property. He's a contractor, so he knows a lot more than I do about that stuff. Of course he is our leader in that, and all questions about anything related go to him. His wife, Kathryn, is a CPA and our accountant. I have no

---

* *Hebrews 5:12*

idea how much money is coming through around here. People know to go to Kathy if there is a money question. I trust them both wholeheartedly and know the Spirit has given them gifts and passions entirely different from mine. On the other side, of course, is the risk of being wishy-washy and not leading where I'm called to lead. I'm called to raise up others, but also be raised up myself. This isn't about being wishy-washy or indecisive, it's about focusing on who the Spirit has made me to be and leading in those areas. This lets me focus on the things I have been called to do."

"Which is?"

"I am a teacher, Luke, among my other gifts. Also, as the pastor here I need to pray for people, and follow up with people, and encourage them, along with my teaching during various events through the week. Being concerned with all the other stuff means my mind is elsewhere. I've gone months in prior positions where my mind was everywhere except the places God had called me to be. That is a sin. That's why seeing the Spirit leading everyone into leadership is a gift. It frees me to do the things my community needs me to do, while also encouraging everyone to be invested in what we are doing here. The disciples gave up leadership responsibilities to the seven men, like I mentioned before, so that people could be fed and also so the disciples could focus on what they needed to focus on."

"Prayer and Scripture."

"Exactly. But that's not all a church does. That's not all we do. If I am to do those things, and be who I'm supposed to be, that means I have to let others lead, let each person lead within his or her calling. To find that freedom I have to do one of the hardest things any leader can do. Let go."

"It gives you freedom to give them freedom."

"That's it! And by leading they begin to invest. By knowing their opinions count—really count not just figuratively count—they will take note of our broader mission, invest more of themselves and their resources. That's a major cause of nominality you know?"

"Nominality?"

"Meaning 'in name only.' Christians with the title but not the actions. What happens when someone gets too old for the milk but isn't allowed the meat. That's what I'm trying to prevent here. And that means giving people the real responsibilities as the Spirit has called them."

"Do I hear a distinction there? As the Spirit has called them."

"Yeah," Nate says and laughs. "That's my caveat. Just because you might want to lead us in worship singing, that doesn't mean you are supposed to lead us, especially if you have a terrible singing voice. What that means is you are missing your calling in order to do something you're not very good at. Just doing 'something' isn't discernment. It's sloppy spirituality. The Holy Spirit comes on everybody who believes in Christ, just like in Acts 10. That provokes me to see each person as empowered by the Spirit for leading us in some way. First Corinthians 12, however, tells us that people are empowered in distinct ways. Paul and Kathryn Evans, for instance, are extremely gifted in service and giving. So in the ways they are empowered—in service and other ways—I trust them, and have to learn to trust them, and I have to let go of my desire to be the boss. Others in our community—Melissa for instance—have an amazing eye and ear for helping plan our worship services. I let them plan our primary Sunday evening service, with my input shifting week to week according to how the Spirit is leading me. They listen if I have something to say, but I don't insist on having my say. Larry Nguyen, like I said, is in charge of our social outreach. Karl, the waiter over there—I should introduce you when he gets a moment—leads us in singing and musical worship. Go down the list of people here and I'll tell you how I trust them and have given them room to lead as the Holy Spirit has empowered them to serve."

"So it's not anarchy then? That's what it sounded like at first. Or some kind of idealistic communist group."

"We're an anarcho-syndicalist commune. We take it in turns to act as a sort of executive officer for the week, but all the decisions of each officer have to be ratified at a special biweekly meeting, by a simple majority in the case of purely internal affairs, but by a two-thirds majority in the case of more major issues."

"Really?"

"No," he says and laughs. "That's Monty Python. We try for something more in line with Scripture, which has order but is dynamic in that order, with functional leadership always in tune with charismatic leadership, and vice versa. Which sounds more difficult than it is. Mostly I just try to not do stuff and especially not insist on my way all the time."

"It's not about you."

"No. If I left I would guess everyone would miss me but there's nothing here that insists on me. That's a Spirit thing, I think. People are very useful, vital even, but no one person is essential. If something happens, or the Spirit moves me around, or anyone else around, the Spirit will be providing a plug for the hole. This means I have to make sure to do my part in recognizing each person and helping people step forward into their maturity. Otherwise I become essential and the Spirit becomes less so."

"No offense, but you sound like you keep saying the same sorts of things on each topic."

"It is the same, Luke. Welcoming the new people, encouraging their participation, spurring their creativity, finding their leadership—it's all the same thing, all along the path of their spiritual maturity and their maturity within our community. There's nothing separated here. It's not really even different stages, as participation, creativity, and leadership can simultaneously be developing in a particular person as soon as they are welcomed into the community. This is the path of *being* a Christian, not just identifying as one. It's a spiral, and a spiral that leads the person and the community higher and higher toward heaven. This is the work of the Spirit in the church, which then echoes outward, draws more people in—into the same spiral."

"Always expanding and always rising."

"Like in Acts, 'They broke bread in their homes and ate together with glad and sincere hearts, praising God and enjoying the favor of all the people. And the Lord added to their number daily those who were being saved.'* They expanded in their gifts, in their service, in their worship, and then in their numbers."

"A wonderful idea but only if a church stays small enough to keep doing this."

"Yeah, that's the danger to be sure. Many people think new churches will remain small. More individual congregations but fewer people. Obviously, I'm not at the point of dealing with an oversized church, but I do think about it. While I like our small dynamic I wonder if it's a necessity to always stay small. Instead, we might get broader and broader. If everyone is supposed to lead then we have to keep expanding our outreach. Everything spirals upward and outward. I think that's the key part of this whole process of leadership development."

"We see leadership now in terms of categories instead of how the earliest church saw it," I say, "Clergy and laypeople. Find the leader. Discover the gifted leader. Pick the few out of the many and focus on them so they can rise to the top. And as

---

* *Acts 2:46-47*

the church grows, the spiral carries the best and brightest to the top and they become the paid leaders who run things. Isn't that how it always turns out? Even with the best intentions?"

"Luke, your dire forecast is noted, but I don't think this is how it has to be. I do think the principles in Scripture are designed for a church of any size. Scripture talks about different levels in a community. There are elders and there are pastors and there are apostles who spend their time in prayer and Scripture. The categories we use to identify gifts can become more than a way to identify people. We also use them to limit people. We then expect a pastor—someone who is called to preach or teach or pray—to be the leader in everything, even things they may not have any experience in doing."

"Which leads to a chaos of sorts."

"And worse. Like I said before, the Spirit is calling each of us to become. To become who we are, to become mature, to become whole, to become fruitful. In too many churches, I've seen the emphasis on the *church* becoming, or in some cases on the *pastor* becoming, instead of the priority being on *individuals* becoming."

"Explain that a little more."

"Very few come to church as whole people, Luke. They come to church with doubts or fears or worries or something else. They stay that way a lot of the time. Jesus said these doubts and fears and worries come from our not understanding reality. Jesus said he was the reality, and in his salvation we can find hope and purpose and joy through the power of the Spirit who leads us into fullness."

"Right."

"What happens, however, is that a pastor can easily become a proxy for Jesus. That's a huge problem."

"Why? Doesn't the pastor speak of Jesus and in a way represent Jesus' authority?"

"He speaks, but we all represent the same sort of authority to one another. Functionally pastors have a role, but pastors are people, Luke. We all approach Jesus on the same plane. Pastors can lead us to Jesus, and they often do. A pastor can lead us to Jesus, but the pastor is not some exclusive link for communicating with Jesus. Pastors who have that latter concept, or people who have that concept of pastors, will make a church into something that feeds into their pastor's being."

"I don't get that."

"An ego-driven pastor needs people feeding into him and giving themselves up to him in the process. That's why there are such huge power issues from both pastors and those in the church. That's why a really successful pastor can commit these huge, huge sins, totally insulting Christ, and still have a large number of supporters. That's why pastors can play such vicious politics and be so competitive. They are looking for people to feed into them, and are jealous when others take that. People who are afraid, or unable to find their own wholeness, look for a pastor to pour into so through the pastor they can have some identity. That completely cuts off the real work of the Spirit in each person's life and makes for a very dysfunctional situation, which is often hidden by the apparent success of the church."

"I think I understand. The problem is churches start attracting those who are looking for a charismatic leader. They follow the pastor instead of the Spirit. Then people who don't want to pour themselves into that leader begin to feel alienated. The church starts following the leader instead of focusing on Jesus."

"That's it," Nate replies. "We are called to pour ourselves only into one Person, and that is the Spirit. The Spirit, like I said before, is a member of the Trinity who exists in mutuality. Only the Spirit among us knows how to pour back in fullness as we pour out our fullness. People can't do that. We pour into some regular guy, making him into our "Spirit," and we will be drained empty and he will be falsely filled. As we pour into the Spirit, the Spirit pours back into us, and as this continues we learn how to pour into others. But it all is absolutely dependent on there being no one between us and God, even symbolically or sacramentally. The Spirit then takes us and we become part of Christ, saved by Christ, united with Christ, while also becoming all those things with everyone else the Spirit is filling. That is kenosis, mutually pouring into each other."

"That's why you see everyone as a leader."

"That's why everyone can be a leader and is meant to lead in some way. They are not below me, and often times for this to be grasped people need to be intentionally raised up to discover themselves and who they can be and have been created to be. I let go. They embrace. I become less. They become more. I embrace. They let go. I become more. They become less. The process repeats. We all dance."

"Toward heaven."

"Toward Christ and his kingdom."

"Thanks, Nate. This has been a very helpful conversation. Hey, I have to run off now to another meeting, but I really appreciate all the time you've spent talking with me."

"My pleasure, Luke. It's good for me to talk through this stuff. I appreciate your interest. Keep in touch."

"I will."

"By the way," Nate says as I stand up, "to answer your earlier question. We have a lot going on throughout the week, casual stuff, a lot of it unplanned, but our main gathering—if you want to call it that—is Sunday at six o'clock."

"The Love Feast."

"Yeah," he laughs. "You are totally welcome if you're interested."

"I'd like that, Nate," I say. "Well, it's more that I need it. I'll see you Sunday then."

"May peace be with you, Luke," he says as I leave.

" *Our worship, our gathering here, is a reflection of our lives, and our lives are a reflection of our worship. We have to be in all our hours the same people we are in the few hours tonight.*"

||

Uniting Us through Worship

Relationships are hard, especially when two people seem to be going entirely different directions. I've been married for six years now. Well, five years. I'm not sure what to call this last year. Other than the legal definition, nothing of this past year has any sense of marriage to it. We're both wrong, I know that, only I don't know how to be right. I don't even know what right looks like with the two of us. I'm pretty certain Heather feels the same way. That's why we had such a bad afternoon. It's been a lot easier to avoid talking. With her constant work-related travel this has been pretty easy. But today we got into it. We both said things. Five o'clock came and I was about to give up going to the Upper Room altogether.

"Don't you have that church thing tonight?" she asks, wiping tears from her eyes and cheeks.

"Yeah. I'm not going to go," I say.

"No," she replies. "Go."

"You want me out?"

"I want to go with you. I feel like I need to go to something."

I honestly feel the same way. So we get ready and leave. Our fifteen-minute drive is mostly silent.

"Where is it?" she asks when we arrive. I hadn't told her much about the Upper Room, only some of my thoughts about Nate. I had also told her Mike's story. It seemed fitting when another paper broke the story about a television preacher caught with a prostitute.

"Across the street." I say as I get out of the car.

I can feel her staring through the window at the Columba, deciding whether she wants to get out. I really expect her to ask me to drive her home again.

But the car door opens. She gets out, smoothes her black dress, and looks both ways along the street. We both trot across during a lull in the traffic.

There's a small crowd of people at the Columba. All sorts of people—young college kids to older couples sharing a Sunday-night meal. Most of the tables are taken. I don't recognize any of the staff working.

We hear soft guitar and flute music.

"Upstairs," I say, pointing. Before we walk up there, I grab her hand and stop. "Thanks, Heather."

"Alright," she replies and begins walking up.

It is now a little after six.

"Hey, Luke," Nate greets me when we get to the top. "I was beginning to think you weren't going to come. You're usually so prompt." He laughs. I don't think I was on time all week.

"Hi, Nate," I reply. "This is my wife, Heather."

"Welcome to the Upper Room, Heather. As you can tell we don't exactly have a normal layout here. We'll start with a bit of singing and prayer, then we eat. After that we'll do some more prayer and talk a while. It's not too complicated."

He isn't kidding about the layout. There are no chairs. Well, there are two or three chairs in the corner. Other than that I see only large pillows and bean bags and a few couches. Along one wall is a large, low table with carafes and covered plates of all different sizes. The walls are decorated in much the same fashion as downstairs, only a little simpler. And there is nothing representational. There are no pictures of people or scenes or anything recognizable except for a few paintings with text on them. Verses, I imagine. The walls aren't bare; they are painted with different symbols and designs that don't allow my eyes to settle. The room seems to point away from itself.

A simple cross, flanked by two large, red candles, is at the center of the low table along the wall. The candles flicker, and white Christmas lights strung neatly around the top of the walls add to the dim lighting. The windows are closed—I guess to keep out the noise of the traffic. They mostly succeed, but I do hear some loud trucks and other assorted city noise. It is still a little warm. The day has been hot.

About fifteen people gather in small, loose groups. A tall man plays guitar in the far left corner, next to a woman playing the flute. I think the man is the waiter Nate pointed out to me yesterday.

"Hi, I'm Lisa," a woman says to Heather, holding out her hand.

"Nice to meet you," she replies, taking her hand. "I'm Heather. This is Luke"

"Welcome to the Upper Room," Lisa says. "I'm glad you could make it. Let me introduce you to some of the others before we start."

"Alright," Heather says and looks back at me as Lisa leads her away. I begin to follow. Then I stop when someone says my name from the other side of the room. I turn to see Chris, the manager of the Columba, coming toward me.

"He didn't scare you off, I see. Great! I'm glad you came by. This doesn't sum up who we are, but I think it says a lot more about us than long, philosophical conversations."

"I enjoyed them, actually," I reply.

"Hey, Luke," Melissa says behind me. "You came."

"Yeah, I came."

"Good. I hope you and...."

"My wife, Heather."

"I hope you and Heather feel the peace of Christ and Spirit tonight."

"We need it."

"I can feel that," she says. "I have to go help set up. Talk afterward?"

"Yeah, okay."

"Luke, this is my wife, Nicole," Chris says. "Nicole, this is the guy who has been hanging out all week."

"Nice to meet you, Luke," she replies. "Welcome to the Upper Room. Hope it's not too different for you."

"It's different," I say and laugh. "Whether it's *too* different I'll let you know at the end."

"I'm sure you'll get into it," she replies, laughing with me.

I look around for Heather. She's on the opposite side of the room talking with two or three other women, and a couple of guys.

The music begins to get louder. Something is about to start. People stop their conversations and begin to stare toward the musicians. I notice many people close their eyes and bow their heads. Some lift their heads and their hands. Lips move in silent prayer. Another couple comes in from downstairs, with two kids. The woman is Natasha, who I had met earlier in the week. It's my first time here, and I'm already seeing people I know walk through the door. Mike waves when he and his wife come into the room. They take a seat off to the side. Karl—I think that's his name—begins to sing. But not the usual kind of chorus. It sounds more like a chant, like he's chanting one of the Psalms. The woman with the flute stops playing while he sings.

I hear a loud whir and a door opens up along the wall not too far from them. A man in a wheelchair rolls out of what I now realize is an elevator. He balances a large tray on his lap, with a plate and a goblet on the tray. While Karl continues to chant, this man—the only man here dressed in a suit and tie— rolls over to the large table. A woman helps him set the tray down on the table. The man stops for a moment and stares at the table before rolling to an open spot next to it. Nate stands with his head bowed near the door where we came in.

The chanting continues for a little while, then the flute begins again. Karl begins to sing a more contemporary song of praise to God—Father, Son, and Spirit. I haven't heard it before but apparently it is known to everyone else. Others quietly begin to join in. The low murmur in the room soon crescendos to a gentle chorus. I realize I'm focusing too much on what's going on. I'm watching the people and checking out the room, not really participating. But I'm starting to feel like this isn't about my article anymore. I need to participate. For myself. I close my eyes and listen. I try to find prayer. The music is calming my emotions, reminding me of something I have not felt for a while during worship. Peace? Hope?

My shoulders relax. I didn't realize they had been tense. While I listen I increasingly feel lighter, almost like I'm swimming with the music. After a little while of this singing—one song flowing into another—I realize I have been feeling a breeze. My hair rustles with it. My skin tingles. I open my eyes, which for whatever reason immediately focus on the top of the heads of the people across from me. The windows are still closed.

Oh. Someone has turned on a fan. The candles on the table flicker wildly, casting dancing shadows on the walls and ceiling. I watch the shadows for a long moment, enjoying their dance before I close my eyes again and begin to sing the chorus as it comes by the second time. The room becomes brighter. I peek again and notice the sun has sunk low in the sky so that it is shining through the west-facing window. Shining right onto the group of people across from me. Shining on Heather. She stands out to me in the sun's light. We used to enjoy watching the sun set when we went camping. It's been a long time since we did that.

We all continue to sing, "Praise be, Praise be to the Holy One...."

I don't know how long the singing continues. It feels like five minutes but I know it must be longer. It's dark outside by the time we finish. We sang through the sundown. That feels important to me for some reason, a reason that doesn't resolve itself in my mind.

The song hasn't really finished, it is easing toward a close. Karl stops singing but continues strumming his guitar as the flute carries the melody. Both become softer as they continue, until the noise of the fan stands out. One of the men begins to pray.

I expect the sort of prayer that often follows a time of singing. A prayer of transition thanking God and so on, a prayer that starts lofty and then brings us down to earth again, generally followed by a joke and announcements. It isn't that at all. If anything, the man's prayer sounds like the verses of the songs we just sang, like a psalm of praise and worship continuing to echo in the room.

The words slip by me, but their tone, their beauty, fill me—reminding me of who God is, and who I am before God. I realize I am praying with him. Not aloud, but inside—my words join with his like we are playing different parts of a song. Other people pray when he falls silent. They pray for many things— for the community, for the Columba, for Pasadena. They pray for the government and for some of the events in the news. Others follow by praying for specific local needs, and people. All while praising God and thanking him for the work he has already done. Each prayer seems as unique as the individual speaking.

I don't notice the time passing like I often do during long prayers. After a while everyone joins in the prayer as the first man begins, "Our Father, who is in heaven, Holy be your name…"

When we all finish, there is a long pause, a potent silence, and I continue to pray, feeling like I need to pray for forgiveness. The words I said this afternoon to Heather come back to me. They feel like weights. *God, cleanse me and help me see your light.*

It isn't only God who comes to mind. I open my eyes and look across the room. Heather is staring at me.

I mouth, "I'm sorry. I'm so sorry."

She whispers back, "I'm sorry too. Thank you."

I don't know what she is thanking me for, but saying those words and her response help me feel clean again. I feel free and ready for the evening to continue.

I lean over to Chris next to me and whisper, "Who was that man who prayed? Another pastor?"

He leans back and whispers, "Nah, that's Steve. He's a plumber, his wife, Tanya, teaches, um, third grade. That's their son Connor. Great people. Prayer warriors."

Four people stand up and walk over to the table, where they take the lids off the dishes. They pull some plates from underneath the table. On the dishes are rice, vegetables, bread, and assorted entrées I can't quite identify.

Nate says loudly, "Shall we eat?"

"Yeah!" Connor yells out loud. Everyone laughs. He is about five, I guess.

"Yeah!" Nate yells back and walks over to the table. Everyone follows. I guess they eat during their service.

The young boy clings to Steve as they walk over, their eyes wide with expectation. Natasha and her husband have two daughters—maybe around eight and ten years old. Debbie has a son as well, it seems, maybe around twelve. I don't see her husband. It occurs to me she probably doesn't have one. She wasn't wearing a ring when she served us.

While in line I listen and watch some more, noticing some of the people staring at the stairs. Not everyone has shown up tonight. Somehow I expect that before anyone goes to bed those people will be found.

I'm not lost in my thoughts for long. Chris introduces me to others, and we begin talking about ourselves. Apparently they've heard about me and are curious about my thoughts so far. I'm curious about them, so there's a lot of polite deflecting of the topic. This continues as we find a seat somewhere in the room, and eat. Drinks are poured and passed out. People laugh and talk. Others seem very serious as they pick at what's on their plates. The casual or not-so-casual conversations continue for about twenty or thirty minutes, maybe longer. I'm not sure because there aren't any clocks in the room, and I think it would be rude to pull out my cell phone to check the time.

Heather laughs with the same group of people she met when we first walked in. I haven't seen her laugh like that in a long time. It seems she has found some friends. For that matter, after talking with Chris and the others I've met, I think I might have found friends too. Through the meal men and women wander over to where I'm sitting and briefly introduce themselves before getting another piece of bread or some rice or some more of that wonderful chicken dish. The man in the wheelchair, it turns out, is Larry Nguyen, who is in charge of the social outreach.

While we're talking I hear Nate talking a little more loudly, like he is wanting everyone to focus his direction. I expect this is when the sermon will begin.

"So where were we last week?" he says.

"Philippians 2," a man replies. That same man begins reading from what I assume is Philippians 2.

If you have any encouragement from being united with Christ, if any comfort from his love, if any fellowship with the Spirit, if any tenderness and compassion, then make my joy complete by being like-minded, having the same love, being one in spirit and purpose. Do nothing out of selfish ambition or vain conceit, but in humility consider others better than yourselves. Each of you should look not only to your own interests, but also to the interests of others.

Your attitude should be the same as that of Christ Jesus: Who, being in very nature God, did not consider equality with God something to be grasped, but made himself nothing, taking the very nature of a servant, being made in human likeness. And being found in appearance as a man, he humbled himself and became obedient to death—even death on a cross! Therefore God exalted him to the highest place and gave him the name that is above every name, that at the name of Jesus every knee should bow, in heaven and on earth and under the earth, and every tongue confess that Jesus Christ is Lord, to the glory of God the Father.

Therefore, my dear friends, as you have always obeyed—not only in my presence, but now much more in my absence—continue to work out your salvation with fear and trembling, for it is God who works in you to will and to act according to his good purpose. *(Philippians 2:1-13)*

"Do we?" Nate asks. "Do we have any encouragement from Christ? I know we are supposed to say we do. What is it?"

While people still pick at the food on their plates and drink from their cups, they all discuss Nate's question and other questions. But it's not just a free-for-all. Nate is doing something more. He's leading the conversation. During lulls, he makes a point about a word's meaning. Or he has someone else open a Bible and read from a passage in Jeremiah or the Gospels. There is a free form to the discussion but with a curious quality that I can't quite put my finger on.

Maybe it's a dance. It feels like a dance with the text. Everyone who wants to participates. Some remain silent but occasionally Nate directs a question to a particular person who hasn't said anything. Even the kids jump in, and Nate takes their comments just as seriously, sometimes even bouncing off the question to carry the conversation to another level. Unlike when he and I were talking, he isn't giving very many answers. Mostly questions. He peels back the layers and gets us—gets me—to look behind the surface. Others ask questions as well, and Nate smiles when they do. How many times have I read this passage? Who knows? This is the first time, I think, I've really looked at it.

Do I have any encouragement from Christ? That should mean something then. That should mean everything. Only it hasn't. If I have that encouragement then I should be like-minded? With whom? Christ? And those Christ has called.

My whole life, my whole week, my whole day flash before me as I realize I have been trying to claim something for myself. What? I have no idea. But it hasn't been Christ. Nothing about my afternoon had any regard for Christ. What should that mean then?

Nate asks me a question, and I have no idea what he asked. Mike jumps in after a moment with an answer, saving me from a little embarrassment. It feels a lot like high school, except instead of my mind wandering far afield, it had wandered more deeply, into myself, into my life. I start listening again as others wrestle with what is meant by "fear and trembling." Nate gives what I assume is a condensed study of what scholars think, though he makes it sound very approachable and fits it into the suggestions others are making.

I realize what he's doing. It's a sermon in the form of a conversation.

There is a lull after we finish talking about the last verse. Karl begins strumming his guitar. Then one of the women I haven't met begins to sing.

"Jen," Chris leans over and whispers to me.

"Thanks," I whisper back. I realize just then she is singing some of the words from the passage we just discussed.

"...made himself nothing..." she sings, with Karl following up with the guitar by itself before she continues. Earlier Nate had mentioned this passage may have been a common hymn that Paul adapted. I guess Jen and Karl took that and reattached the music. It is haunting and beautiful. The words bury themselves into my soul.

When they come to the end, there is more silence. They then start again, this time a little bit faster. Someone is now playing a small drum. I can't see who. A few people stand up and walk over to the table where they pick up the platter and goblet which Larry Nguyen had brought in. I watch them uncover the platter and I see a large loaf of bread. Two other people get up and walk out. Nate breaks the loaf in half and hands a half in each direction where people break off their own piece. The two people who had left return, this time carrying large, lit candlesticks, which they place in the center of the room. The lights are dimmed and we sit in the light of dancing flames.

With the singing we celebrate the Eucharist. We all pause when Nate speaks the appropriate words. Then we continue again with the hymn.

Lisa, the woman who first introduced herself to Heather, gets up and walks out, returning after a moment with a large bowl and towel. She sits down and dips her hands in the bowl, then dries them with the towel. She passes the bowl and towel to Heather next to her and whispers a few words. Heather dips her hands, dries them, and whispers something to the woman sitting on her other side as she passes the bowl to her.

Lisa then opens her Bible and says, "Ezekiel, in 36:24-27":

> **For I will** take you out of the nations; I will gather you from all the countries and bring you back into your own land. I will sprinkle clean water on you, and you will be clean. I will cleanse you from all your impurities and from all your idols. I will give you a new heart and put a new spirit in you; I will remove from you your heart of stone and give you a heart of flesh. And I will put my Spirit in you and move you to follow my decrees and be careful to keep my laws.

I look at Chris.

"Ablutions," he leans over and whispers to me. "We dip our hands as a sign of cleansing, reminding us of our baptism, our constant forgiveness, and new start."

As the bowl continues around the room, Lisa opens up a notebook and reads a poem, prefacing it by saying she wrote it the other day. It is a reflection on Christ's work as shown in the passage we discussed. It is really good.

When she finishes she leans over to Heather and whispers something. Heather stares at the ground for a moment then nods. Lisa opens up her Bible, thumbs through it for a moment and hands it to Heather, pointing to a verse.

Heather then begins to read:

> **All night long** on my bed I looked for the one my heart loves; I looked for him but did not find him.
>
> I will get up now and go about the city, through its streets and squares; I will search for the one my heart loves. So I looked for him but did not find him.
>
> The watchmen found me as they made their rounds in the city. "Have you seen the one my heart loves?"
>
> Scarcely had I passed them when I found the one my heart loves. I held him and would not let him go....
> *(Song of Solomon 3:1-4)*

She stops and puts down the Bible. I can see light from the candles reflecting off the tears in her eyes. Then she closes her eyes and lowers her head. Her lips move in silent prayer.

The woman next to her picks up the Bible and turns the pages back and reads a psalm. The man next to her reads a reflection he wrote earlier in the day, a response to the Philippians passage. Each person contributes something he or she wrote or a passage from the Bible. I feel Chris tapping me with the bowl of water.

He leans over and whispers in my ear, "The peace of Christ be with you, Luke." Then he hands me the bowl and the towel. I dip my hands, dry them off, and hand the bowl to Natasha, who is sitting next to me.

"The peace of Christ be with you, Natasha," I whisper.

"And also with you," she replies as she takes the bowl and towel.

While another person reads his work, I see Melissa stand up and walk across the room toward me, with an open Bible in her hands.

"Read this," she says, handing me the Bible and pointing at highlighted verses. It is Ephesians 5. Melissa returns to her seat without another word.

When Chris finishes a song he apparently wrote, I wait for a moment and then read:

> **Husbands,** love your wives, just as Christ loved the church and gave himself up for her to make her holy, cleansing her by the washing with water through the word, and to present her to himself as a radiant church, without stain or wrinkle or any other blemish, but holy and blameless. In this same way, husbands ought to love their wives as their own bodies. He who loves his wife loves himself. After all, no one ever hated his own body, but he feeds and cares for it, just as Christ does the church—for we are members of his body. 'For this reason a man will leave his father and mother and be united to his wife, and the two will become one flesh.' This is a profound mystery—but I am talking about Christ and the church. *(Ephesians 5:25-32)*

I don't hear what Natasha sings after me. My mind has gone elsewhere. Why did Melissa give me this passage? I begin to pray with whispered words. I lose myself in those words for a little while. When I start paying attention again a man is speaking. I choose to keep my eyes closed and just listen.

Voices change every few minutes, with each person present making some sort of contribution. This continues until I recognize Nate's voice. He reads through the Philippians passage again and when he reaches the end he pauses for a long while. The only sound is the whir of the fan.

He begins to pray. This prayer is one for the community. He mentions everyone by name and prays even for Heather and me. He stops and a woman continues the prayer. Her prayer is one of praise and thanksgiving, honoring God for all he has done in the past week and for what he is still doing. After a while she too stops. No one says anything. I open my eyes and look around. Everyone has their eyes closed still. This must be an expected pause.

"Amen," Nate finally says.

This must be it. Everyone stands and begins to mingle again, just like at the beginning. Some talk with more serious expressions while others nearby laugh. I see a few people laying hands on one of the women and praying for her. Then I realize the woman is Heather.

"I'm glad you two could come," Nate says in a somewhat subdued voice.

"How did you get to doing all of this?"

"What do you mean?"

"I mean it is a curious service, you have to admit. Very free and yet very formal."

"I suppose. I think it is more a part of our willingness to be free in the Spirit. The Spirit isn't about letting us run around wildly. The Spirit frees us and constrains us, as has always been the case. But, in doing this the Spirit frees us to live in the way we are supposed to live, and be constrained from those things which destroy life. I like what Isaiah says."

He opens his Bible and turns to Isaiah.

"Isaiah 63, verse 11 through 14"

> **Then his people** recalled the days of old, the days of Moses and his people—where is he who brought them through the sea, with the shepherd of his flock? Where is he who set his Holy Spirit among them,
>
> who sent his glorious arm of power to be at Moses' right hand, who divided the waters before them, to gain for himself everlasting renown,
>
> who led them through the depths? Like a horse in open country, they did not stumble;
>
> like cattle that go down to the plain, they were given rest by the Spirit of the Lord. This is how you guided your people to make for yourself a glorious name.

Nate continues, "God has always led by his Holy Spirit and so we want to listen to what the Holy Spirit is doing now and learn what the Holy Spirit has always done, so that the full work of the Spirit is reflected in our lives and in our worship."

"Which is the same thing," Chris says, joining us.

"It is the same thing," Nate replies. "Our worship, our gathering here, is a reflection of our lives, and our lives are a reflection of our worship. We have to be in all our hours the same people we are in the few hours tonight."

"Nate!" someone yells from across the room.

"Always busy," he says and laughs. "You free this week?"

"Yeah, but I think I have enough to work with."

"I want to hear more about your journey. We've talked too much about mine already," he replies, then walks over to the person who yelled his name.

"We have to run off now," Chris says to me. "But I wanted to catch you before we left. I talked with Nicole and we'd really like to have you and Heather over for dinner this week. If that's okay. At our place."

"Not here?" I ask and laugh.

"No, I know the kitchen too well to eat here," he laughs. "Just kidding. But yeah, our place. Here's our number. Talk to Heather and see if it works out."

"Thanks, Chris."

"Talk to you this week," he says then joins Nicole by the stairs. She waves goodbye to people, and me, before they disappear down the stairs.

"Hey, Luke, nice you could join us," Mike says to me, as we shake hands. "This my wife, Rachel. My blessing from God."

"Nice to meet you, Rachel," I reply.

"Mike says you and he had a great conversation this week," Rachel says.

"We did. Very interesting to hear how God works."

"And we know," Rachel says, "that in all things God works for the good of those who love him, who have been called according to his purpose."

"Just takes a bit to discover his purpose at times," Mike laughs. "Will we see you next week?"

"I think so," I reply. They walk down the stairs, holding hands and laughing.

Heather is still talking with others. I look over and she glances my way, giving me a smile. A smile. I know that smile. I love that smile.

Melissa walks by and says while she is walking, "I think you got what I was going to say."

"Yeah. Thanks."

"Don't thank me," she replies, and points upward, looking back at me as she, too, goes down the stairs.

I turn around and look at a painting behind me which goes from floor to ceiling. It has the look of one of the old illuminated manuscripts, and is decorated with intricate patterns and whorls. Very Celtic but with other designs mixed in as well. They look African. The title at the top says "The Tradition." The words below are written in a flowery script but are quite readable:

> We are a body knit together as such by a common religious profession, by unity of discipline, and by the bond of a common hope. We meet together as an assembly and congregation, that, offering up prayer to God as with united force, we may wrestle with Him in our supplications. This violence God delights in. We pray, too, for the government, for their ministers and for all in authority, for the welfare of the world, for the prevalence of peace, for the delay of the final consummation. We assemble to read our sacred writings, if any peculiarity of the times makes either forewarning or reminiscence needful.

> However it be in that respect, with the sacred words we nourish our faith, we animate our hope, we make our confidence more steadfast; and no less by inculcations of God's precepts we confirm good habits. In the same place also exhortations are made, rebukes and sacred censures are administered. For with a great gravity is the work of judging carried on among us, as befits those who feel assured that they are in the sight of God; and you have the most notable example of

judgment to come when any one has sinned so grievously as to require his severance from us in prayer, in the congregation and in all sacred intercourse.

The tried men of our elders preside over us, obtaining that honor not by purchase, but by established character. There is no buying and selling of any sort in the things of God. Though we have our treasure-chest, it is not made up of purchase-money, as of a religion that has its price. On the monthly day, if he likes, each puts in a small donation; but only if it be his pleasure, and only if he be able: for there is no compulsion; all is voluntary. These gifts are, as it were, piety's deposit fund.

For they are not taken thence and spent on feasts, and drinking-bouts, and eating-houses, but to support and bury poor people, to supply the wants of boys and girls destitute of means and parents, and of old persons confined now to the house; such, too, as have suffered accident; and if there happen to be any in the mines, or banished to the islands, or shut up in the prisons, for nothing but their fidelity to the cause of God's Church, they become the nurslings of their confession.

But it is mainly the deeds of a love so noble that lead many to put a brand upon us. See, they say, how they love one another, for themselves are animated by mutual hatred; how they are ready even to die for one another, for they themselves will sooner put to death. And they are wroth with us, too, because we call each other brethren; for no other reason, as I think, than because among themselves names of consanguinity are assumed in mere pretense of affection. But we are your brethren as well, by the law of our common mother nature, though you are hardly men, because brothers so unkind.

At the same time, how much more fittingly they are called and counted brothers who have been led to the knowledge of God as their common Father, who have drunk in one spirit of holiness, who from the same womb of a common ignorance have agonized into the same light of truth! But on this very account, perhaps, we are regarded as having less claim to be held true brothers, that no tragedy makes a noise about our brotherhood, or that the family possessions, which generally destroy brotherhood among you, create fraternal bonds among us.

One in mind and soul, we do not hesitate to share our earthly goods with one another. All things are common among us but our wives.

Our feast explains itself by its name. The Greeks call it *agapè*. Whatever it costs, our outlay in the name of piety is gain, since with the good things of the feast we benefit the needy; not as it is with you, do parasites aspire to the glory of satisfying their licentious propensities, selling themselves for a belly-feast to all disgraceful treatment,—but as it is with God himself, a peculiar respect is shown to the lowly.

If the object of our feast be good, in the light of that consider its further regulations. As it is an act of religious service, it permits no vileness or immodesty. The participants, before reclining, taste first of prayer to God. As much is eaten as satisfies the cravings of hunger; as much is drunk as befits the chaste.

They say it is enough, as those who remember that even during the night they have to worship God; they talk as those who know that the Lord is one of their auditors. After manual ablution, and the bringing in of lights, each is asked to stand forth and sing, as he can, a hymn to God, either one from the holy Scriptures or one of his own composing,—a proof of the measure of our drinking. As the feast commenced with prayer, so with prayer it is closed.

We go from it, not like troops of mischief-doers, nor bands of vagabonds, nor to break out into licentious acts, but to have as much care of our modesty and chastity as if we had been at a school of virtue rather than a banquet. Give the congregation of the Christians its due, and hold it unlawful, if it is like assemblies of the illicit sort: by all means let it be condemned, if any complaint can be validly laid against it, such as lies against secret factions.

But who has ever suffered harm from our assemblies? We are in our congregations just what we are when separated from each other; we are as a community what we are individuals; we injure nobody, we trouble nobody. When the upright, when the virtuous meet together, when the pious, when the pure assemble in congregation, you ought not to call that a faction, but the court of God.

Below this main text, written a little larger, are the words, "Tertullian—Carthage, North Africa c. A.D. 200."

Interesting.

I feel hands placed on my shoulders. I turn around to see Nate looking at the painting with me.

"The same Spirit, Luke," he says. "Then and now. Doing the same thing. Always doing the same thing, drawing people to God, so that we may be truly one with him and one with each other. May we all listen. May we all continue to listen and respond as the Spirit leads us toward eternity."

So be it.

May the grace of the Lord Jesus Christ, the love of God, and the fellowship of the Holy Spirit be with you all.*

---

*2 Corinthians 13:14

Bibliography

Basil of Caesarea. *On the Holy Spirit*. Crestwood, NY: St. Vladimir's Seminary Press, 1980.

Burge, Gary M. *The Anointed Community: The Holy Spirit in the Johannine Tradition*. Grand Rapids, MI: Eerdmans, 1987.

Burgess, Stanley M. *The Holy Spirit: Ancient Christian Traditions*. Peabody, MA: Hendrickson, 1984.

———. *The Holy Spirit: Eastern Christian Traditions*. Peabody, MA: Hendrickson, 1989.

———. *The Holy Spirit: Medieval Roman Catholic and Reformation Traditions*. Peabody, MA: Hendrickson, 1997.

Cassian, John. *The Conferences*. Trans. by Boniface Ramsey. New York: Newman Press, 1997.

Fee, Gordon D. *God's Empowering Presence*. Peabody, MA: Hendrickson, 1994.

———. *Paul, the Spirit, and the People of God*. Peabody, MA: Hendrickson, 1996.

Frost, Michael and Alan Hirsch. *The Shaping of Things to Come*. Peabody, MA: Hendrickson, 2003.

Gibbs, Eddie and Ryan K. Bolger. *Emerging Churches*. Grand Rapids, MI: Baker Academic, 2005.

Grenz, Stanley J. and John R. Franke. *Beyond Foundationalism*. Louisville, KY: Westminster John Knox Press, 2001.

Hawthorne, Gerald F. *The Presence and the Power*. Eugene, OR: Wipf & Stock, 2003.

Kärkkäinen, Veli-Matti. *Pneumatology: The Holy Spirit in Ecumenical, International, and Contextual Perspective.* Grand Rapids, MI: Baker Academic, 2002.

———. *Toward a Pneumatological Theology: Pentecostal and Ecumenical Perspectives on Ecclesiology, Soteriology, and Theology of Mission.* Ed. by Amos Young. Lanham, MD: University Press of America, 2002.

Lossky, Vladimir. *The Mystical Theology of the Eastern Church.* Crestwood, NY: St. Vladimir's Seminary Press, 1998.

Moltmann, Jürgen. *The Spirit of Life.* Minneapolis, MN: Augsburg Fortress Press, 1992.

———. *The Source of Life.* Minneapolis, MN: Augsburg Fortress Press, 1997.

Pagitt, Doug. *Church Re-Imagined.* Grand Rapids, MI: Zondervan, 2005.

Pagitt, Doug and Tony Jones, eds. *An Emergent Manifesto of Hope.* Grand Rapids, MI: Baker, 2007.

Pannenberg, Wolfhart. *Systematic Theology.* Trans. by Geoffrey W. Bromiley. 3 vols. Grand Rapids, MI: Eerdmans, 1991-1998.

The Philokalia. Trans. by G.E.H. Palmer, Philip Sherrard, and Kallistos Ware. 4 vols. London: Faber and Faber, 1983-1999.

Pinnock, Clark H. *Flame of Love.* Downers Grove, IL: InterVarsity Press, 1996.

Volf, Miroslav. *After Our Likeness.* Grand Rapids, MI: Eerdmans, 1998.

Welker, Michael. *God the Spirit.* Trans. by John F. Hoffmeyer. Minneapolis, MN: Augsburg Fortress Press, 1994.

About these sources

In a book on theology—for that is what this is—the tradition is generally to include copious notes and references, so as to acknowledge the source material and to give credit for ideas that are not fully original. It is, to be sure, extremely important to ground any thoughtful work within the context of learning and research, both to avoid the charge of possible plagiarism and to establish the work as something more than a personal fancy. If we affirm that in fact the Holy Spirit does "teach us all things" we also must affirm that the key word in that phrase is not *me* it is *us*. If I am the only person who affirms a point about the Spirit then it is quite likely I have missed the mark in one way or several.

Yet in attempting to establish the body of writings that underlie a book on theology, something else is often lost: readability. While the work may be well-grounded and established as part of the wider academy, the rhythm and flow of the work is marred by constant interruption, whether this be through footnotes or through imbedded interactions with the various sources and related ideas.

So a choice has to be made: Risk credibility by limiting interruptions and emphasizing style, or risk losing readers by insisting on noting all the particular arguments, sources, influences, or perspectives on each particular topic.

As someone who loves the intricacies of academic discussion and has a passion for the renewal of the church, I found myself in a bind. The fact is I claim very little originality in any of the ideas presented here. Had I chosen a style more in keeping with a standard academic work, the footnotes would have been many and the discussions would have most certainly delved much more deeply into concepts and discussions that are certainly applicable. I did not, however, choose that style.

Instead I chose to journey farther back in time before the constraints of academic argumentation had been formalized.

Quite a bit farther back, in fact. My inspiration for the style, in which a student has a conversation with a teacher, came from *The Conferences* by **John Cassian**. In this early fifth-century work the author relates a series of twenty-four conversations he and a friend had with the religious radicals of his day, the monastics of Egypt. Instead of giving a systematic list of right belief and behavior, Cassian instead shares with us casual interactions consisting of questions and answers that help the students best pursue purity of heart and the kingdom of heaven.

The conversation breaks up the difficult considerations and allows for questions to be asked—questions that are often on the readers' mind. It also makes the theology into a story. This is not a removed set of philosophical statements but instead people living the life God has called them to live. We remember the story, the characters, the conversation much better than we remember details and notes. Cassian's strong emphasis on Scripture as the primary source of authority for all topics related to the Christian life was also very influential in my writing.

In Cassian's conversation it was clear he was not basing his thoughts on his own authority but instead gave clear attribution to a group of fifteen men who would have been considered authorities in his time. It is also very much the case this present work has been influenced greatly by the thoughts of others.

One book stands out as a primary reference. This is **Emerging Churches** by **Eddie Gibbs** and **Ryan K. Bolger**. The authors sought a more coherent understanding of the emerging church movement and so interviewed those leading various communities around the world. As the conversations continued they began to note certain emphases that seemed to define these new churches, and they found there were roughly nine of these emphases. Gibbs and Bolger arranged their book around these nine traits. These traits also form the foundation of *It's a Dance*.

The reason for this has little to do with wanting to follow a new trend or jump onto a bandwagon of contemporary church thinking. Instead, it occurred to me very early on in reading the book that these emphases are not unique to the emerging churches. Indeed, the more I read the more I was reminded of the thoughts of others, and these others were not talking about cutting-edge church ministry. They were talking about the Holy Spirit.

John Cassian helped me with the style. Gibbs and Bolger provided a framework. The following books helped steer the content and provided the foundations for much of the discussion in this book. While not nearly a complete list of worthwhile books related to the Holy Spirit, these select texts were particularly influential in my developing thought. I heartily recommend each of these for further study on the topics I raise.

SCRIPTURE: A key help for my scriptural exegesis was **Gordon D. Fee,** *God's Empowering Presence.* In writing an article about the Holy Spirit, Fee realized very little had been written about Paul's understanding of the Holy Spirit. He decided to remedy this situation by putting together a text in which he exegetes every Pauline passage related to the Holy Spirit. At the end he sums up his discoveries. This necessarily lengthy and detailed book would not, however, appeal to a broad audience, so he gathered together his conclusions in the book *Paul, the Spirit, and the People of God.*

Also very helpful were **Gary M. Burge,** *The Anointed Community: The Holy Spirit in the Johannine Tradition* and **Gerald F. Hawthorne,** *The Presence and the Power.*

THEOLOGY: The formal study of the Holy Spirit is called pneumatology, *pneuma* being "spirit" in Greek. While the study is certainly not new,

> ### Gordon D. Fee:
>
> THE ONLY worthwhile theology, after all, is one that is translated into life; and Paul's understanding of the Spirit is ultimately a matter of lived-out faith. The experience of the Spirit was how the early believers came to receive the salvation that Christ had brought, and how they came to understand themselves as living at the beginning of the end times. For them, the Spirit was both the evidence that God's great future for his people had already made its way into the present and the guarantee that God would conclude what he had begun in Christ. Thus, the Spirit is foundational to their entire *experience* and *understanding* of their present life in Christ.
>
> *Paul, the Spirit, and the People of God* (pp. 2-3)

it is only rather recently that works specifically devoted to the topic of the Holy Spirit have been written. Generally, the topic of the Holy Spirit was for the most part contained in other categories such as church or salvation or various other emphases—never quite emerging as a distinct focus.

One noteworthy exception is a wonderful book by **Basil of Caesarea** called *On the Holy Spirit.* Basil wrote this near the end of the fourth century during the era when the concept of the Trinity was being sorted out. In this book, Basil sets forth the

---

Basil of Caesarea:

IT IS THE UNIQUE FUNCTION of the Holy Spirit to reveal mysteries, as it is written, "God had revealed them to us through the Holy Spirit" (1 Cor. 2:10). One cannot see the Father without the Spirit! It would be like living in a house at night when the lamps are extinguished; one's eyes would be darkened and could not exercise their function. Unable to distinguish the value of objects, one might very well treat gold as if it were iron. It is the same in the spiritual world; it is impossible to maintain a life of holiness without the Spirit.

It would be easier for an army to continue its maneuvers without a general, or for a choir to sing on key without its director. How can the Seraphim sing, "Holy, holy, holy," without the Spirit teaching them to constantly raise their voices in praise? If all God's angels praise Him, and all His host, they do so by cooperating with his Spirit. Do a thousand thousands of angels serve Him? Do ten thousand times ten thousand stand before Him? They accomplish their proper work by the Spirit's power. All the indescribable harmony of the heavenly realm, whether it be the praise of God or the mutual concord of the bodiless powers, would be impossible without the authority of the Spirit....

If we are illumined by divine power, and fix our eyes on the beauty of the image of the invisible God, and through the image are led up to the indescribable beauty of its source, it is because we have been inseparably joining to the Spirit of knowledge. He gives those who love the vision of truth the power which enables them to see the image, and this power is Himself.

On the Holy Spirit (p. 64)

argument of why the Holy Spirit can and should be emphasized along with the Father and the Son.

To understand how other writers of that era or later understood the Spirit, however, we generally have to pull out passages from less Holy Spirit-oriented works. It is, then, a bit of a process to determine what has been taught on the Holy Spirit over the centuries. Fortunately, **Stanley M. Burgess** has provided us with an overview of historical thought in his three-volume set on the Holy Spirit. Burgess starts with *The Holy Spirit: Ancient Christian Traditions*, continues with *The Holy Spirit: Eastern Christian Traditions*, and ends with *The Holy Spirit: Medieval Roman Catholic and Reformation Traditions*.

Among the other benefits of living in our era, the oft-neglected focus on the Holy Spirit is now realized and there has been a wonderful selection of works in recent decades trying to come to terms with how the Spirit fits into the broader theological spectrum.

Clark H. Pinnock's book *Flame of Love* is a great place to begin a study of pneumatology. It is quite readable and introduces important concepts and ideas without getting bogged down in a lot of heavy theological wording. It is, in his own words, "a systematic theology of the Spirit that examines the Christian vision from the vantage point of the Spirit" (p. 18). A very stimulating examination indeed. This is the first theology book devoted to the Holy Spirit that I read and so I give it a great deal of credit for my developing thought.

Clark H. Pinnock:

BECAUSE MISSION is holistic, it must be empowered—it simply cannot be carried out by our human wisdom and strength alone. Actions have to be initiated and empowered by the Spirit. The Shepherd has to go on ahead of us. There is a partnership in which the Spirit is the leading player and we are junior partners and instruments. It is God's mission, and we are being caught up in it. The Spirit bears witness, and you also (Jn. 15:26-27)....If there was greatness in the disciples, surely it was not their ability but their openness to the Spirit. It was baptism in the Spirit that enabled them to give testimony to Jesus Christ.

Flame of Love (p. 145)

Jürgen Moltmann:

FOR THE CHRISTIAN faith, true freedom is found neither in insight into a cosmic necessity or a necessity of world history, nor in the autonomous right of disposal over oneself and one's property. It means being possessed by the divine energy of life, and participation of that energy. Through trust in the God of the Exodus and the resurrection, the believer experiences and partakes of this liberating power of God which raises to new life. "All things are possible with God", so "All things are possible to those who believe" (Mark 9:23). God manifests his creative energies in these confronting historical events, and the people touched by them are interpenetrated by these energies.

Through faith, the hitherto unexplored creative powers of God are thrown open in men and women. So faith means becoming creative with God, and in his Spirit. Faith leads to a creative life which is life-giving through love, in places where death rules and people resign themselves, and surrender to it. Faith awakens trust in the still unrealized possibilities in human beings—in oneself and in other people. So faith means crossing the frontiers of the reality which is existent now, and has been determined by the past, and seeking the potentialities for life which have not yet come into being. "All things are possible to him who believes'; and this being so, believers become what Musil calls "possibility people".

The Spirit of Life (p. 115)

WHAT SERVES the discipleship of Jesus, and can be put to use there, comes from the Holy Spirit, and what comes from the Holy Spirit leads us along the way of Jesus Christ and into his discipleship. What the synoptic Gospels call the discipleship of Jesus, the apostle Paul calls life in the Spirit. So personal and public, political and economic discipleship of Jesus is the practical criterion for 'testing the spirits'.

The Source of Life (p. 18)

More importantly for this present work, however, were the writings of two German theologians. It was in the reading of these two great thinkers I began to realize there were traits in the contemporary church scene that reflected a significant work of the Holy Spirit.

The most important is **Jürgen Moltmann** and *The Spirit of Life*. This book is the culmination of a decades-long realization of the work of the Holy Spirit, which permeates all of theology. Again and again, the topic of the Holy Spirit would emerge from Moltmann's other writings, taking on increasing importance until he felt he had to add this book on the Holy Spirit to his planned series of contributions to systematic theology.

More approachable to a popular audience is Moltmann's much smaller work *The Source of Life*.

It should be added, however, that the whole body of Moltmann's work seems to touch on the Holy Spirit, so for the more stalwart I would recommend all his books.

I also found *God the Spirit* by Moltmann's colleague **Michael Welker** to be extremely helpful.

> **Michael Welker:**
>
> THE ACTION of the Spirit does not flee from the world, but overcomes the world, delivering and renewing life. The Spirit does not cause a flight from the world, but rather the resurrection of the flesh and participation in eternal life— and thus a reformation and transmutation of that which is perishable (cf. 1 Cor. 15:49-50). God's power acts on earthly life so that it becomes a bearer and a mirror of God's glory, and so that it acts in turn on other earthly life....The Power of the Spirit is in fact superior to the world, changing the world.
>
> *God the Spirit* (p. 263)

Yet another German theologian helped add a different perspective on the work of the Spirit—**Wolfhart Pannenberg**. Though in agreement on much, Pannenberg differs with his particular emphases and topics of interest, and is more interested in a systematic approach to theology. His *Systematic Theology*, three volumes, is translated by Geoffrey W. Bromiley. The third volume is especially rich in considerations of the Holy Spirit involved in eschatology.

Throughout *It's a Dance* I am open to sharing terms that might be unusual even to long-time church-goers. One example of this is the word *perichoresis*. This word, however, is just one instance of a broader influence in my thought provided by the Eastern Orthodox tradition, which has developed strands of theology in many ways very different from what we in the West are used to. While retaining the same emphases on all the essential doctrines, those in the East have asked different questions, focused on different realities, and in general provided a unique theology worth discovering. Those in the East have a much more substantive understanding of the Holy Spirit in general, and along with this they have what I consider a better-developed understanding of the Trinity as well.

A key book for my understanding of Eastern Orthodox theology was **Vladimir Lossky, *The Mystical Theology of the Eastern Church.*** Also very influential were the four volumes of ***The Philokalia*** translated by G.E.H. Palmer, Philip Sherrard, and Kallistos Ware.

I am not, however, Eastern Orthodox, so there remain distinctions in my theology that place me still within the broadly evangelical tradition. Though focused more on ecclesiology (the study of the church), ***After Our Likeness*** by **Miroslav Volf** helps emphasize some distinctives.

Wolfhart Pannenberg:

PNEUMATOLOGY and Eschatology belong together because the eschatological consummation itself is ascribed to the Spirit, who as an end-time gift already governs the historical present of believers. Conversely, then, eschatology does not merely have to do with the future of consummation that is still ahead; it is also at work in our present by the Spirit. Hence the presence of the Spirit also means already the overcoming of sin and death. If sin and death are to be finally overcome only in the eschatological consummation, victory over them is already in process in the present work of the Spirit, and above all in his presence as a gift in believers.

Systematic Theology, v. III (p. 553)

> **Miroslav Volf:**
>
> THE CHURCH is not a club of universally gifted and for that reason self-sufficient charismatics, but rather a community of men and women whom the Spirit of God has endowed in a certain way for service to each other and to the world in anticipation of God's new creation....
>
> The Spirit works, first, as the Spirit chooses; no church, neither an entire (local) church nor any stratum in the church, can prescribe which gifts the Spirit is to bestow on which members. Furthermore, the Spirit works *when* the Spirit chooses; the church cannot determine at which time the Spirit is to bestow its gifts. This clearly reveals that the church lives from a dynamic not deriving from itself. The problem of who is to do what in the church is in an important sense not a church matter at all. It is not the church that "organizes" its life, but rather the Holy Spirit.
>
> *After Our Likeness* (p. 231-232)

For an excellent overview of what these theologians and other recent theologians have to say on the topic of the Holy Spirit, I heartily recommend **Veli-Matti Kärkkäinen,** *Pneumatology: The Holy Spirit in Ecumenical, International, and Contextual Perspective.* See also his collection of essays titled *Toward a Pneumatological Theology: Pentecostal and Ecumenical Perspectives on Ecclesiology, Soteriology, and Theology of Mission,* edited by Amos Young. For this present work, however, it is not enough to note the books of Veli-Matti Kärkkäinen. It was in his classes and under his tutelage I first engaged the study of pneumatology and learned many trails of study that were heretofore hidden. His teaching and his introduction to other teachers (including most of the previously mentioned books) has been immensely influential in every way.

CHURCH: While I consider *It's a Dance* to be primarily a book on pneumatology rather than a text on ministry or church leadership, a particular perspective on ministry is deeply imbedded in these pages. This perspective did not arise from a vacuum. Many of the issues and traits came out of my own experiences as both a participant and as a leader in a variety of churches, including some of the earliest emerging churches. Much of my perspective also came from the experiences of many friends who likewise have participated in many ways in a variety of settings. I did not want to simply project my own experiences onto a church, however. I sought instead to understand my experiences and background within a broader conversation of church ministry. Therefore, much of what is portrayed in this present work is a composite of my own efforts and the efforts of others. Not only did Gibbs and Bolger provide a framework of traits, they also shared the stories of many participants, helping me to have a broader understanding of what is going on in the church during our era.

Stanley J. Grenz and John R. Franke:

THE CHRISTIAN conception views God as the one who in grace shares the divine life with us. That is, ultimately we enjoy the fullness of community as, and only as, God graciously brings us to participate together in the fountainhead of community, namely, the life of the triune God. The agent of this participation is the Holy Spirit, through whom we become the children of God and through whom we thereby share in the love present within the eternal triune God. For this reason, the communal fellowship we have together as members of the church goes beyond what is generated by a common experience or even by a common narrative. The community we share is our shared participation, or participation together, in the perichoretic community of trinitarian persons.

Beyond Foundationalism
(p. 228)

The Shaping of Things to Come by Michael Frost and Alan Hirsch and *Church Re-Imagined* by Doug Pagitt were very helpful as this book began to take shape, helping me to understand the present thinking on the church, especially in regards to a renewed missional approach. Though published after I was well along in the editing stage I found *An Emergent Manifesto of Hope*, edited by Doug Pagitt and Tony Jones to be another great overview of contemporary church thought.

One additional book worth noting as helping me get a grasp of the broader philosophical climate in which we all reside—happily or not—was *Beyond Foundationalism* by Stanley J. Grenz and John R. Franke.